Sexual SHAKESPEARE

Sexual SHAKESPEARE

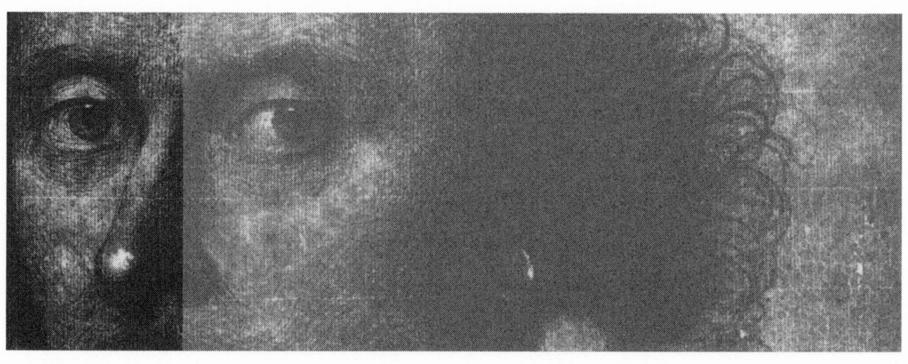

Forgery Authorship Portraiture

Michael Keevak

Wayne State University Press Detroit

Manufactured in the United States of America.
05 04 03 02 01 5 4 3 2 1

Library of Congress Cataloging-in-Publication Data
Keevak, Michael, 1962–
Sexual Shakespeare : forgery, authorship, portraiture / Michael Keevak.
p. cm.
Includes bibliographical references and index.
ISBN 0-8143-2953-5 (cloth) (alk. paper)
ISBN 0-8143-2975-6 (paper) (alk. paper)
1. Shakespeare, William, 1564–1616. 2. Shakespeare, William, 1564–1616—Views on sex. 3. Dramatists, English—Early modern, 1500–1700—Sexual behavior. 4. Homosexuality and literature—England—History. 5. Shakespeare, William, 1564–1616—Authorship. 6. Shakespeare, William, 1564–1616—Forgeries. 7. Shakespeare, William, 1564–1616—Portraits. 8. Sex in literature. I. Title.
PR2894 .K38 2001
822.3'3—dc21 00-011801

TO MY STUDENTS AT
NATIONAL TAIWAN UNIVERSITY

Contents

List of Illustrations

Acknowledgments

I HAVE many people to thank for the completion of this book. I am grateful to the National Science Council in Taiwan for ongoing financial support. Without this repeated generosity I can safely say that this work could not have been finished—or even begun. I owe Patricia Parker for her kindness and encouragement when the idea of a book was only beginning to take shape. Stephen Orgel and Stephen Nichols read parts of the manuscript in its early stages and helped me to revise it. Thanks to Arthur Marotti for suggesting Wayne State in the first place, and to Arthur Evans and Adela Garcia of the press for their kindness and professionalism. An anonymous reader for another press graced me with many tightly packed pages of incisive criticism, forcing me to rethink the project as a whole; I only wish I could identify the author in order to thank him or her personally.

More than anyone else, however, I must extend thanks to Richard Burt for recommending the project and for suggesting ways to make it better at a time when few others, myself included, seemed to believe in it any more. This book would certainly not have been published without his support and his guidance at every stage.

I am lucky to have friends like Brandy Alvarez, Bart Cornelis, Leif Dahlberg, Jody Greene, Elmer Kolfin, Mia Mochizuki, David Ogawa, George Schoolfield, Brigham Taylor, Kirill and Beni Thompson, Tad Turner, Lisa Venezia, Jude Wheway, Rishona Zimring, and Dawn Hillmayr. I am especially happy to thank Eric Jan Sluijter and Nicolette Sluijter-Seijffert for their friendship and hospitality. The staff at the National Taiwan University Library endured my requests without flinching: special thanks to Kuo Bih-fen. The staff at the Folger Shakespeare Library helped me to obtain bibliographical information and illustrations with amazing speed and accuracy: special thanks to Georgianna Ziegler and Lori Johnson. Huang Su-ching and Hsueh Yu-i forwarded materials to me on the other side of the world. Lastly, I could have accomplished nothing without my invaluable research assistants, each a delight in their own way: Anne Elizabeth Sheu, Brian Lin, Tsai Yu-fen, Su Chiu-hua, and, above all, Laura Jane Wey, my Chinese tutor, trusted assistant, and friend. There are many things that I will continue to owe her.

Acknowledgments

An earlier version of chapter 1 appeared in *Criticism* 40 (1998): 167–89. Reprinted with permission from Wayne State University Press.

Unless otherwise noted, all quotations from Shakespeare correspond to *The Riverside Shakespeare,* 2d ed., ed. G. Blakemore Evans et al. (Boston: Houghton Mifflin, 1997).

INTRODUCTION

"*French* Dancers and *Italian* Eunuchs": Bardolatry and Its (De)Sexualization

SINCE THE eighteenth century, Shakespeare studies have been characterized by amazingly persevering and manifold preoccupations with establishing the authentic, the biographical, and the originary Shakespeare.[1] And yet, as we are so relentlessly reminded, we really don't know anything about him. Or do we? We probably know more about Shakespeare than any other early modern author, but there will obviously never be enough facts for a figure who is (or until very recently, was) the English national poet, "universal" high-culture icon, and, indeed, "the greatest writer of all time."[2]

But if the relative amount of information available is clearly not the problem, still readers have consistently been trapped by a circular need to embody a figure about whom nothing else *can* be known: the result being that the notoriously unsatisfying biographical vacuum has itself given rise to a remarkable variety of personal and cultural fantasies that, to a large extent, are the "biography" of Shakespeare. The history of "Shakespeare's lives," to borrow the title of the standard book on the subject by Samuel Schoenbaum,[3] is also a history of forgery, whether the intent has been consciously to deceive the public or merely to memorialize the Swan of Avon.

This book will argue, however, that the authentic Shakespeare cannot escape being a sexual one as well, whether it is ever acknowledged or whether the polymorphous realities of sexuality are praised, blamed, bracketed, or simply suppressed. Amazingly enough, this aspect of Shakespearean authenticity has so far escaped serious consideration, despite the fact that all biographical reconstructions (life stories, critical editions, visual representations)[4] cannot seem to avoid the desire or the need to sexualize not only the undeniably sexy works that bear his name, but also some idea of the "man himself."

Even in the very first biography, Nicholas Rowe's *Some Account of the Life &c. of Mr. William Shakespear* of 1709, the sexual seems to bubble up from beneath the surface of a text whose concern does not seem to be sexual at all. Frustrated by the lack of reliable information, Rowe supposedly sent retired actor Thomas Betterton on a pilgrimage to Stratford to interview locals who might be able to support or add to the growing body of legends that already surrounded the poet's life.[5] One of the new "facts" that turned up, via the ubiquitous William Davenant, was that the earl of Southampton, Shakespeare's alleged patron (and dedicatee of both *Venus and Adonis* and *The Rape of Lucrece*), had presented the poet with a gift of £1,000:

> There is one Instance so singular in the Magnificence of this Patron of *Shakespear's,* that if I had not been assur'd that the Story was handed down by Sir *William D'Avenant,* who was probably very well acquainted with his Affairs, I should not have ventur'd to have inserted, that my Lord *Southampton,* at one time, gave him a thousand Pounds, to enable him to go through with a Purchase which he heard he had a mind to. A Bounty very great, and very rare at any time, and almost equal to that profuse Generosity the present Age has shewn to *French* Dancers and *Italian* Eunuchs.[6]

Southampton was already an attractive figure for biographers who felt a need to de-emphasize Shakespeare's disturbingly humble origins, but one is struck by the suggestiveness of Rowe's unexpected comparison between Shakespeare and "*French* Dancers and *Italian* Eunuchs," since the poet is likened not only to performing women (assuming that the "*French* Dancers" were female) but—most shocking of all?—to castrated males. Students of early modern queer studies will immediately be reminded of stock diatribes about the "effeminacy" of Renaissance actors (and not just the boys who played women's roles) as well as the "effeminization" of anyone who attended plays, both of which had been common features of antitheatrical complaints in the previous century and a half.[7] But Rowe's reference to castrati seems very much a product of the early eighteenth century. The story itself may have come from Davenant, but surely not the reference to eunuchs, even though castrati singers were introduced to the English public shortly after the Restoration, and, although officially banned, were not unknown even in Shakespeare's day.[8] Nonetheless, the vogue for performing eunuchs was still in its early stages in 1709 (and still a long way from the theatrical triumphs of the likes of Farinelli in the mid-1730s).[9] Moreover, Rowe's allusion to specifically foreign dancers or singers is clearly not expressing the same kind of xenophobic and demonizing sentiment so often featured in harangues about "sodomitical" foreigners (including eunuchs), or their pernicious influence on English culture as a whole.[10]

On the contrary, Rowe's comment is meant as unadulterated praise for the bard and the "great and uncommon Marks of Favour and Friendship"[11] that he inspired in his noble patron, but it is not hard to imagine that even in

1709 readers might have been rather uncomfortable with other conceivable implications. One such reader was Alexander Pope, who, in his edition of Shakespeare published in 1723–25, silently rewrote and reorganized Rowe's text, and the suggestive or even scandalous allusion to dancers and castrati was altered, although not entirely excised. The phrase now read "*French* Dancers and *Italian* Singers."[12] Pope was evidently disturbed by Rowe's choice of words, although one might wonder why he did not remove the comparison altogether (or does the whole thing in fact remain intact, since Italian singers might have been castrati anyway?). At any rate, when referring to eunuchs or Italian opera elsewhere in his works, Pope does so with the utmost contempt,[13] and he is much better known for a more circumspect reaction to another Shakespearean scandal, which will be the subject of chapter 2, that this same William Davenant might have been Shakespeare's illegitimate child. This one neither he nor Rowe deigned to mention in print at all.[14]

Perhaps the vogue for Italian castrati was still a relatively "safe" subject in the mid-1720s, or at least free from the kind of sexual (and nationalistic) implications that became increasingly complex in the following decades. Yet surely Pope wanted to *avoid* certain associations as well: besides the infelicitous likening of the bard to a castrated man, and a castrated performer at that (and bardolators could never shake off the ignominy that the Swan of Avon was a player as well as a dramatist), Rowe's allusion could easily bring to mind other unpleasant insinuations about prostitution,[15] sodomy,[16] effeminization,[17] and eunuchs as freakish "ravishers" of male and (especially) female auditors.[18] Rowe's and Pope's rich reference to dancers, eunuchs, and singers, in other words, is entangled by a constellation of historically fluid, vague, and often contradictory notions connected not only with sexuality, but also with the theater, theatrical tradition, and contemporary social satire.

Yet I would argue that Shakespeare as a eunuch is an oddly appropriate, if half-concealed, image for the unavoidably sexual terrains of bardolatry itself. To be sure, the notion of a castrated bard has never, to my knowledge, been taken literally, and indeed never even pursued in traditional Shakespeare criticism,[19] but yoking together castrati and Shakespeare might actually help us to bring into clearer focus the kinds of confusion surrounding the poet's sexuality that even by Rowe's time were already beginning to present a real problem—and that, like the "utterly confused category" of sodomy itself,[20] have yet to be resolved. Indeed, the total effect of Pope's revision remains rather muddled, but tellingly so, since this is not just a question of a fashion that had not yet bloomed into a pervasive and inescapable cultural force. For the physical and sexual puzzle literally embodied by eunuchs, whose atrophied genitals were the constant objects of titillation and mystery precisely by virtue of their being hidden from view,[21] also finds an analogue in the present-absent sexuality of the authentic Shakespeare himself, who can be known only from a very few dry legal and financial records or distinctly unrevealing contemporary allusions. We should recall that in *Twelfth Night* Viola announces that she will disguise herself as a (singing) *eunuch* when entering Orsino's service (1.2.56),[22] for like so many other boy heroines, from Rosalind to Cleopatra, she is a supposedly desexualized figure who is at the same time the subject or the object of considerable suggestiveness and bawdy innuendo.[23]

I argue that the very idea of an embodied Shakespeare is also both a concealment and a provocation, an act of simultaneous suppression and titillation that seems to encompass all erotic possibilities even as it appears to have nothing to do with sexuality at all. Shakespeare cannot be isolated from the vast variety of sexual or erotic arrangements that can be imagined, celebrated, or feared for him, even as he ends up being unsexed entirely: becoming not so much a eunuch, perhaps, as merely a non-gender-specific singer (or "*French* Dancer"). Put another way, authenticating Shakespeare often takes the form of a sexual/desexual dynamic in which readers' seemingly ineluctable need to embody him is countered by an even more powerful tendency to render him "impersonal" and ultimately free from any kind of sexuality at all—forcing readers once again to fantasize about the truth of an authenticity or an authorship that, in the end, remains indeterminate and indeed indeterminable. In a word, as I will try to show in the following chapters, bardolatry is effectively *inseparable* from its own (de)sexualization.

For example, it is no accident that Rowe's inadvertent foray into the realms of the sexual occurs only in the context of a discussion of Southampton, about whom various surmises were soon to become one of the flash points for the bard's presumed "homosexuality" (although, of course, that term was never used). One only has to look at other biographies and editions of the poems to see that Southampton has always been a touchy subject, and that his relationship to the poet has accordingly been routinely marginalized or ignored. An early Rowe plagiarizer, for instance, focused instead on the supposition that Shakespeare made reference to Southampton's gift in the dedication to *The Rape of Lucrece,* which refers to "the warrant I have of your Honourable disposition."[24] Later readers, beginning with Edmond Malone, simply rejected the story altogether, although they believed that £100 might seem a more likely sum.[25] E. K. Chambers agrees, hypothesizing that such a figure may have been paid to buy a share in the Lord Chamberlain's company in 1594; in any event, "the aggregate of Shakespeare's known purchases in real estate and tithes throughout his life does not reach £1,000."[26] Hyder Rollins's variorum edition of the *Poems* cites a number of readers who also disputed the amount of Southampton's largesse: "If the tradition is true," one of them comments, "the gift has no equal in the history of patronage."[27] On the other hand, Sidney Lee's 1898 *Life* accepted the tale as a "trustworthy tradition."[28] And yet in all of this flurry of words, there is not a single one about eunuchs (or even singers).

I have not undertaken to provide anything like a survey of the reception of the Southampton story, but I suspect that a thorough analysis of it would only produce the same kind of result that this book will try to show in a number of different ways: that sexual suggestiveness is kept out of sight as much as possible, and that, like all incursions into the dangerous territory of the bard's embodiment, accompanying worries about his sexuality will just as powerfully be desexualized (if not castrated) in favor of other details. The obvious anxieties inherent in the earl's "Marks of Favour and Friendship" must be channeled into less worrisome areas—namely, whether the amount of the "Bounty" has been exaggerated, whether the "warrant" mentioned in the dedication to *Lucrece* is a reference to such a gift, and, finally, whether the two men had any real contact at all. One is reminded here of a parallel set of questions regarding the young man sonnets. Are he and the speaker just friends? Are the poems merely following a well-worn convention? Or—as a last resort—are the poems even autobiographical?

Indeed, it is not accidental that so much of this book centers on Shakespeare's tantalizingly first-person sonnets, just as so many of our discussions about authenticity will have to take the eighteenth century—and, specifically, Malone—as their starting point. For he more than anyone else single-handedly ushered in the concept of the authentic Shakespeare that still holds sway today, and once an unaltered and unexpurgated text of the sonnets was republished, also by Malone in 1780, the floodgates of Shakespeare's "true" life story had finally been opened.[29] The standard text since 1640 had been a bowdlerized edition combining and rearranging the sonnets into a different order, mixing them with other Shakespearean and pseudo-Shakespearean poems, and occasionally altering pronouns in order to make everything conform more closely to the standardized Petrarchan paradigm of love poems to a mistress.[30] Malone's "recovered" Shakespeare, however, was also a "sodomite": not only because of the poet's relationship with a "dark" mistress (also a form of sodomy as far as the early modern period was concerned), but also because of a large number of love poems apparently addressed to another man. In the words of one particularly anxious contemporary, the poet was now "a miscreant, who could address amatory Verses to a man, 'with a romantic platonism of affection.'"[31] Hardly an insignificant or marginal issue, these sexual "discoveries" produced increasingly panicky reactions that culminated in the well-known controversy between Malone and the other great Shakespeare editor of the day, George Steevens, over whether the poems should be published at all.[32]

We will begin our inquiry with a group of forgeries—documents, letters, plays—made at exactly the same time by an ambitious teenager, William Henry Ireland, not merely because it is a convenient means to point out the difficulty of achieving an absolute separation between archival details and mere forgeries, but also because the Ireland case, too, takes an unexpectedly sexual turn. On the surface the forgeries may appear to be less interested in Shakespeare's sexuality than with contentions about authorship and authenticity, including Ireland's own dreams of putting himself forward as a new young bard. But the bardolatrous environment in which the documents were produced and received was positively suffused with fears about the newly sexualized Shakespeare of the sonnets, and I will show that one particularly vociferous believer spoke for an entire generation when he refused to believe that the true-love object of the poems was male.

Once the "facts" had been unearthed and the sonnets had been "authentically" reread, in other words, then sexual conclusions—whatever they might be—would appear to be unavoidable. And yet, as I will argue in chapter 2, the complex notion of a "sodomitical" Shakespeare had actually been brewing long before its eruption in the context of Malonian Shakespeare-worship. It was, rather, a reputation that in a certain sense had only been reborn, although one kind of sodomy associated with his name had largely displaced another, earlier one. This pre-Malone Shakespeare, sometimes called W. S., was much more a sodomite with women than with men: Shakespeare the cynical wooer, the wencher, the gallant.[33] It is a reputation based not so much on the sonnets (despite the dark lady group) as on the early narrative poems, *Venus* and *Lucrece,* among Shakespeare's most popular works during his own lifetime.[34]

Yet this "other" reputation, strangely enough, has also never received the critical attention one might expect, particularly with respect to the broader and more recent cultural concerns of queer studies, perhaps because there has always been a much greater sense of urgency to explain (or celebrate) suspicions about sodomy with the fair young man of the sonnets than with any of its other forms—for example, an adulterous affair with a mistress.[35] Already by 1800 Shakespeare's sexual life was conceived in two rather different directions (unless one simply decides, and this view seems to hold sway in a great deal of popular criticism, that the "solution" to everything is bisexuality);[36] today he is a central figure in both *The Norton Anthology of English Literature* and *The Penguin Book of Homosexual Verse.* The question, however, is not to determine what his sexuality "really was," as if to uncover such a fact would in itself be a useful or meaningful piece of information (although, I suppose, in one sense it certainly might be). This caveat, of course, has never deterred anyone, from forgers to biographers and everyone in between, and although the facts are so few, exceedingly long Shakespeare biographies will surely continue to appear.[37] But this study is not really concerned with providing a list of William Shakespeare's possible sexual "orientations," the number of which would be limited only to the number of sexual orientations one could imagine. I am interested, rather, in examining the contradictory forces of Shakespearean (de)sexualization itself, which we will be able to see more fully at work in two long-standing debates that will occupy the second half of this book: the controversies over authorship and the poet's true likeness.

By questions of authorship I am not thinking primarily of the often-troubled boundaries of the Shakespeare canon (whether "Shall I Die" or *Edward III* should be attributed to him; which parts of *The Two Noble Kinsmen, Sir Thomas More, Henry VIII,* or *Titus Andronicus* are Shakespearean; the evidence of collaboration in general; and so on). One can indeed follow these debates, particularly the ones surrounding the collaborative conditions of early modern playwriting and play production, and produce very interesting results regarding questions of sexuality.[38] Chapter 3, rather, tackles the amazingly persevering claim that William Shakespeare was really a pseudonym for someone else, the candidates ranging from Francis Bacon to Queen Elizabeth. The relevant bibliography on this subject is so large as to cause dismay in even the stoutest hearts, and it may well be more extensive (or rather repetitive) than any other single aspect of Shakespeare studies—no small achievement. Yet no one, so far as I know, has ever attempted to account for or even summarize this tumultuous controversy from the perspective of "Shakespeare's" sexuality.

We will see, in fact, that sexual details, sodomitical or otherwise, are absolutely fundamental to the basic contours of the debate itself, and that the same anxieties that continue to plague standard biographies must be confronted or explained away in substitute narratives featuring alternative authors like Bacon, Marlowe, or the earl of Oxford. *Someone* wrote the plays and the sonnets, replete with bawdy jokes, gender crossing and recrossing, sexual "reversals," and sodomitical innuendo of many kinds. Not surprisingly, then, Bacon, Oxford, and the other candidates end up being desexualized just as Shakespeare is, and one is indeed hard-pressed to find an anti-Stratfordian contribution that makes an attempt to confront (or even describe) the very idea of a sexual Shakespeare. On the contrary, the debate is sidetracked by relentless class bias and the impossibility that Shakespeare's plays could have been written by a common player and boor from the Stratford hinterland. This sort of prejudice is often accompanied by a presupposition (although almost never explicit) that sodomy *is* acceptable for the elite courtly class to which the real Shakespeare must belong. The irony here is that the very same sexual suggestiveness that is kept at bay in most traditional Shakespeare studies reenters as evidence for the works' true aristocratic origin. But, again, even this kind of argument usually remains underground, and I have yet to find a queer-identified critic who has argued that Bacon or somebody else is Shakespeare (although, to be sure, examples are out there somewhere).

A similar story can be told via discussions of the alleged Shakespeare portraits, another of Malone's bardolatrous obsessions that seems to die surprisingly hard. The only universally accepted likenesses are the Droeshout print on the title page of the First Folio and the half-length tomb statue in the Shakespeare monument in his parish church in Stratford. Both of these representations are posthumous (although the Droeshout may have been copied from an earlier image now lost), and their relative plainness (prints and busts aren't generally appealing to modern eyes anyway) seems to frustrate our desire to get a glimpse of Shakespeare's more "human" side. Put another way, we want him to be embodied, but we find it especially challenging to do so from within the confines of Droeshout's print or the Stratford bust. While the amount of criticism on the portraits is a great deal more manageable than parallel debates over authorship, we will see in chapter 4 the degree to which discussions of the poet's likeness also shy away from all sexual topics.

This is somewhat unexpected, perhaps, given that the traditional third-place candidate, the Chandos portrait now in the National Portrait Gallery in London, has always been considered—in one way or another—a very sexy image. This painting, one of many contenders supposedly taken from life, has regularly been characterized and indeed romanticized as showing Shakespeare the bohemian artist, with expressive eyes, slightly parted lips, and gleaming earring. But just as frequently the picture has given rise to derision, indignation, and even xenophobia (its "swarthy" complexion being associated with Italians and Jews). The fact that the Chandos might appear to show a more "human" Shakespeare, in other words, is exactly the problem, since any embodiment at all will imply the very same sexual (and racial?) possibilities that must ultimately be pushed to the margins or canceled out.

We will conclude with a short epilogue on the highly successful recent film, *Shakespeare in Love,* placing it alongside a myriad of new popular introductions to Shakespeare's life and work, in order to provide a highly encapsulated glimpse of the fate of sexual Shakespeare for today's self-described sexually "aware" general audiences. We will see that here, too, a great deal of anxiety remains, even in our purportedly "liberal" sexual contexts, since the poet/dramatist must simultaneously be a figure who is conceivably responsible for so much bawdry in the works, and yet still framable as the bard beyond time and beyond the body. Who was Shakespeare? What did he look like? What kind of a man was he? However naive or peripheral these questions may seem at first glance, they yet stand at the center of Shakespeare studies far more firmly than most of us would like to admit. To produce the authentic Shakespeare one either has to include or deny the kaleidoscopic domains of sexual reality, even as the sexuality that one does seem to "find" does not correspond very comfortably with modern preconceptions with sexual orientations. All portraits of the artist are equally grounded in the realms of fantasized forgery, whether the result is an edition, a painting, or an absent *Life,* and any of these will at some point have to confront the fact that, in the end, we really don't seem to know anything at all.

Finally, I cannot hope to encompass everything that the title of this study might be thought to include or suggest. The following chapters have been composed, rather, with an eye to their separability, and I would like to offer them as examples or highlights of a field much too large for one slim volume—but also a field that, paradoxically enough, has remained almost totally unexplored.

CHAPTER 1

Queer Sonnets and the Forgeries of William Henry Ireland

In 1795 at the age of eighteen, a young man named William Henry Ireland fabricated a series of Shakespearean forgeries that, for the space of few months at least, were enthusiastically believed by both the educated English public and some of the leading scholars and critics of the day. By the end of his meteoric career, Ireland's portfolio of impostures included legal deeds, promissory notes, receipts, letters both to and from Shakespeare, a portrait sketch, and even a "lost" tragedy, *Vortigern*, written in the bard's own hand. After his exposure, Ireland tried to defend his actions, first in a pamphlet and then in a rather "improved" version in his 1805 *Confessions,* and he reiterated the story many times before his inconspicuous demise thirty years later.[1] In each instance, we are presented with the figure of a teenager driven mainly by a desire to please his unresponsive and greedy father, Samuel Ireland—antiquarian, book publisher, fervent bardolator—who often reminded his son that he would gladly give away his entire collection in return for just one authentic example of Shakespeare's handwriting.[2] The story becomes more and more incredible as it unfolds, and it becomes increasingly clear that Ireland's eventual aim, which failed disastrously, was to put himself forward as a new young bard. The few pieces of modern criticism devoted to him give us a fuller picture of the scandal, both of the moral and psychological character of the perpetrator(s), and of the cultural and literary climate in which so many men and women willingly believed in the impostures.[3] In some sense the papers are interesting wish fulfillments, late-eighteenth-century bardolatrous versions of what the poet "should" have been like (the sophisticated and urbane author of *Romeo and Juliet* or *Venus and Adonis,* or the passionate gentleman depicted in the Chandos portrait, particularly popular in the eighteenth century),[4] and not, in other words, the poet of the distinctly uncomplimentary legends that had by this time grown up around him: deer poacher, holder of horses, Stratford yokel. Ireland thus furnishes a more Protestant "Profession of Faith" to counteract the disturbingly Catholic or "papist" one left by the poet's father; a gushing and proto-romantic love letter to "Anna Hatherrewaye" (including an effusive poem and even a lock of his hair); "Deeds of Gift" that sound much more generous and intellectual than Shakespeare's actual will; and very informal letters from Southampton and even the queen herself, which in the words of one enthusiast proved once and for all that Shakespeare was "the Garrick of his age."[5]

The documents make a certain kind of sense in 1795, in other words, but as is often the case with forgeries, it seems surprising in hindsight that anybody could actually have been fooled.[6] For the papers are ridiculously suspect on too many counts, with their dubious source in the house of an invented Mr. H., who freely gave them, one by one, to the young man (and who even began to correspond with the elder Ireland without the latter recognizing his son's own handwriting); their errors of diction and historical anachronism (a promissory note mentioning the Globe theater ten years before it was built); their laughably exaggerated "Elizabethan" spelling (in the words of Edmond Malone, "the orthography of no age whatsoever")[7]; and their often preposterous subject matter (a Deed of Gift in which the poet professes his undying gratitude to a contemporary William Henry Ireland who saved him from drowning in the Thames!). By the same token, however, the very speed with which the discoveries had been made—within the space of a couple of months only—was probably the most convincing proof for Ireland's contemporaries that the documents were real (or that they must be the work of more than one person). Actually, the praise the papers received and the ease with which each new item was accepted astonished even their maker—despite his own self-perception as a neglected poetic genius—particularly since he had produced them so quickly, and since in many cases one document often necessitated the composition of another in order to explain or correct it.

For instance, the Deed of Gift to Ireland's Elizabethan namesake included all the profits from several plays (an anachronism, since playwrights did not own their work in this way),[8] including *King Lear,* a phony manuscript version of which Ireland had just "discovered"—a ploy clearly designed both to authenticate the play itself and to provide a justification for Ireland to be able to publish or produce the treasure once it had been unearthed. An impossible coincidence, perhaps, but it was nonetheless believed, just as it was not necessarily too good to be true that this same sixteenth-century W. H. might be the same as the W. H. addressed in Thomas Thorpe's mysterious dedication of the sonnets![9] Similarly, Ireland's climactic imposture, another Deed of Gift, conveniently referred to other unauthenticated finds such as the love letter and *Vortigern,* the latter not coincidentally being in preparation for production at the Drury Lane theater. But even more audaciously, the rights to this play were (again anachronistically) granted to an unnamed and presumably illegitimate child of Shakespeare left in the care of John Heminges, fellow player and coeditor of the First Folio, thus making a number of enticing insinuations about possible family ties between Heminges and Ireland's Mr. H., or a possible connection between this child, "of whome wee have spokenn butt who muste nott be named here," and Ireland's fictive namesake.[10] In some way, in other words, the forger seems to be attempting to fashion himself as a true descendant of Shakespeare, both genealogically and artistically.

Such a plethora of ridiculous lies, however, inevitably caught up with their perpetrator, and despite the care Ireland employed to use authentic paper from the period, an ink that looked old when the documents were held before a flame, and seals cleverly remade from Elizabethan ones, Malone had little trouble demonstrating the documents' many inconsistencies and inaccuracies in his scrupulously thorough *Inquiry into the Authenticity of Certain Miscellaneous Papers* of 1796, one of the first examples of "professional" Shakespeare criticism and the chief force behind Ireland's exposure. As Malone concludes, those involved in the forgery "know nothing of the history of Shakspeare, nothing of the history of the Stage, or the history of the English Language."[11] Within the space of a few days, *Vortigern* was laughed off the stage, and there was nothing left to do but for young William Henry to confess. The elder Ireland, however, stubbornly refused to believe that his son was capable of such acts, nor of such elevated artistic creations, and continued to insist on the papers' authenticity until his death four years later.[12] William Henry went on to write many more books, sometimes pseudonymously, but was never again to rise from obscurity.

The whole case remains a fascinating and important piece of evidence relating to the history of Shakespeare-worship, which at this time was just beginning to take shape, as well as a family drama that ultimately becomes, in the words of Samuel Schoenbaum, "invested with an almost unendurable pathos."[13] But it is rather more difficult to concur with Brian Vickers that the Ireland episode, other than the fact it managed to fool so many people for a time, "has no significance for the history of the interpretation of Shakespeare."[14] I will argue that the Ireland forgeries indicate a great deal not only about the way that Shakespeare—player, playwright, poet, cultural icon—was regarded by the late eighteenth century, but also about how more modern preoccupations have grown out of the very same debates. The center of this obsession, then as now, is the Shakespeare biography, or rather lack thereof. It is by now somewhat cliché to be reminded that we know next to nothing about Shakespeare's life, that our knowledge is confined mainly to dry legal records or unsatisfying contemporary references, and that so little about him is "revealed" in his works.[15] Readers are thus forced to find their own answers for understanding the national poet, and the sonnets have predictably become a favorite site for those searching after more intimate details, since they tempt us to read in them a very provocative "story." In fact, the sheer number of controversies that have grown up around the poems is spectacular, and it is worth our while to enumerate them briefly here.[16]

I count at least ten, although they inevitably overlap somewhat, and each of them has inspired its own industry of subsequent comment. (1) Were the poems authorized by Shakespeare or published without his consent by Thomas Thorpe? If Shakespeare gave them for publication himself, why would he choose not to include any prefatory matter, such as a dedicatory letter addressed to a patron, as he had done with his earlier narrative poems? How did Thorpe acquire the manuscript? (2) Why do so few copies of the text remain (only thirteen), if Shakespeare was already famous by 1609, and why are there so few contemporary references to the poems from other writers? Does this indicate that the poems were somehow withdrawn from publication (by Shakespeare or someone else) after they appeared (because they had been pirated; because they were somehow an embarrassment), or is it merely the case that the text did not sell very well? Are thirteen copies of a quarto, in fact, an unusually large number to have survived? (3) Are the 154 poems in the correct order, or might they have been rearranged by Thorpe—thus obscuring (or creating) the poems' "story"? What kind of manuscript did Thorpe have to work from? Should modern readers try to alter the poems' arrangement in order for them to make more sense? (4) The poems were published in 1609, but what are their real dates of composition? Why would Shakespeare (or Thorpe) have waited until 1609 to publish them, presumably long after many of them were written and long after the sonnet vogue of the 1590s had passed? How do the poems fit into the once-fashionable Elizabethan genre of the sonnet sequence? What were Shakespeare's sources or major influences? (5) Are the poems autobiographical or merely fictitious, exercises in a poetic tradition? What kind of "story" do they tell? (6) Who is the "Mr. W. H." addressed in Thorpe's epigraph, and is he identical with the young man presumably addressed in the first 126 poems? (7) Who *is* this young man whom Shakespeare seems to love so dearly (and sexually)? Can he (or the "rival poet") be identified with someone from the period? (8) Do the sonnets describe a relationship that we would today call "homosexual" or merely fall into the relatively safe category of Renaissance "friendship"? How do we account for the fact that so many of the poems are addressed to a man? (9) Who is the "dark lady" addressed in the final twenty-eight poems? What "really happened" between her and the speaker? Was Shakespeare an adulterer? And lastly, we must mention the bugbear debate of them all, since it too will have a bearing on the aftermath of the Ireland forgeries and their relationship to problems of authenticity: (10) Is "William Shakespeare" merely a pseudonym for another author who wished to remain unknown, and thus are the sonnets in fact an autobiographical record of someone else? Who is Shakespeare if not the man from Stratford?

A number of these controversies are of course rather hollow and irrelevant, and it has often been lamented how many false questions and crackpot theories have grown up around the poems; as E. K. Chambers famously put it, "more folly has been written about the sonnets than about any other Shakespearean topic."[17] But the extent to which these debates depend on conjectures about Shakespeare's "real life" is extraordinary, and it is no accident that the sonnets stand at the center of this sort of biographical game. The problem hinges on the extent to which the poems can serve as "evidence" for the life of Shakespeare (or somebody else), and it is in precisely the same way that the Ireland forgeries—and the supposed letter from Queen Elizabeth, which will be our focus here—relate to these discussions. For both the impetus and the result of the documents was their presumed ability to fill in some of the large gaps that existed in the Shakespeare biography; in a letter to the *Gentleman's Magazine* of February 1795, even Malone made an appeal for more "ancient papers" that might be "illustrative of the history of this extraordinary man."[18] Indeed, Ireland describes a similar motivation for his own creations.

We have already mentioned the Profession of Faith, the letter to Anne Hathaway, and the Deeds of Gift as representative of this sort of biographical fantasy, but it is the queen's letter that unwittingly produced the most telling "story"—and the most telling response from one former believer, George Chalmers.[19] "Wee didde receive youre prettye Verses goode Masterre William through the hands off oure Lorde Chambelayne," Elizabeth is made to write, "ande wee doe Complemente thee onne theyre greate excellence." She continues: "Wee shalle departe fromme Londonne toe Hamptowne forre the holydayes where wee Shalle expecte thee withe thye beste Actorres thatte thou mayste playe before oureselfe toe amuse usse bee notte slowwe butte comme toe usse bye Tuesdaye nexte asse the lorde Leycesterre will bee withe usse. Elizabeth. R."

The letter is addressed "For Master William Shakspeare atte the Globe bye Thames." Finally, on an attached piece of paper the poet was made to add, obviously to provide an explanation for the fact that the letter itself has survived: "Thys Letterre I dydde receyve fromme mye moste gracyouse Ladye Elyzabethe ande I doe requeste itte maye be kepte withe all care possyble. Wm. Shakspeare."[20] William Henry's chaotic spelling and seeming disinterest in punctuation are just two of the more noticeable features in the forgeries, but here the chattiness of the queen is positively astonishing.[21] Malone had many other objections, however. Would Elizabeth have misspelled Leicester's name in such a way (even if standard orthography

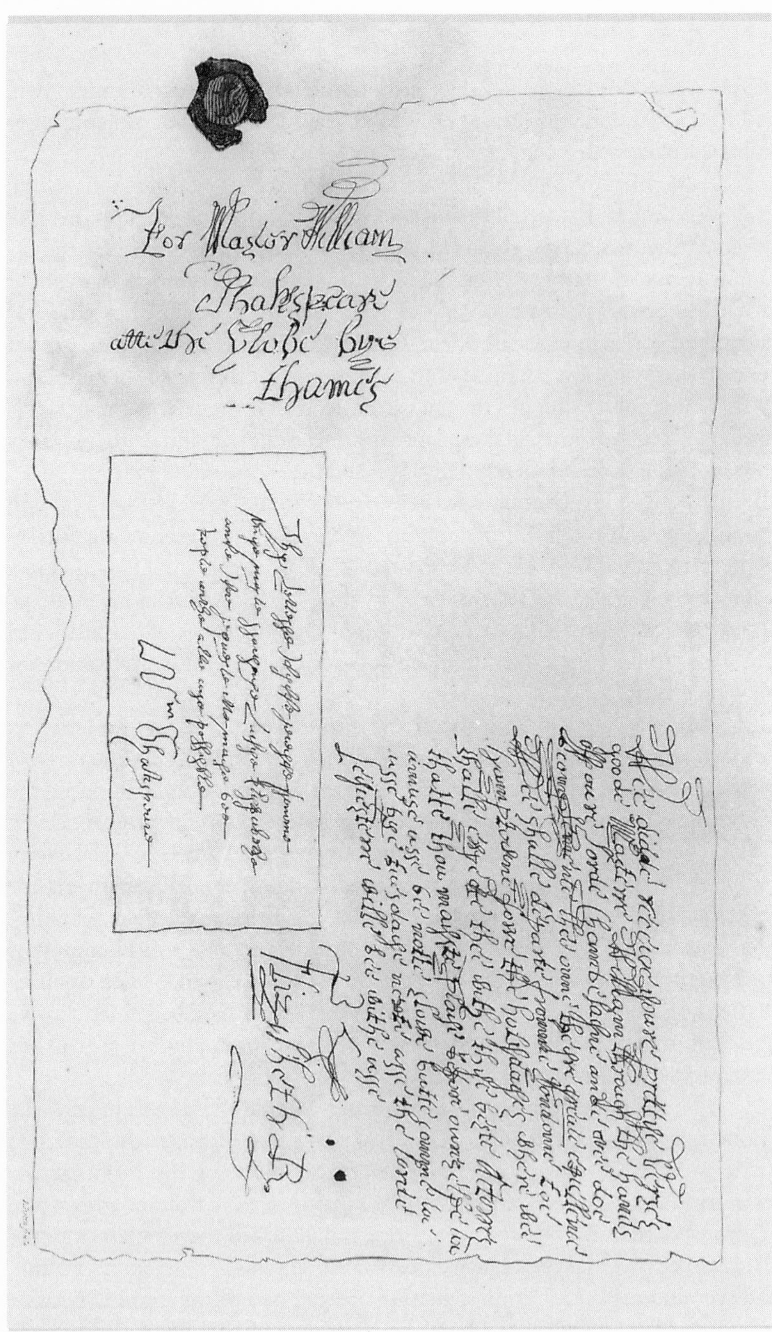

For Master William
Shakspeare
atte the Globe bye
Thames

William Henry Ireland, forged letter from Queen Elizabeth to "Master William Shakspeare atte the Globe bye Thames," thanking him for his "prettye Verses." Facsimile engraving included in Samuel Ireland, *Miscellaneous Papers and Legal Instruments under the Hand and Seal of William Shakspeare . . .* (London, 1796). By permission of the Folger Shakespeare Library.

did not yet exist), not to mention London or Hampton Court? Why should the letter have survived when so many other documents, not to mention the "prettye Verses" themselves, have not? Perhaps the reference to Leicester was designed to give the note an added air of authenticity, but since he had died in 1588 it would have to have been written when Shakespeare was at most twenty-four years old, and (unluckily) in that year the Globe did not yet exist.[22]

According to Ireland's subsequent account, the idea of a letter from the queen was suggested to him by a legendary missive from James I, which (it was hoped) might turn up with the other papers. "My principal object in the production of this letter was to make our bard appear of so much consequence in his own time as to be personally noticed by so great and politic a princess as our Elizabeth," but "as to the verses alluded to in my gracious epistle, they certainly never had existence, to the best of my knowledge."[23] But the letter had already worked its intended effect, to herald Shakespeare as "the Garrick of his age," and it was the chief piece of evidence that, in 1797, led Chalmers to posit his own theory, published in his *Apology for the Believers in the Shakspeare-Papers,* which we will need to examine in some detail: that the "prettye Verses" were none other than Shakespeare's sonnets, and that all of them were in fact addressed to the queen![24]

To be fair, when Chalmers's hypothesis is placed beside the vast legion of fantastic, ridiculous, and lunatic theories in the long and varied history of Shakespeare criticism, and that of the sonnets in particular, his conclusion might seem rather tame and perhaps even arguable.[25] It certainly ranks higher than George Elliott Sweet's contention that Elizabeth *was* "Shakespeare,"[26] but even this position could be said to grow out of the very same set of biographical problems that have plagued all readers. Chalmers simply offers another version of the "story" behind the poems' composition: essentially that Shakespeare was attempting to praise his monarch after the example of Spenser (who was quite successful in obtaining preferment in this way), and that one should read the first seventeen poems—the "procreation sonnets," which urge a young man to marry and reproduce—as in fact rhetorical proposals to the Virgin Queen. So far so good, perhaps, but Chalmers will have to perform a lot of verbal gymnastics in order to prove that all the poems are addressed to only one person, and that the rest of the sequence, especially the markedly denigrating poems in the "dark lady" group, are also designed to appeal to the queen.[27] As a matter of fact, Chalmers has little to say about these final poems.

But it is vital to understand that Chalmers does not claim that the Ireland forgeries are authentic; rather, he offers an "Apology for the Believers" in the documents, which is to say an attempt to explain why he and others *had* been fooled, and why the documents had made sense as new evidence relating to the life of the bard.[28] Chalmers's real target is not the forger at all but Malone's recently published *Inquiry*, which in Chalmers's view is too sarcastic and snobbish in its demonstrations. "If Mr. Malone had written, instead of his *Inquiry*, a pamphlet in plain prose," writes Chalmers in his preface, "stating his objections without irony, and submitting his documents without scoffs; . . . no one would have answered what few would have read; since a cheat exploded is a cheat no more" (*A*, iii). Chalmers endeavors to show just how many times this (as he felt) self-proclaimed authority on Shakespeare was misleading or mistaken; perhaps he does manage to correct Malone on a few occasions,[29] but there is also an overwhelming pointlessness to most of Chalmers's 628 pages, since, although he begins by admitting his own gullibility, he has to spend so much time proving how it might have been possible, and the tedious legalistic paragraphs that open the book concerning the distinctions between possibility and probability are hardly enlivened by the bitter attack on "the public accuser" that follows. What is really the difference if Malone's detection has turned out to be "right by chance" rather than "convincing by argument" (*A*, 123)?[30]

Let us here recall that the monarch's letter is actually rather modest when compared with some of Ireland's more reckless creations to come. Moreover, Chalmers's treatment fills only the first ninety or so pages of the book, and his theory regarding the sonnets soon gives way to other considerations. But this does not lessen the importance of that theory for the history of Shakespeare criticism, or rather the history of his sexuality, despite the fact that ridicule was both immediate and potent.[31] For Chalmers continued to assert that the poems were addressed to the queen *even after* he admitted that her letter itself was spurious. In some sense, then, his reading of the sonnets must have existed before the letter was even forged. At first glance, this might seem farfetched or illogical, since is it really likely that Chalmers could have "guessed" beforehand that Elizabeth is the poems' true addressee? Isn't it clear, in other words, that the forged letter produced the theory rather than the other way around? Perhaps his reading had not been fully or even explicitly formulated before the letter actually appeared, but there were undoubtedly certain "problems" regarding the meaning of the poems—and thus regarding Shakespeare's biography—that had been bothering readers ever since the 1609 text was restored (also by Malone). Ireland's letter, that is, merely served as a convenient means (or an excuse or a justification) to explain or unravel a particular mystery *already* in place, and we have begun to see that many of the forgeries themselves represent similar kind of "solutions."[32]

Chalmers's theory, in a word, is a response to something other than the debate over Elizabeth's letter; the main issue, then as now, is the (apparently undeniable) fact that most of the 154 poems are addressed to a man.

This has always been the Sphinx's riddle of Shakespeare sonnet criticism. Was Shakespeare engaged in a sodomitical relationship with another man? On presumably these grounds George Steevens had notoriously refused to publish the poems at all, saying that "the strongest act of Parliament that could be framed, would fail to compel readers into their service."[33]

When other early authorities broached the subject of the poems' sexual suggestiveness, it was only in order to render them somehow innocent (or completely desexualized), for the sonnets, we are told, describe not a love affair between men but only an idealized friendship (Coleridge); their praise of a young man merely represents a tradition and is not really sexual (Malone); and they are not autobiographical poems anyway (James Boswell, Jr.). Peter Stallybrass has acutely noted how in all of these comments the possibility or reality of sodomy between men is always central but never explicitly named,[34] and Chalmers's theory is clearly one more attempt to circumvent this same unnamed danger—that the bard is guilty of this particular form of sodomy—simply by showing that the addressee is really a woman. If the poems are addressed to someone of the opposite sex, in other words, then all their problems can be made to disappear, just as one would have nothing more to worry about if Shakespeare "himself" were really a woman in disguise. Chalmers is neither the first nor the last to change the gender of the addressee to suit contemporary tastes; Coleridge succumbed to the same tendency,[35] and it had also occurred in what is arguably the first "reading" of the sonnets we possess, Benson's bowdlerized edition of 1640. Hardly a marginal phenomenon or an isolated publication, however, Benson's text was the basis for all new versions of the sonnets for nearly a century and a half—until, that is, Malone.[36]

Chalmers's book is thus responding not only to Malone's *Inquiry,* but also to prevailing tastes and contemporary judgments regarding Shakespeare's poems. The need for an authoritative biography had become acute, and bardolatry naturally required a fuller picture of the newly proclaimed national poet; the Ireland forgeries helped to supply the same demand. In his *Inquiry,* Malone announced that a definitive *Life of Shakespeare* was forthcoming, and his recent edition of the poems (1790) had included a biographical sketch that was probably the first to search the sonnets for biographical evidence.[37] But utilizing the sonnets in this way also carried with it certain sexual anxieties, and it is in this very area that Malone disagreed most violently with Steevens. The infamous sonnet 20 was the main source of contention even then, for while here the poet seems to say that his "passion" for the male "master mistress" is purely platonic (since the speaker relinquishes the "prick'd . . . out" friend to the "use" or sexual pleasure of women only), this rhetorical act is achieved via the most titillating and suggestive sexual language of the entire sequence.[38] Steevens had grumbled that "it is impossible to read this fulsome panegyrick, addressed to a male object, without an equal mixture of disgust and indignation," and Malone replied with the now-familiar defense that "such addresses to men, however indelicate, were customary in our author's time, and neither imported criminality, nor were esteemed indecorous."[39] Implicitly, then, Chalmers is arguing not merely that the great Shakespeareans had not found the correct solution to the sonnets, but also that the poems could be rescued from "fulsome," "disgusting," "indignant," "indelicate," "indecorous," or indeed "criminal" readings. For if the addressee of all the poems is really the queen, Chalmers says, would it not be appropriate for Shakespeare to refer to her as his "master mistress," since she was both his "love" and his sovereign, both a woman and a prince (*A,* 51–52, 58)? Malone, he says, faulted the poems for "professing too much love . . . to a man," but when readers realize the truth "they will be happy to find that the poet was incapable of such grossness." "Ought we to wonder," he concludes, "that in performing this great operation [of praise], he should confound the sexes?" (*A,* 60–61).[40]

This seems, at best, a rather thickheaded reading, but at the same time Chalmers is fantasizing a biography for Shakespeare built up around the poems' newly understood "story" (*A,* 51):

> The fact is that Shakspeare had not leisure to write one hundred and twenty such sonnets to any man; being wholly occupied in providing for the day, which was passing over him; that the poet had no love, but a teeming wife to whom he was strongly attached by early ties; and for whom he could hardly provide by any means: Add to these circumstances that in another sonnet, Shakspeare maintains the unity of his object by saying to his idol, Elizabeth:
>
> For to no other pass my verses tend,
> Than of your graces and your gifts to tell;
> And more, much more than in my verse can sit,
> Your own glass shows you, when you look in it.
> [103.10–13]

The only thing remarkable about this (exceedingly bad) reading is that it is arguably the first of its kind, the first explicitly autobiographical reading of the sonnets in the history of Shakespeare criticism—despite the fact that Malone had initiated the trend in many of the glosses included in his 1780 and 1790 editions.[41] Moreover, Chalmers can now make any of the poems contribute to this same "story," which, circularly, the poems are said to describe. In this sense, he is also setting a precedent that will (unfortunately) be followed by so many other critics, both scholarly and otherwise. Only eleven years later the sonnets were already being described as "paint[ing] most unequivocally the actual situation and sentiments of the poet," and by 1838 there was no turning back after the appearance of a volume titled *Shakespeare's Autobiographical Poems.*[42]

But the debate between Chalmers and Malone did not end here, even though Malone, probably wisely, declined to respond. For Chalmers refused to let matters stand as they were. Rather than simply allowing the fuss over the Ireland case to run its course and be forgotten, in the way that many such controversies soon die away, two years later Chalmers produced another volume, *A Supplemental Apology for the Believers in the Shakspeare-Papers,* also more than six hundred pages, which is surely one of the oddest things about this whole rather odd affair. For the title page tells us that the volume was written in "reply to Mr. Malone's answer, which was early announced, but never published."[43] If the first *Apology* was more about Malone than about the Ireland forgeries themselves, even though they were the book's ostensible subject, the second volume does not even need a response from Malone to keep the debate alive. Chalmers now has only "news-paper paragraphs, magazine essays, and monthly criticisms" to contend with (*SA,* vi), but it hardly seems to make any difference. Moreover, having had two years to work out his initial theory in more detail, Chalmers now needs the space for his "supplemental" proofs: since, as he now argues, Spenser's *Amoretti* were addressed to Queen Elizabeth as well (an equally surprising claim), and since Shakespeare was influenced by Spenser (as was also argued in the first *Apology*), one must reread Shakespeare's poems in the light of Spenser's, which were both Shakespeare's chief model and the best evidence that Shakespeare's were also addressed to the queen (*SA,* 21). There is more than just a little circularity in this reasoning, for the main proof that Shakespeare addresses the queen is the fact that Spenser does so as well, and the main evidence that Spenser does so is his similarity to Shakespeare—not to mention the fact that the female addressee of the *Amoretti* is also idealized. As in Chalmers's first book, we are rhetorically asked to consider who else but Elizabeth could possibly fit the kind of exaggerated description found in Spenser's poems. Like Shakespeare, "it is . . . extremely improbable that Spenser, living with his Wife and family at Kilcolman . . . should have addressed such a body of Amatory Sonnets to a private Woman, whom to address in such encomiastic strains would have been dangerous in him and unsafe in her" (*SA,* 31). The shadow of sex between men may be absent here, but the biographical reading techniques are unchanged.

And yet this is not all, for once Chalmers attempts to flesh out his theory by actually examining individual poems, it is evident that such a demonstration is by no means easy to accomplish. It is all well and good to claim that the poems' many references to "he" or "him" could also refer to Elizabeth as a prince (even if this already seems a bit farfetched), but what about the poems' many erotic or bawdy details, which would seem to lose much of their rhetorical force if they were not really directed toward another man? In sonnet 20, how could the queen be "prick'd . . . out for women's pleasure," even if it were possible that she qualified as "the master mistress" of the speaker's "passion" (unless of course the poems are what we would now call lesbian, a possibility that Chalmers certainly does not entertain either)? Or when sonnet 16 suggests to the addressee that "many maiden gardens, yet unset, / With virtuous wish would bear your living flowers," how would this apply to a proposed marriage for the queen? Or in another vein, in sonnet 69, how could Shakespeare have gotten away with claiming that Elizabeth's "fair flower" had been given "the rank smell of weeds," and that she therefore "dost common grow"?[44] One could extend these questions indefinitely, but these three poems are actually used by Chalmers to prove his point (*SA*, 58–59, 70, 77). This struggle against male-male sodomy becomes panicky and even hysterical, and Chalmers is forced to resort to ever more remote interpretive claims to make his theory work.

But the real meat and substance of the argument concerns the definition of "normal" gender designations, and a rather complicated problem of what we might call gender crossing.[45] For a great many of the sonnets refer to the addressee—and sometimes the speaker himself—"as" a woman. For instance, the friend has a woman's face, heart, and eye in sonnet 20, he is compared to both Adonis and Helen in 53, and to Eve in 93 (where the speaker is also "a deceived husband"). The speaker likens himself to an unwed mother in 36, to a widowed one in 97, to Philomela in 102, and to "a careful huswife" in 143. But more generally, in terms of the whole genre of the Petrarchan sonnet sequence, one of the most interesting and unusual things about Shakespeare's poems is precisely the fact that the speaker's "mistress" is really (or at the same time) a "master," and that this male addressee is an *object* of beauty and indeed "passion." An analogous "reversal" of genders is also at work in *Venus and Adonis* and a number of poems in *The Passionate Pilgrim.* But this is also what bothers readers like Chalmers so much, and what seems to compel him to prove that all the "feminine" references to the male beloved are in fact references to a woman—or rather the queen. This last distinction is important, for if the poems already cross gender lines by associating the male addressee with a mistress, Chalmers's reading takes the addressee's "feminine" position literally by (as it were) crossing back to make the poems refer not only to a real woman, but also to someone who is "more than a woman." If the "master mistress" is the queen, we have crossed lines of rank as well as of gender. A related idea is read back onto the addressee of the *Amoretti* as well, since both poets, "in their situations as married men and in their circumstances as to wealth," certainly would not have "addressed such Sonnets to ordinary Women (and much more to ordinary Men)" (*SA*, 51). The proof (in Shakespeare) is that one cannot "apply to [a] man the feminine epithet 'tender churl,' and the womanish epithets 'unthrifty loveliness' and 'beauteous niggard'" (*SA,* 53n). Indeed it is neither fit nor proper "to apply such sentiments . . . to a man, or indeed to any woman, except Elizabeth" (*SA,* 54n). In which gender category, then, is the queen said to reside?

Chalmers's reading of sonnet 20, however, is predictably the most revealing. A number of critics have remarked how often this poem, the bawdiest and (apparently) most sodomitical of the entire sequence, at least with respect to another man, has ironically become the center of interpretations in precisely the opposite direction: most commonly that the speaker and his addressee are "just friends."[46] But if the addressee is a woman, and indeed the queen herself, the problems only intensify. "Master mistress" only means "chiefest" mistress, Chalmers says; this is perhaps fair enough, and was even suggested by Malone.[47] "A man in hue" may also refer to Elizabeth's "masculine" quality of "lofty pride," but how likely is it that the obviously bawdy phrase "prick'd thee out" merely means "marked" (*SA,* 59n)?[48] In this reading, Elizabeth is merely "marked" as a woman, and therefore she is "prick'd . . . out for women's pleasure" in the sense that she is "marked" with "the pleasure which *belongs to* woman" (*SA,* 60n; my emphasis). The "love" that the speaker gets is supposedly only that of virtue.[49] But why would the "use" of the queen, in this sense, be appropriate for other women? Chalmers says that "thy love's use" is the "treasure" of other women in the sense that "chastity is the appropriate treasure of women." If this already seems a bit hard to follow, one will wonder what the queen is "prick'd . . . out" with. "It will after all be asked, what additional circumstance was it which nature, in her doting, superadded, and which defeated the poet from possessing his master-mistress. I will not shrink from the question. . . . Elizabeth was sprung of heavenly race" (and he cites Spenser to prove it). The "one thing" added by nature is her "divine origin, or high birth"; this was "the additional circumstance that dashed all his hopes: For she was only a man in hue; and she was more than a woman, by addition" (*SA,* 60–61n). Although this reading, he claims, has the advantage of "clearing obscurities by the context" (*SA,* 61), such a tortuous theory has understandably won little support. For all of the poem's dynamic eroticism—and especially the "one thing" with which the friend is "prick'd . . . out for women's pleasure"—has been deflated or distilled into simplistic praise of the Virgin Queen. Like the friend, she may also be "more than a woman," but his/her "love's use" has been primly de-eroticized, and the bawdy jest in which the friend's "one thing" is called a "nothing"—an unmistakable sexual pun—is quietly expurgated.

It is perhaps only in this way that Shakespeare can be saved from the charge that had already been leveled against him by one of Chalmers's contemporaries: that he was "a miscreant, who could address amatory Verses to a man, 'with a romantic platonism of affection'" (cited in *SA,* 73). But now, having been "freed . . . from this stain," "darkness brightens into light, order springs out of confusion, and contradiction settles into sense" (*SA*, 73–74). Never mind that pronouns are changed from his to her and back again (for example, *SA*, 68–69), or that Chalmers's only proof is a list of "feminine" labels that "cannot be properly applied to a man": "unthrifty loveliness," "beauteous niggard," "dear my love," "outward fair," "grace of person," "beauty of eye," and so on (*SA*, 72n, 76n, 78n, 79). And how, he rather blindly asks, could a man possibly "be exhibited as an object for the eyes of men" in sonnet 16 (*SA*, 78)? Shakespeare must be saved at any cost from "the odious imputation of platonism" (*SA*, 89n), much as the fictive William Henry Ireland had been made to rescue him from the Thames. And as for the twelve-line sonnet 126, with its seemingly irrefutable male invocation ("O thou, my lovely boy"), Chalmers remarks that since the poem lacks its final two lines, "the printer had before him a very imperfect Manuscript" (*SA*, 86). This is no doubt a last resort, and from this point on the argument abruptly dies away, if it ever had any life to begin with, by apologizing for the fact that it is not possible to treat every poem in the sequence with the same level of attentiveness (*SA*, 81). This is hardly surprising, since the break occurs just when the text comes to the dark lady poems, even though it might seem necessary to "rescue" the poet from them (and her) as well.

One may wonder why we should even bother with Chalmers's theories after two hundred years. Do they reside merely in "the by-ways of eighteenth-century letters,"[50] or is it possible to argue that these thick volumes are more than just an effect of an antique milieu in which bardolatrous forgeries were so readily accepted? Although the Ireland case has received its share of analysis, far too little attention has been paid to Chalmers's involvement in the controversy, and to the manner in which his texts have much to teach us about larger critical questions—and about the effects of sodomitical sexuality in particular. In this sense, we must orient our understanding of Chalmers's response to contemporary queer studies debates, and especially to the way that the term "sodomy" was used in the early modern period.[51] The sonnets are unquestionably queer or sodomitical poems, either in terms of their (supposed) relationship with a man or a married woman, but clearly it is much more urgent for Chalmers to free Shakespeare from the possibility of same-sex desire than from an adulterous affair.[52] Just as the forged letter from Elizabeth may simply have given Chalmers an opportunity to relieve Shakespeare from the graver charge of "platonism," the whole theory about a female addressee is a belated rescue operation whose "solution" stems from a cultural anxiety about sodomy between men just as much as from the letter itself. Even in the first *Apology*, the forgeries had already moved into the background. But Chalmers also looks "backward" in the way in which he endeavors to define a normatively sexual Shakespeare that will counteract an anxiety about male-male sodomy already being felt[53]—as well as an alternative anxiety, which we will examine in the next chapter, of Shakespeare's seventeenth-century reputation as a gallant and cynical wooer of women. This is one reason why the Ireland affair is such a valuable and instructive piece of evidence for modern queer studies. Yet let us also recall that Chalmers's reading is also the first predominantly autobiographical one of Shakespeare's poems, and we should pause to ask why the initial foray into this sort of criticism should have taken this particular form rather than any other. Is it important, in other words, that the *first* autobiographical reading should have the avoidance of "platonism" at its center?

In terms of queer studies, I am reminded of the now-classic opening of Eve Kosofsky Sedgwick's *Epistemology of the Closet,* where we are told that "an understanding of virtually any aspect of modern Western culture must be, not merely incomplete, but damaged in its central substance to the degree that it does not incorporate a critical analysis of modern homo/heterosexual definition."[54] This statement seems to apply equally well to Chalmers's own form of definitional crisis, for one cannot understand what is really at stake in the eighteenth-century imaginary of (a "normal") Shakespeare without also understanding the different kinds of sodomy that bardolatry had to work against even as it was being fashioned. Moreover, the main consequence of the lack of biographical information relating to the poet was that that one had to rely so heavily on his works for an understanding of the author "himself," and, of course, a group of first-person poems was inevitably the most alluring treasure trove of all. But this also meant that one had to account for (or deny) what the poems appeared to say—that the speaker had addressed "amatory verses" to another man. But once the "true" Shakespearean text had been rediscovered, it also had to be integrated into the bard's official biography. Thus, the issue of bardolatry itself, and the question of biographical criticism in general, cannot be entirely separated from the (then newly forming) definition of a Shakespeare who was, in one way or another, *sexual.* Indeed, the homo/hetero definition was also at work in 1795—even if the terms themselves had not yet been invented—in the ostensibly desexualized terrains of bardolatry and autobiography.

Yet what of more modern, self-aware, queer readings? Can anyone really be said to have fared any better? One of the most enlightening things about Chalmers's theory, in fact, is just how representative it is as a moral vindication of Shakespeare based on his sexual "orientation," and many (if not most) later readers have also concentrated on the homo/hetero distinction despite the fact that the poems can be read or divided in a number of other ways, and indeed the real "scandal" of the sonnets might lie in their descriptions of promiscuity with a woman rather than some form of pederasty.[55] Joseph Pequigney was the first to provide a detailed review of the way in which the sonnets' male-male sexuality has been consistently whitewashed throughout their modern critical history—up to and including Stephen Booth's still-standard edition.[56] Such bowdlerization can even be accomplished under the aegis of historical or cultural difference, since if one misreads or oversimplifies Alan Bray's foundational arguments, that male "friendship" took on particular and to us surprising forms in Renaissance society,[57] or that an individual sodomite would not have conceived of him/herself in a way that would correspond to a modern "gay" (or even queer) identity,[58] wouldn't it be possible to say that the sonnets are not "gay poems" at all but something that one can no longer understand or recognize? This is part of the message of Pequigney's book, for critics' long-standing refusal to read what is "really there" in the poems blinds them to a narrative that would be not only homoerotic but "sexual in both orientation and practice."[59] Or is it, in Chalmers's words, "for impure minds only to be continually finding something obscene in objects that convey nothing obscene, or offensive, to the chastest hearts" (*SA*, 63)? Put another way, at what point does one's "dirty mind" pursue sexual puns or innuendoes that are no longer appropriate for a Renaissance poem, as if at some point such readings had crossed over into distinctly modern sexual slang?

We have already examined the speaker's preoccupation with the "one thing" (or "nothing") that the male "master mistress" is "prick'd . . . out" with in sonnet 20, but this is by no means our only example. What of the pointed references to masturbation in the opening poems, particularly in sonnets 1 and 4? The male body is provocatively described as a "sweet up-locked treasure" in sonnet 52, its value being continually renewed by the "unfolding" of phallic "imprison'd pride" (52.12). Or sonnet 56, which is an expression of the fulfillment and reawakening of sexual desire, seems (contextually speaking, at least) to refer only to male bodies. Or the bawdy language of sonnet 80 (one of the "rival poet" group) likewise seems to be an all-male affair:

> My saucy bark (inferior far to his)
> On your broad main doth willfully appear.
> Your shallowest help will hold me up afloat,
> Whilst he upon your soundless deep doth ride,
> Or (being wrack'd) I am a worthless boat,
> He of tall building and of goodly pride.
> (80.7–12)

Pequigney also points out that a number of words in sonnet 33 suggest references to fellatio,[60] even though the opening of the poem is also a rather conventional periphrasis of the dawn:

> Full many a glorious morning have I seen
> Flatter the mountain tops with sovereign eye,
> Kissing with golden face the meadows green,
> Gilding pale streams with heavenly alcumy;
> Anon permit the basest clouds to ride
> With ugly rack on his celestial face[.]
> (33.1–6)

But can this sort of erotic playfulness be accounted for merely by saying that these are examples of premodern male "friendship," or that praise of a young man is merely a well-worn tradition? Does it matter if a paradigmatic marriage poem like sonnet 116 ("Let me not to the marriage of true minds / Admit impediments") is in context not only addressed to another man, but has rhetorical force only when its homoeroticism is set against the less idealized sexuality of the dark lady poems? Or is it merely an "impure mind" that leads one astray into the dangerous and heretical world of (male-male) sodomy? Where shall we *stop* reading?

It is remarkable how many of the controversies that surround the sonnets are inextricably bound up with the issue of sexuality, and with sodomy between men in particular. Again, why should this be so? Arguably, any of the points of debate outlined above is affected by the question of the poems' queerness, precisely because of the scandalous "story"—whatever its specifics—that the speaker appears to tell. Aren't most readers tempted to say that the sonnets were unauthorized largely because of the sodomitical relationships they appear to trace, and therefore that the poems must not have been intended for publication? Similar fantasies seem to lie behind long-standing claims that they might have been suppressed soon after their publication. Or to what extent is the search for the identity of the young man, Mr. W. H., the rival poet, or the dark lady really more interested in the fact that any or all of them could have been the speaker's sexual partner(s)?[61] The point is that modern readers, too, seem titillated or disturbed—culturally speaking—by the poems' queer suggestiveness, and in this sense any "apologetic" theory, although couched in very different-sounding terms, really seems to take its cue from Chalmers.

The question of whether or not the period could be said to have had any sort of self-identified sodomitical (sub)culture remains a vexed one.[62] Whether or not Shakespeare "himself" was (or should have been) "gay," the sonnets are nonetheless queer, and perhaps a lot queerer than most modern critics have been willing to allow. But more importantly, the poems have just as frequently served as a pretext for readings that seek to leave the speaker without a sexuality at all—he and the young man are just friends; their love is only a literary tradition; the poems aren't autobiographical anyway—despite the apparently more explicit sexual language of the dark lady poems. The point is that it really makes little difference if the sonnets "really are" "gay" poems, since modern culture continues to respond to them—or apologize for them—as if they were. The poems present a certain burden or a challenge that must be answered or defended, forcing one once again to define them as "normal" in spite of the possibility or the fear that they might be the contrary. One of the most popular options is to turn them into a group of miscellaneous poems with no "story" at all. In any case, the poems tell us less about Renaissance "homosexual" identities than about what has come to be defined as normative and heterosexual in our own time. It is the roots of this kind of *production* of heterosexual normality that queer theory, of course, seeks to analyze; it represents a challenge not only to the sexual subject (in both senses) of Shakespeare's sonnets, but to normative sexuality as well, and one hopes that such analysis, much like other forms of cultural study, is capable of producing—at the very least—a less exclusionary mode of criticism.

CHAPTER 2

Shakespeare My Godfather: William Davenant and the "Pre-Queer" Bard

ALTHOUGH PERHAPS no longer the most familiar episode in that curious mixture of fact and fiction known as the biography of Shakespeare, standard treatments of the life and work of Sir William Davenant (1606–68) regularly begin with the rumor or the legend that he was Shakespeare's illegitimate son. Even *The Oxford Companion to English Literature* introduces Davenant in this way.[1] Such rumors were particularly popular in the middle of the eighteenth century, just before the sonnets were "rediscovered" by Malone in 1780, although by 1750 the Davenant story had already been in circulation for at least seventy-five years. It was tantalizingly first laid out in John Aubrey's gossipy and thoroughly unreliable manuscript notes compiled in 1681:

> His father was John Davenant a Vintner . . . , a very grave and discreet Citizen: his mother was a very beautifull woman, & of a very good witt and of conversation extremely agreable. . . . Mr. William Shakespeare was wont to goe into Warwickshire once a yeare, and did commonly in his journey lye at this house in Oxon: where he was exceedingly respected. . . . Sr. Wm. [Davenant] would sometimes when he was pleasant over a glasse of wine with his most intimate friends . . . say, that it seemed to him that he writt with the very spirit that [*sic*] Shakespeare, and . . . seemed contentended [*sic*] enough to be thought his Son: he would tell them the story as above, in which way his mother had a very light report, whereby she was called a whore. (*WS*, 2:254)[2]

It is, of course, possible that Davenant only wanted "to be thought his Son" in the sense of being a literary follower after the example of the Tribe of Ben; as Samuel Schoenbaum sensibly observes, Davenant wouldn't have "casually defamed his parents and sacrificed his legitimacy in order to maintain descent from a writer who, after all, had not yet been deified."[3] But by the same token, it is likely enough that he did little to deny such a rumor. According to Pope, the suggestion of being "more than a poetical child only of Shakspeare was common in town; and Sir William himself seemed fond of having it taken for truth" (*WS,* 2:271–72).

Indeed, Davenant may well be our first bardolator. He is also either involved in or the source of many other enduring Shakespeare legends: holding horses outside the theater, accepting a gift of £1,000 from Southampton, receiving an "amicable" letter from the king himself (*WS,* 2:266–67, 270, 284–86). He was, in short, "the acknowledged custodian of the Shakespeare tradition" and "the repository of a greater and more authentic mass of Shakespeareana than any other living man."[4] But when rumors about the bard and Mrs. Davenant were picked up by later commentators, they became both more elaborate and—as might be expected—more interested in his relationship with the beautiful, witty, and agreeable innkeeper's wife. In 1698, Charles Gildon wondered whether the bard's regular visits to Oxford were "for the beautiful mistress of the house or the good wine."[5] Even Anthony Wood, whose staid entry on Davenant, in 1691, declined to repeat so many of Aubrey's insinuations (the sentence referring to Mrs. Davenant as a whore was even crossed out, perhaps by Wood himself), continued to describe her as "a very beautiful woman, of a good wit and conversation" (*WS,* 2:258). Nicholas Rowe's *Life* (1709) doesn't mention the story at all, claiming that "what particular Habitude or Friendships [Shakespeare] contracted with private Men, I have not been able to learn" (*WS,* 2:267). But in the same year, a diary entry by Thomas Hearne added plenty of new grist for the rumor mill:

> 'Twas reported by Tradition in Oxford that Shakespear as he us'd to pass from London to Stratford upon Avon . . . always spent some time in ye Crown Tavern in Oxford, which was kept by one Davenant who had a handsome Wife, & lov'd witty Company. . . . He had born to him a Son who was afterwards Christen'd by ye Name of Wm. who prov'd a very Eminent Poet, and was knighted (by ye name of Sr. William Davenant) and he said Mr. Shakespear was his God-father & gave him his name. (In all probability he got him.) 'Tis further said that one day going from school a grave Doctor in Divinity met him, and ask'd him, *Child whither art though going in such hast?* to wch the child reply'd, *O Sir my God-father is come to Town, & I am going to ask his blessing.* To wch the Dr. said, *Hold Child, you must not take the name of God in vaine.* (*WS,* 2:269–70)

The godfather story, although hardly hilarious, seems to have had special appeal for the mid-eighteenth century, when it was repeated with small variations in anecdotal manuscripts by Joseph Spence, William Oldys, and Joseph Wight—all of whom refer to Pope (who cites actor Thomas Betterton) as their source (*WS,* 2:272, 277–78, 284). William Chetwood was the first to allude to the scandal in print, in 1749, asserting that "Sir William Davenant was by many, suppos'd the natural Son of Shakespear" (*WS,* 2:285).

But then the tale seems to have died away just as quickly as it came. Steevens and Malone were well acquainted with it, but only Malone included it in an appendix of "Additional Anecdotes of the Life of Shakespeare" for his 1790 edition.[6] Thereafter, the affair was driven to the periphery of Shakespeare studies, ironically returning to biographies of Davenant only. Sir Walter Scott made use of it in a novel of 1826, in which "there were no bounds to [Mrs. Davenant's] complaisance for men of genius,"[7] but for the most part the legend was rarely taken seriously again. It is not merely a coincidence that this is exactly the same period when, as we saw in our last chapter, a "gay Shakespeare" was born.

Why, then, did the story become marginalized only at this particular time? Wouldn't it, from a certain perspective, seem far preferable to that other, newer reputation of having written a group of love poems to another man—especially since biographical information about Shakespeare had always been so frustratingly scarce, and since the situation was increasingly exacerbated by the growth of bardolatry as the eighteenth century progressed? Is this simply a case where, in Stephen Orgel's apt phrasing, "the love of men for men . . . appears less threatening than the love of men for women, [since] it had fewer consequences, it was easier to desexualize, [and] it figured and reinforced the patronage system"?[8] If there was so much fuss over Shakespeare's same-sex "amatory verses" in the 1790s, why not gleefully "return" to the legend of the godfather story and others like it, in order to rescue him from the dangerous specter of sodomy with another man?

Clearly, the situation is not so simple, and this is not merely a question of deciding on one or the other sexual "orientation" for Shakespeare, the whole idea of which would also be quite alien with respect to the period(s) in question. For the real problem here seems to lie in the fact that Shakespeare was sexual *at all*, and the contention that he was Davenant's biological father seemed no more "preferable" than the idea that he had addressed sonnets to a male lover. Surely, it is also not enough to say that editors simply refused to believe in this particular scandal's veracity, since other equally sensational and potentially embarrassing legends about poaching deer or holding horses were almost universally repeated. When Oldys reported having found an anonymous version of the godfather story in a 1630 book of jests by John Taylor (*WS*, 2:282), perhaps the Davenant one began to appear as nothing more than the distant echo of an old joke: "A boy, whose mother was noted to be one not overloden with honesty, went to seeke his godfather, and enquiring for him, quoth one to him, Who is thy godfather? The boy repli'd, his name is goodman Digland the gardiner. Oh, said the man, if he by thy godfather, he is at the next alehouse, but I fear thou takest God's name in vain" (*WS*, 1:573–74). But the discovery obviously didn't deter Oldys himself, and when he inquired of Pope why he had declined to publish such "choice fruits of observation" in his 1723–25 edition, Pope discreetly replied that "there might be in the garden of mankind such plants as would seem to pride themselves more in a regular production of their own native fruits, than in having the repute of bearing a richer kind of grafting" (*WS*, 2:277–78). In other words, it might be better if this particular item, which Wight had described as being "generally supposed or whispered in Oxford" (*WS*, 2:284), were left unmentioned, even if Pope, too, hardly seems to have had any qualms about offering it in conversation. Was it in fact even worse, or harder to explain away, than the apparent story of the sonnets?

As the godfather legend became more and more about Shakespeare rather than Davenant, more and more about the national poet rather than a mere adapter of his inviolate masterpieces, it inevitably became more and more concerned with imaginary reconstructions of the personality of the bard himself and his relationship with the vivacious Mrs. Davenant. But there is also an accompanying need to apologize for his apparently loose moral character and indeed sexual impropriety. Perhaps, as Margreta de Grazia has suggested, even in the sonnets the real scandal concerned the dark lady's "promiscuous womb" and not the young man.[9] One could, of course, always blame the woman herself as being of "very light report" (Aubrey), "noted to be one not overloden with honesty" (Taylor). Or one could attribute to Shakespeare an overpowering charisma, as in Walter Whiter's 1794 *Specimen of a Commentary on Shakespeare:* "The truth is, that the *great beauty* and *sprightly wit* of the lady would easily afford a subject of scandal to the censorious, when the *melancholy gravity* of her husband was contrasted with the pleasantry, the accomplishments, and the genius of the *gentle Shakespeare.*"[10]

It may be that Shakespeare really was Davenant's godfather, although even this idea could have been influenced by another legend mentioned in at least two manuscripts from about 1650: that Shakespeare was godfather to one of Jonson's children (*WS*, 2:243, 247).[11] Rumors and legends tended to mix together anyway, making it difficult to determine the point at which any one of them might trail off into the realms of fantasy. Yet whatever the truth about the scandal, whether it embarrassed biographers or simply strained their credulity, it is vital to understand that as a legend it fits quite well with a certain reputation surrounding Shakespeare that one might say traces back to the very earliest allusions that have come down to us. This is a mythology that *precedes* the gay or rather queer Shakespeare, author of (for example) apparently introspective and homoerotic first-person sonnets. Although queer moments can indeed be found throughout the Shakespeare canon,[12] the sonnets have been the focus of nearly all biographical interpretations since Malone first reprinted the 1609 quarto text in 1790 (as we discussed in chapter 1). Yet what we still need to understand is a very different idea of

"Shakespeare the man" already in circulation before the sonnets were even published: a character for whom the suggestion of having an illegitimate child could be incorporated without difficulty. This is a personality that appears to grow out of his earliest published work, namely the narrative poems, and one of the most startling facts for the modern reader is to learn that Shakespeare's early fame seems to have been based just as much—if not more—on his poems as on his plays.

The measure of this popularity is hard to gauge, since on the one hand playwriting was viewed as a much less respectable literary activity, and on the other hand authorship of a play was a much more fluid and flexible concept than it is today. Plays were owned by the companies that produced them and not by their authors, and the vast majority were also collaboratively written, revised, and performed before they were ever printed (if indeed they were). Most of these were then published anonymously or with more than one author listed on the title page. Shakespeare's name does not even appear on a play until the 1598 quarto of *Love's Labour's Lost,* where the text is described as being "newly corrected and augmented" by him.[13] Yet the name William Shakespeare is proudly, explicitly, and even ostentatiously appended to the obsequious dedications to Southampton that precede the narrative poems *Venus and Adonis* (1593) and *The Rape of Lucrece* (1594). As Hyder Rollins puts it, Shakespeare "apparently expected that his permanent reputation as a man of letters would rest upon *Venus, Lucrece,* and possibly the *Phoenix and Turtle.*"[14] Moreover, *Venus* and *Lucrece* were extremely influential and went through multiple editions during Shakespeare's lifetime (at least ten for *Venus,* six for *Lucrece*). Rollins includes lengthy commentary on the contemporary vogue of the two poems,[15] and if one consults collections like *The Shakspere Allusion-Book,* one can see that before his death in 1616 there were surprisingly numerous references to *Venus* or to *Lucrece.* This is particularly evident for the 1590s, when the poems were first published, even though a number of extremely popular plays date from the same period (the *Henry VI* plays, both parts of *Henry IV, Romeo and Juliet, Richard II, Richard III, Love's Labour's Lost,* and so on), and the poems' popularity remained strong even after the First Folio was printed in 1623. According to totals given in the *Allusion-Book,* quantitatively dubious though they may be, *Venus* comes in fourth place and *Lucrece* sixth of all references to Shakespeare's works before 1700, and before 1650 *Venus* even takes second (*AB,* 2:540).[16] E. A. J. Honigmann has pointed out that "apart from Greene's citation of a line from *3 Henry VI,* all but two of the early tributes to Shakespeare's works before 1598 are to *Venus and Adonis* and *Lucrece.*"[17] Only at the end of the seventeenth century was Shakespeare described as "the Great Genius of our English Drama" (*AB,* 2:282), and by then the poems are barely mentioned in lists of his works (for example, *AB,* 2:422). In 1709 Rowe published just the plays, and by 1810—after the quarto text of the sonnets had reappeared—the narrative poems are erroneously described as "hav[ing] never been favourites with the public."[18] Even today one often gets the impression that they are included in editions merely for the sake of completeness.

But exactly what kind of reputation did Shakespeare acquire during this early period? One of our first references is a ribald and sensational story in John Manningham's diary from 1602:

> Upon a tyme when Burbidge played Rich. 3. there was a Citizen grewe soe farr in liking with him, that before shee went from the play shee appointed him to come that night unto hir by the name of Ri: the 3. Shakespeare overhearing their conclusion went before, was intertained, and at his game ere Burbidge came. Then message being brought that Rich. the 3d. was at the dore, Shakespeare caused returne to be made that William the Conquerour was before Rich. the 3. (*AB*, 1:98)

Tales about the libidinous atmosphere of the theater were evidently something of a cultural stereotype; a satirical character sketch of a player from 1628 quips that "waiting women Spectators are over-eares in love with him, and Ladies send for him to act in their Chambers."[19] But in Shakespeare's case, it is also likely that such biographical delicacies were themselves an effect of his early notoriety as the author of *Venus* and *Lucrece.* Although Aubrey also noted that Shakespeare "was not a company keeper" and "wouldn't be debauched" (*WS,* 2:252), this information does not seem to have been used when writing the poet's life, as if it had been discarded precisely because it failed to fit a preconceived idea of the passionate bard. Indeed, there are a great many references and allusions that indicate that in terms of his literary output, Shakespeare was above all known as a poet of love—and by the first decade of the seventeenth century, as a poet specifically versed in love's discourse and the arts of verbal seduction. This fame may also help to explain why the sonnets were even published in 1609, in a presumably unauthorized edition, long after the vogue for them had come to an end.[20]

Aside from the announcement in the dedication to *Venus* that the "first heire of [his] invention" would be followed by "some graver labour" like *Lucrece,* it is clear that the two poems are also meant to complement each other in terms of their differing registers of erotic rhetoric and its attendant ironies (Venus woos Adonis but fails to persuade him and he is killed; Tarquin woos Lucrece but rapes her instead and feels immediate guilt and shame).[21] As John Lane put it in 1600:

> When chast *Adonis* came to mans estate,
> *Venus* straight courted him with many a wile;
> *Lucrece* once seene, straight *Tarquine* laid a baite,

With foule incest her bodie to defile:
Thus men by women, women wrongde by men,
Give matter still unto my plaintife pen. (*AB*, 1:71)

Early commentators tended to stress some combination of the poems' stylistic "sweetness," apparently a cliché term from the very beginning, as well as their striking treatments of carnal passion. A marginal note in 1595 refers to "All praise worthy Lucrecia," "Sweet Shakspeare," and "Wanton Adonis" (*AB*, 1:23). Richard Barnfield, whose *Affectionate Shepherd* (1594) and *Cynthia* (1595) contain some of the earliest imitations of Shakespeare's narrative poetry, also praises his "hony-flowing Vaine" in 1598 (*AB*, 1:17–20, 51). John Weever, another early imitator, composes an epigram on "Honie-tong'd *Shakespeare*" in 1599:

Rose-checkt *Adonis* with his amber tresses,
Faire fire-hot *Venus* charming him to love her,
Chaste *Lucretia* virgine-like her dresses,
Prowd lust-stung *Tarquine* seeking still to prove her:
Romeo-Richard; more, whose names I know not,
Their sugred tongues, and power attractive beuty
Say they are Saints, althogh that Sts they shew not
For thousands vowes to them subjective dutie:
They burn in love thy children *Shakespear* het [heated] them,
Go, wo[o] thy Muse more Nymphish brood beget them.
(*AB*, 1:24)

The sonnets (and the appended *Lover's Complaint*), at least some of which must have been written during the same period, could be described in much the same way. In 1598, Francis Meres refers to "mellifluous & hony-tongued" Shakespeare's "sugred Sonnets," along with *Venus, Lucrece,* and a number of plays (*AB*, 1:46). We know that at least two of the sonnets were in circulation by 1599, since they appear in that year at the beginning of a collection published under Shakespeare's name called *The Passionate Pilgrim.* And in 1607, William Barksted wrote a "prequel" to *Venus* tellingly called *Myrra, the Mother of Adonis, or Lustes Prodegies.*[22]

Sweet, honeyed, sugary, rosy, fiery-hot, charming, lust-stung, attractive, wanton, passionate, nymphish, burning in love—these are the adjectives that quickly become associated with Shakespeare's poetic style. As Thomas Freeman notes in a sonnet "To Master W. Shakespeare" in 1614, "vertues or vices theame to thee all one is: / Who loves chaste life, there's *Lucrece* for a Teacher: / Who list read lust there's *Venus* and *Adonis,* / True modell of a most lascivious leatcher" (*AB*, 1:245). Shakespeare's poetic work, and

Venus and Adonis in particular, coincided with a vogue for highly eroticized Ovidian verse (whether he initiated or merely followed the trend), the most common theme being passionate desire—wooing or being wooed—and as in Weever's poem, dramatic characters like Romeo and Richard are included in the same category. His figures are hardly saintly, yet "thousands [vow] to them subjective dutie."

Perhaps the clearest indication of this popularity can be found in the many parodies of Shakespeare's erotic language. In one of three *Parnassus* plays produced at Cambridge University between 1598 and 1601, a simpleton tries to court a lady by inaccurately quoting from *Venus* and *Romeo.* "Let this duncified worlde esteeme of Spencer and Chaucer," he bombastically declares, "I'le worshipp sweet Mr. Shakspeare, and to honoure him will lay his Venus and Adonis under my pillowe." In the same play, "Mr. Shakspear's veyne" is pilloried in a ludicrous stanza in praise of Venus:

> Faire Venus, queene of beutie and of love,
> Thy red doth stayne the blushinge of the morne,
> Thy snowie necke shameth the milkwhite dove,
> Thy presence doth this naked worlde adorne;
> Gazinge on thee all other nymphes I scorne.
> When ere thou dyest slowe shine that Satterday,
> Beutie and grace muste sleepe with thee for aye!
> (*AB*, 1:68)

A few years later, Thomas Heywood's *The Fair Maid of the Exchange* (1607) presents a fatuous wooer who declares that he "never read any thing but *Venus* and *Adonis.*" "Why thats the very quintessence of love," his encourager replies, "if you do remember but a verse or two" (*AB*, 1:177–78). In Lewis Machin and Gervase Markham's *The Dumb Knight* (1608), a lawyer's clerk is discovered reading and quoting from the same poem, which he calls "maides philosophie" and the "best booke in the world" (*AB*, 1:188). Stock comic figures in James Shirley's *The Ball* (1632), Lewis Sharpe's *The Noble Stranger* (1640), and Thomas Durfey's *The Virtuous Wife* (1680)—and surely there are more examples than these—all refer to or cite *Venus and Adonis* (*AB*, 1:360, 448, 2:256).

Not all early allusions are complimentary. "Almost from the first they fall into two fairly well defined groups," Rollins remarks, "on the one hand are the writers who lavish praise almost without qualification; on the other, those who find the poems an invitation to loose living or bawdry."[23] One of the earliest criticisms might be Gabriel Harvey's marginal note from around 1600, now lost, alleging that "the younger sort take much delight in Shakespeare's Venus and Adonis; but his Lucrece, and his tragedy of Hamlet,

Prince of Denmarke, have it in them to please the wiser sort" (*AB*, 1:56). A university wit in the *Parnassus* plays comments that Shakespeare's "sweeter verse" would be better if "a graver subject him content, / Without loves foolish lazy languishment" (*AB*, 1:69, 102). John Davies remarks around 1611 that "fine wit is shew'n" in *Venus and Adonis* (if it is indeed Shakespeare's poem that is being referred to), "but finer twere / If not attired in such bawdy Geare." The "Art of Love" in such a work, he adds, is merely "how to subtilize" (*AB*, 1:220). In a satire by Richard Brathwait from 1615, a courtesan uses very Shakespeare-like language when offering herself to the speaker:

> Ile be thy *Venus*, pretty Ducke I will,
> And though lesse faire, yet I have farre more skill,
> In Loves affaires: for if I *Adon* had,
> As *Venus* had: I could have taught the lad
> To have beene farre more forward then he was,
> And not have dallied with [s]o apt a lasse.
> (*AB*, 1:256)

In 1622, one can also read of a lecherous man who would "after supper . . . reade a little of *Venus* and *Adonis*, the jests of *George Peele*, or some such scurrilous booke: for there are few idle Pamphlets printed in *England* which he hath not in the house" (*AB*, 1:290). And Peele's jest book itself (1607) refers to a tapster who "was much given to Poetry: for he had ingrossed the Knight of the Sunne, *Venus* and *Adonis*, and other Pamphlets which the strippling had collected together" (*AB*, 1:171).

A further aspect of the poems' early reception (and again, especially with regard to *Venus and Adonis*) is the idea that they were popular but dangerous reading for women. In Middleton's *A Mad World, My Masters* (1608), a newly married husband boasts that he has "conveyed away all [his wife's] wanton pamphlets; as *Hero and Leander*, *Venus and Adonis;* O, two luscious marrow-bone pies for a young married wife!" (*AB*, 1:189). Brathwait's *The English Gentlewoman* (1631) mentions *Venus* as one of several "unfitting Consorts for a Ladies bosome" (*AB*, 1:354), and in *The English Gentleman* (1630), he also laments:

> alas; to what height of licentious libertie are these corrupte times growne? When that *Sex*, where Modesty should claime a native prerogative, gives way to foments of exposed loosenesse; by not only attending to the wanton discourse of immodest Lovers, but carrying about them (even in their naked Bosomes, where chastest desires should only lodge) the amorous toyes of *Venus* and *Adonis:* which Poem, with others of like nature, they heare with such attention, peruse with such devotion, and retaine with such delectation, as no subject can equally relish their unseasoned palate, like those lighter discourses. (*AB*, 430n)

In *The Converted Courtesan* (1635), Thomas Cranley describes the title character's room as containing:

> a heape of bookes of thy devotion
> Lying upon a shelfe close underneath,
> Which thou more think'st upon then on thy death.
> They are not prayers of a grieved soule.
> That with repentance doth his sinnes condole.
> But amorous Pamphlets, that best likes thine eyes,
> And Songs of love and Sonets exquisit.
> Among these *Venus,* and *Adonis* lies,
> With *Salmacis,* and her Heraphrodite:
> *Pigmalion's* there, with his transform'd delight.
> (*AB,* 1:398)

One of the "sorrows of Cornelius," in Thomas Randolph's *Cornelianum Dolium* (1638), is that his daughter carries "wanton" *Venus and Adonis* in her bosom and has learned things from it that she shouldn't know ("*Venerem* etiam & *Adonidem,* petulantem satis Librum / In sinu portat, eoque multò peritior evasit / Quàm probae necesse est") (*AB,* 1:430). Finally, John Johnson's *The Academy of Love* (1641) includes, in Love's library, the poet Shakespeare, "who (as *Cupid* informed me) creepes into the womens closets about bed time, and if it were not for some of the old out-of-date Grandames (who are set over the rest as their tutoresses) the young sparkish Girles would read in *Shakespeere* day and night, so that they would open the Booke or Tome, and the men with a Fescue in their hands should point to the Verse" (*AB,* 1:471).[24]

Both Schoenbaum and G. E. Bentley remind us that not all these allusions necessarily refer to Shakespeare rather than to another poet or to the stories of Venus or Tarquin in general.[25] Those that mention Venus and Lucrece in the same breath seem indisputably Shakespearean.[26] Yet it is remarkable the degree to which, as a group, the comments fit with a certain *idea* of Shakespeare as a love poet, an idea that began to grow up around him even in the early 1590s. Whatever the truth of Schoenbaum's contention that "scattered references to Shakespeare, many of them from manuscript sources, hardly add up to a very impressive testimonial to his contemporary reputation,"[27] it is the fashion for Shakespearean poetry itself that is important and not to what degree he rather than someone else really stands at the center of it. Indeed, some of our most revealing evidence comes from pseudonymous or dubious works, which have been unjustly ignored in this context, such as *The Passionate Pilgrim* and the anonymous *Willobie His Avisa* (1594). The preface to *Willobie* actually contains the earliest printed reference to Shakespeare by name:

> Though *Collatine* have deerely bought,
> To high renowne, a lasting life,
> And found, that most in vaine have sought,
> To have a *Faire,* and *Constant* wife,
> Yet *Tarquyne* pluckt his glistering grape,
> And *Shake-speare,* paints poore *Lucrece* rape.
> (19)[28]

According to its preface, *Willobie* was found among the papers of one Henry Willobie, but published by his friend Hadrian Dorrell (5). It tells of five "trials" or temptations of a chaste wife named Avisa, who resolutely refuses all of her wooers. A very popular work, it appears to have gone through six editions by 1635.

It is important to recognize that this very theme of rhetorical resourcefulness—a series of would-be suitors who unsuccessfully try every available means to woo a steadfastly chaste wife—accords with a larger body of contemporary amatory verse that also includes, and perhaps features, Shakespeare's narrative poems. This is not merely because *Willobie* shares a certain thematic similarity with Shakespeare's work (its editor even concluding that "*Willobie His Avisa* is the sequel to Shakespeare's *Lucrece*" [231]), but also because of a curious figure called W. S., the "familiar friend" and adviser of H. W. (or "Henrico Willobego"), Avisa's fifth and last wooer. For this W. S. is specifically described as being well versed in the arts of seduction. One would be foolish, of course, simply to assume that the initials must stand for William Shakespeare (or that H. W. is Southampton), as if no other W. S. could have existed in the late sixteenth century. But it also seems rather hasty to claim that the identification of this W. S. is nothing more than a comparatively recent aftereffect of bardolatry (the text wasn't even noticed until 1858), for the character type that W. S. represents, however colored that figure may be by four centuries of mad pursuit of ever more Shakespeareana, is remarkably consistent with a certain conception of an amorous and lusty Shakespeare that seems to begin even in the first decade of his career. This is part of the reason why the idea that W. S. is Shakespeare has seemed so attractive; as C. M. Ingleby remarked very early on in the controversy, "W. S. appears in this 'imaginary conversation' as a standard authority on Love; and assuredly Shakespeare was *the* amatory poet of the day."[29] There is also the fact that three apocryphal plays were published as "By W. S."—in 1595 (even before the publication of a play with Shakespeare's full name), 1602, and 1607—all of which were included in the Third Folio of 1664.[30]

Admittedly, it is difficult to decide which of these preceded the other, the figure of W. S. or an incipient myth about William Shakespeare as a W. S. figure, and there was certainly enough overlap to make such a distinction impossible to uphold in any absolute sense.[31] But we will see that it is not our only example of a related body of legends, rumors, and interpretations that quickly become associated with Shakespeare's name (even if the *Willobie* reference might have come first). It is possible, in other words, to see *Willobie* as itself an early example of Shakespearean biographical mythmaking, even if this was not its express intention, and there is evidence to suggest that even at the beginning, there was already some debate about whether its characters represented actual people and who they might be. *Willobie*'s modern editor reminds us that in 1599 it was one of several books to be "stayed" or called in by the censors (185), which implies that it was read as a contemporary satire on particular individuals. And the text itself repeatedly tempts us to wonder about just this sort of thing, not only in the way that three of the suitors are referred to only by their initials (the other two being a nobleman and a "cavaliero"), but also in the way that the first canto conveniently provides numerous clues about the twenty-year-old Avisa's real identity—that she lives in the west of England, that her father was mayor of the town, that she lives at an inn with the sign of St. George, and so on (23, 27, 121). And yet the introductory letter signed by Dorrell begins by claiming that Avisa represents no one woman in particular (5–6), and adds that few such chaste women even exist in England. Dorrell goes on to say, however, that he has "at least heard of one in the west of England" who remains "unspotted, and unconquered. . . . Whether my Author knew, or heard of any such I cannot tell, but of mine owne knowledge I dare to sweare, that I know one. A. D. that either hath, or would, if occasion were so offered, indure these, and many greater temptations with a constant mind, and setled heart" (8–10). Regarding H. W., "it seemes that . . . the author names himselfe, and so describeth his owne love, [but] I know not, and I will not bee curious." And as for the various suitors, they are "so rightly described according to their nature, that it may seeme the Author rather meant to shew what suites might be made, and how they may be answeared, then that there hath bene any such thing indeede." Yet "when I do . . . deepely consider of it, &. . . weigh every particular part, I am driven to thinke that there is some thing of trueth hidden under this shadow" (8–9).

Is it any wonder that readers would be drawn to wonder about the "solution" to all of this, beginning perhaps with the obvious supposition that Avisa and A. D. might be one and the same? There was, in fact, an almost immediate response, for in 1596 Peter Colse's *Penelope's Complaint* appeared, also cited in the modern edition of *Willobie,* which claimed to be an answer to the latter's affront to Englishwomen by "over-slipping so many praiseworthy matrons" in favor of Avisa alone, whoever she might be (234). Subsequent editions of *Willobie* included an "Apologie," also dated 1596, in which Dorrell addresses himself to "one P. C.," claiming that "there is no particular woman in the world, that was either partie or privie to any one sentence or word in that booke" (238). He goes on to give a number of arguments for the name Avisa—that it is equivalent to "non visa," that it represents chastity itself—and concludes by claiming once again that "the Author intended in this discourse, neither the description or prayse of any particular woman; nor the naming or cyphering of any particular man" (243–44). The apology is followed by a poem in praise of English ladies (245–53), which argues once again that England has virtuous wives and that Avisa is no one woman in particular.

Later readers have understandably been drawn to other matters than defending the relative chastity of the English, but despite *Willobie*'s repeated claims to the contrary, modern critics have always been drawn into the very game of "naming or cyphering" that the author both discourages and provocatively holds out to us. As with the story of Davenant the godson, however, later readers become much more interested in the figure of W. S. than in Avisa herself, at the same time hopelessly confusing literary reputation with an idea of "Shakespeare the man." As one reader argued in 1921, "beyond question he was a man of strong passions and a recognized master in the art of love, as is proved by the curious poem, 'Willobie His Avisa.' "[32] The identity of Avisa became the subject of a great deal of research and debate as well, but only after it had been resolved that W. S. was William Shakespeare. Such an identification is tempting enough, not only because of the exceptionally vivid prose section in which H. W. and W. S. are introduced, but also because of a number of seemingly irresistible theatrical metaphors:

> H. W. being sodenly infected with the contagion of a fantasticall fit, at the first sight of *A,* pyneth a while in secret griefe, at length not able any longer to indure the burning heate of so fervent a humour, bewrayeth the secresy of his disease unto his familiar frend W. S. who not long before had tryed the curtesy of the like passion, and was now newly recovered of the like infection; yet finding his frend let bloud in the same vaine, he took pleasure for a tyme to see him bleed, & in steed of stopping the issue, he inlargeth the wound, with the sharpe rasor of a willing conceit, perswading him that he thought it a matter very easy to be compassed, & no doubt with payne, diligence & some cost in time to be obtayned. Thus this miserable comforter comforting his frend with an impossibilitie, eyther for that he now would secretly laugh at his frends folly, that had given occasion not long before unto others to laugh at his owne, or because he would see whether an other could play his part better then himselfe, & in vewing a far off the course of this loving Comedy, he determined to see whether it would sort to a happier end for this new actor, then it did for the old player. But at length this Comedy was like to have growen to a Tragedy, by the weake & feeble estate that H. W. was brought unto, by a desperate vewe of an impossibility of obtaining his purpose. (115–16)

Modern decipherers have been quick to assume that W. S. had at one time been in love with Avisa as well (the whole thing becoming once again more about Shakespeare than anyone else), but it is equally likely that W. S.'s experiences are supposed to lie elsewhere. "Yonder comes my faythfull frend," H. W. begins, "That like assaultes hath often tryde, / On his advise I will depend" (119). "Well, say no more: I know thy griefe," W. S. replies,

> And face from whence these flames aryse,
> It is not hard to fynd reliefe,
> If thou wilt follow good advyse:
> She is no Saynt, She is no Nonne,
> I thinke in tyme she may be wonne.
> (121)

While certainly this is rather tired and cliché language, it is significant that there are a number of similar passages in the Shakespeare canon; Chambers suggests sonnet 41.5–6, *1 Henry VI* 5.3.78–79, *Titus Andronicus* 2.1.82–83, and *Richard III* 1.2.227–28,[33] as well as a thematically similar poem in *The Passionate Pilgrim,* which we will discuss in a moment (*WS*, 1:569). "At first repulse you must not faint," W. S. continues:

> Nor flye the field though she deny
> You twise or thrise, yet manly bent,
> Againe you must, and still reply:
> When tyme permits you not to talke,
> Then let your pen and fingers walke.
>
> Apply her still with dyvers thinges,
> (For giftes the wysest will deceave)
> Sometymes with gold, sometymes with ringes,
> No tyme nor fit occasion leave,
> Though coy at first she seeme and wielde,
> These toyes in tyme will make her yielde.
> (122)

There is more, but clearly W. S. is presented as something of a cynical cavaliero himself (to utilize a term from the poem), but instead of passing judgment on this sort of rhetoric or wondering in what way it is meant to be satirical (of Shakespeare), we need to remember that this is not the only example of such a character being in one way or another connected to the bard. There is also a W. S. mentioned in a nearly contemporary manuscript by J. M. called *The Newe Metamorphosis* (c. 1610):

who hath a lovinge wife & loves her not,
he is no better then a witlesse sotte;
Let such have wives to recompense their merite,
even Menelaus forked face inherite.
Is love in wives good, not in husbands too?
why doe men sweare they love then, when they wooe?
it seemes 't is true that W. S. said,
when once he heard one courting of a Mayde—
Beleve not thou Mens fayned flatteryes,
Lovers will tell a bushell-full of Lyes!
(*AB*, 1:89)

This W. S. is not himself the purveyor of antifeminist counsel, but rather a figure or an author who is once again cited as being able to see through male hypocrisy. The compilers of the *Allusion-Book* wonder whether this W. S. and the one in *Willobie* might be the same, and they also suggest a parallel with Polonius's advice to Ophelia (*Hamlet* 1.3.123–31). But it is not clear why he should be described as having once overheard rather than written about such deceptive wooing, a detail that places the whole episode more in the realm of personal experience than the citation of a literary authority.

The Passionate Pilgrim is a group of twenty poems published as "By W. Shakespeare" in 1599, including three poems taken from *Love's Labour's Lost* (4.2.105–18, 4.3.58–71, 99–118) (a quarto version of the play, "By W. Shakespere," having already appeared in 1598). The text begins with two alternative and presumably earlier versions of Shakespeare's sonnets 138 and 144. Although the publisher was clearly trying to flesh out the few authentic poems that he could obtain by including a pastiche of other verses on amatory subjects, it is clear that as a group they could be successfully attributed to some idea of "W. Shakespeare" in the contemporary marketplace. Moreover, when another (third) edition was published in 1612, "newly corrected and augmented," a generic subtitle was added, *Certaine Amorous Sonnets betweene Venus and Adonis.*[34] Once again it is clear that Shakespeare was a well-known figure (and still recognized as such in 1612) who specialized in a particular sort of erotic poetry. The poems dramatizing the Venus and Adonis story (poems 4, 6, 9, 10, and 11) are certainly the most bawdy and suggestive—with Venus "touch[ing] him here and there" (4.7), Adonis standing "starke naked on the brookes greene brim" (6.10), and so on—and they are clearly influenced by Shakespeare's poem on the same subject, as well as by Marlowe's *Hero and Leander,* first published in 1598. One of the most salacious passages occurs at the end of the ninth poem, also a clear variation or imitation of the eroticism in Shakespeare:

Once (quoth she) did I see a faire sweet youth
Here in these brakes, deepe wounded with a Boare,
Deepe in the thigh a spectacle of ruth,
See in my thigh (quoth she) here was the sore,
She shewed hers, he saw more wounds then one,
And blushing fled, and left her all alone.
(9.9–14)

Criticism of this poem, what little there is, has been distracted by authorship questions and a line that appears to be missing. And yet a poem that peeps at Venus's unspecified "wounds" was evidently readily ascribable to Shakespeare, just as the whole collection (with the exception of one or two poems) is still regularly included in editions of the complete works.

It is revealing that Shakespeare's name was removed from the title page in 1612 after Heywood protested because the third edition also included nine poems lifted from his *Troia Britanica* (1609). In a preface to his *Apology for Actors* (1612), he implies that Shakespeare, too, was "much offended" with the publisher who "presumed to make so bold with his name." In other words, it seems to be the case that for thirteen years, and through two editions, the twenty original poems were unproblematically accepted as being "By W. Shakespeare," whoever might have written them, and indeed that the third edition might also have gone unremarked if the borrowing had not been so obvious—or if the author in question had not complained.[35]

Perhaps the most revealing poem of all, in terms of Shakespeare's early reputation, is the eighteenth. Two manuscript versions of uncertain date also exist, one of them signed "W. S." in a later hand, which may indicate that the poem had already been in circulation by the time *The Passionate Pilgrim* appeared.[36] A title, "Wholesome counsell," is also provided in John Benson's 1640 edition of the *Poems,* an even more ambitious pastiche "by Wil. Shakespeare," which, in addition to *The Passionate Pilgrim,* included a rearranged and sometimes altered text of the sonnets, *A Lover's Complaint, The Phoenix and Turtle,* and a number of works by other poets.[37] "When as thine eye hath chose the Dame," the *Passionate Pilgrim* poem begins,

And stalde the deare that thou shouldst strike,
Let reason rule things worthy blame,
As well as fancy (partyall might)
Take counsell of some wiser head,
Neither too young, nor yet unwed.

And when thou comst thy tale to tell,
Smooth not thy toung with filed talke,

Least she some subtill practise smell,
A Cripple soone can finde a halt,
But plainly say thou lovst her well,
And set her person forth to sale.

What though her frowning browes be bent
Her cloudy lookes will calme yer night,
And then too late she will repent,
That thus dissembled her delight.
And twice desire yer it be day,
That which with scorne she put away.
(18.1–12)

After six more stanzas one is indeed reminded of the cynical description of women's gullibility and fickleness offered by W. S. in *Willobie His Avisa.* As one nineteenth-century editor summarized the *Passionate Pilgrim* poem, "let us not think to get the better of a woman by guile, but let us deliver our assault roundly, and trust to that traitor within her fortress who longs to open the gates to the enemy."[38] One is also reminded of the irony at the end of *A Lover's Complaint,* where the lady admits that her male wooer could "yet again betray the fore-betray'd, / And new pervert a reconciled maid" (328–29).

Thematic and formal connections with the W. S. section of *Willobie* have long been noted (they use the same metrical form; both contain sardonic advice to a wooer), but the *Passionate Pilgrim* poem has also been read as explicitly mocking Avisa's continually triumphant chastity. Indeed, the later poem seems to take everything to one further extreme; John Roe points out that it "increases the erotic tempo considerably with its confident prediction that [come] night . . . we shall witness a remarkable turnabout on the lady's part, modesty and chaste denial transforming themselves into unappeasable appetite."[39] Not only will she "repent," but in fact "twice desire" ("thrice" in one version). The poem's most difficult stanza is also its rhetorical climax:

Thinke Women still to strive with men,
To sinne and never for to saint,
There is no heaven (by holy then)
When time with age shall them attaint,
Were kisses all the joyes in bed,
One Woman would another wed.
(18.43–48)

The main point, however, is clear enough: women are just as prone to sin as men are, and they will not even think of heaven until old age shall "attaint" them. The especially misogynistic couplet at the end of the stanza is echoed by, or an echo of, *The Merry Wives of Windsor* (3.2.14–17), when in response to Ford's claim that "if your husbands were dead, you two would marry," Mrs. Page replies: "Be sure of that—two other husbands."

In sum, we might hypothesize that from the very earliest allusions up to the time of Malone's republication of the sonnets, two centuries of bardolatry had produced a cultural notion of a William Shakespeare or a W. S. that was distinctly sexual, but what we would now call "heterosexual." It is hardly surprising that our myriad-minded Shakespeare inspired a correspondingly complex and often contradictory body of personal and literary myths, and indeed there are a number of other legends besides Shakespeare as godfather that could be said to relate to the idea of a bawdy bard. It does not require much imagination to place the slightly more familiar anecdotes about holding horses or stealing deer (for which he was "oft whipt & sometimes Imprisoned" [*WS*, 2:257]) into the same biographical narrative; this is the Shakespeare who, depending on which version one reads, was son of a wool dealer or a glover or a tinker or a butcher, who "from an Actor of Playes . . . became a Composer" (*WS*, 2:257), who had his first child by Anne Hathaway only six months after marrying, and who is suspected of having fathered an illegitimate son with Mrs. Davenant. This is the local boy of inferior rank who made good in the big city, the common player who turned to writing and immediately caught on.[40] Indeed, a number of these legends tellingly share the same provenance, with Davenant once again near the bottom of it all. When introducing the horse-holding story for the first time in print, for example, the author of *The Lives of the Poets of Great Britain and Ireland* (1753) admits that he "cannot forbear relating a story which Sir William Davenant told Mr Betterton, who communicated it to Mr Rowe; Rowe told it to Mr Pope, and Mr Pope told it to Dr Newton, the late editor of Milton, and from a gentleman, who heard it from him, 'tis here related" (*WS*, 2:285). The tale is canonized in Johnson's 1765 edition, which claims that it came from Pope via Rowe, although neither of them actually mentions it in print (*WS*, 2:287–88).

Some of the liveliest related legends concern Shakespeare as a carouser in public houses, often combined with his "natural" or "prodigious" wit (*WS*, 2:249, 253) being demonstrated in extemporaneous epitaphs and other short poems. One wonders to what extent Digland the gardener spending his time "at the next alehouse" in Taylor's joke, or the fact that the Davenants also owned a tavern, might have mingled with or contaminated these other tales, which as a matter of fact tend to date from exactly the same period. The combinations are endless. An anonymous manuscript note from c. 1650 describes Shakespeare completing an epitaph begun by Jonson while both of them were "being Merrye att a Tavern" (*WS*, 2:246); in the same decade, another manuscript twice describes the same epitaph but neglects to divulge where it was composed (*WS,* 2:247–48). A diary from about 1661 remarks that "Shakespear, Drayton, and Ben Jhonson, had a merry meeting, and itt seems drank too hard, for Shakespear died of a feavour there contracted" (*WS,* 2:250). In Aubrey (again despite the claim that the bard "wouldn't be debauched" and moreover that "if invited to writ; he was in paine" [*WS,* 2:252]), we are told the story of an epitaph for John Combe, again conceived in a tavern (*WS,* 2:253), which was repeated by Rowe but without the tavern (*WS,* 2:268–69). Two different Combe epitaphs are mentioned in 1740 and 1742 (*WS,* 2:273, 274).

By 1760, Shakespeare and Jonson are charmingly described "at a tavern-club" entertaining "several lords from the court who went to hear their wit and conversation" (*WS,* 2:286), and in 1780, Steevens notes the relic of an "earthen half-pint mug, out of which [Shakespeare] was accustomed to take his draughts of ale at a certain publick house in the neighbourhood of Stratford, every Saturday afternoon" (*WS,* 2:296). There is also a frequently mentioned tavern at Wincot, reputedly the bard's favorite (*WS,* 2:249, 288, 290). Most entertaining of all is a Stratford legend created around a crabtree described about 1762 as "Shakespear's canopy," so named because the author was forced to sleep there one night after becoming too intoxicated to return home:

> he, as well as Ben Johnson, loved a glass for the pleasure of society; and he, having heard much of the men of that village as deep drinkers and merry fellows, one day went over to Bidford, to take a cup with them. He enquired of a shepherd for the Bidford drinkers; who replied they were absent; but the Bidford sippers were at home; and, I suppose, continued the sheepkeeper, they will be sufficient for you: and so, indeed, they were. He was forced to take up his lodging under that tree for some hours. (*WS,* 2:287)

Twenty years later the tale was further embellished, with the bard now "extremely fond of drinking hearty draughts of English Ale, and glory[ing] in being thought a person of superior eminence in that proffession" (*WS,* 2:291). We are even given the text of four lines composed upon waking up the morning after.

Before the post-Malone Shakespeare of the sonnets, we might conclude, before there was a national bard suspected of a sodomitical relationship with another man for which he must somehow be excused or exonerated, there was a love-poet Shakespeare or a W. S., whose reputation as a lover encompassed much more than mere praise of Adonis figures or erotic situations in which a young man is the object of desire. For he was also a figure who could plausibly have fathered William Davenant (indeed another kind of sodomy as far as the early modern period was concerned), a figure who might also be characterized as a wencher, a gallant, a swaggerer, a roisterer, a toper, a lusty youth, a common player, a bawdy wit, a rowdy ruffian, and so on ad infinitum. Such a reputation could *also* be "homosexual," of course, just as contemporary stereotypes of the figure of the gallant himself did not necessarily present a man who was interested in women alone.[41] And yet the idea of a queer Shakespeare is hardly a product of the sonnets alone. Once again, we would need to look no further than the narrative poems—*Venus and Adonis, A Lover's Complaint,* most of *The Passionate Pilgrim*—to find that in early Shakespearean representations of erotic situations, gender designations or gender roles are often either "reversed" or markedly ironized.

In *Venus and Adonis,* we have not only a man as the object of a woman's wooing, but also a "masculine" female wooer who, for instance, plucks Adonis from his horse, and a "feminized" male object of desire who, unlike the Venus and Adonis story in Ovid, remains unmoved.[42] Such inversions are a marked feature of early *Venus* parodies, and even in the poem itself Adonis's frigidity is satirized by the "correct" way in which his horse woos a mare (*Venus,* 259–324, 385–408). In the Cambridge *Parnassus* plays, the fool Gullio recounts how he attempted to woo his mistress by adopting a few lines from Shakespeare's poem. He begins unproblematically enough by substituting his own name for that of the wooing queen of love, and, after a nice parody of the exaggerations of young Romeo, he imperfectly quotes the second stanza of *Venus and Adonis*:

> Thrise fairer than myself (—thus I began—)
> The gods faire riches, sweete above compare,
> Staine to all nimphes, [m]ore lovely the[n] a man.
> More white and red than doves and roses are!
> Nature that made thee with herselfe had strife,
> Saith that the worlde hath ending with thy life.
> (*AB,* 1:67, cf. *Venus,* 7–12)

The gender switch of courting a woman rather than Adonis becomes the butt of ridicule, as it is perhaps not much of a compliment to call one's mistress "thrice fairer than myself" or "more lovely than a man."

But the most commonly imitated lines from the poem, which one finds cited not only in caricatures but also in ballads and commonplace books,[43] are the stanzas in which Venus titillatingly offers her body to Adonis in terms of metaphors of the hunt, his favorite activity (13–18). In parodies, the male wooer again takes Venus's role, as in Heywood's *Fair Maid of the Exchange*:

> *Bowdler.* Fondling I say, since I have hemd thee heere,
> Within the circle of this ivory pale,
> Ile be a parke.

> *Mall Berry.* Hands off fond Sir.
> *Bowdler.* —And thou shalt be my deere;
> Feede thou on me, and I will feed on thee,
> And love shall feede us both.
> *Mall.* Feede you on woodcockes, I can fast awhile.
> *Bowdler.* Vouchsafe thou wonder to alight thy steede.
> *Cripple.* Take heede, shees not on horsebacke.
> *Bowdler.* Why then she is alighted.
> Come sit thee downe where never serpent hisses,
> And, being set, ile smother thee with kisses.
> (*AB,* 1:177)

In Machin and Markham's *Dumb Knight,* a man reads from the poem and once again transforms Venus into a male wooer:

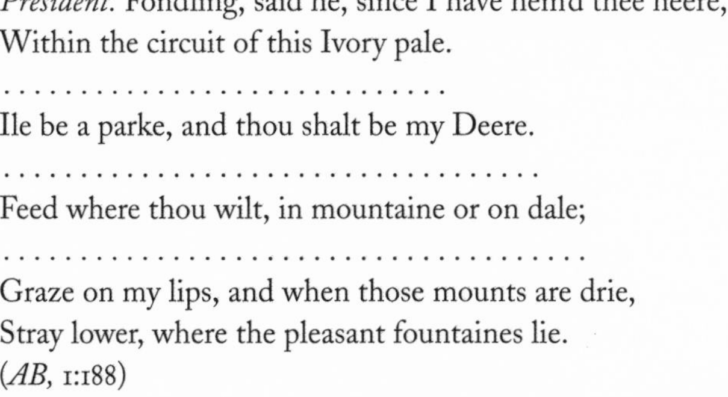

> *President.* Fondling, said he, since I have hem'd thee heere,
> Within the circuit of this Ivory pale.
> . . . .
> Ile be a parke, and thou shalt be my Deere.
> . . . .
> Feed where thou wilt, in mountaine or on dale;
> . . . .
> Graze on my lips, and when those mounts are drie,
> Stray lower, where the pleasant fountaines lie.
> (*AB,* 1:188)

The ellipses mark places where President interrupts his reading to address those who have come to see his master, but notice how the man's *body* has also come to take Venus's place in a potentially ridiculous way, since instead of female breasts, the male lover offers the "mounts" of his own "pleasant fountaines." A similar joke is repeated in Durfey's *Virtuous Wife,* where a forgetful wooer must actually be prompted from Shakespeare's text. Note how a parody of *Venus* still must have had great cultural currency at this late date (1680):

> *Sir Lubberly.* Madam, for ever I'll inclose you here,
> with the Circuit of this Ivory pale—What's next Sirra?
> *Boy.* You'll be the Park—
> *Sir Lubberly.* I'll be the Park, and you shall be the Deer:
> Feed where you will, on Mountain, or in Dale,
> Graze on my lips, and when those Hills are dry—

When those—Hills are dry—hum—are dry,
What's next you Dog?
Boy. Stray farther where the pleasant Fountains lie—
Sir Lubberly. Stay further where the pleasant Fountains lie.
Lady Beardly. Very well—I vow there's a great deal of
pleasure in being Courted.
(*AB,* 2:256)

Queer readings of these parodies seem particularly irresistible, and yet the notion that wooing might "reverse" gender roles also has a larger and more complex place in the Shakespeare canon—and, indeed, perhaps in early modern English culture as a whole. These parodies might also help us to bring together Shakespeare's two "opposite" reputations, both before and after Malone's republication of the sonnets.

In other words, gender "reversibility" is itself an important part of Shakespeare's works, and it is also evident in the early-seventeenth-century fashion for "transgendered" modes of dress or behavior for both men and women. The most famous example of this trend is the 1620 pamphlet controversy between *Hic Mulier; or, The Man-Woman,* and *Haec Vir; or, The Womanish-Man,* where we can glimpse the manifold cultural anxieties surrounding gender boundaries for both sexes.[44] Barnabe Riche's *Farewell to Militarie Profession* (1581) criticizes men attired like "some shamelesse woman" in order "to please Gentlewomen."[45] In Shakespeare, one might think of the fastidious "popinjay" lord disparaged by Hotspur in *1 Henry IV* for speaking "with many holiday and lady terms . . . like a waiting-gentlewoman" (1.3.46, 55), or the wooing Falstaff's claim to Mrs. Ford that "I cannot cog and say thou art this and that, like a many of these lisping hawthorn buds, that come like women in men's apparel" (*Merry Wives* 3.3.70–72). But *Haec Vir* not only accuses men of "ravishing" women's styles and their speech, but also makes specific reference to the Venus and Adonis story: "Goodnesse leave mee," Hic Mulier herself is made to complain, "if I have not heard a man court his mistris with the same words that Venus did Adonis, or as neere as the booke could instruct him" (*AB,* 1:281). The implication here is not merely that men will attempt to woo women by following a previously written erotic narrative ("oh for the book of *Venus* and *Adonis,* to court my Mistres by," yearns a foolish gentleman in Sharpe's *Noble Stranger* [*AB,* 1:448]), but also that they will become "effeminated" precisely with regard to their relationships with women. Both Mario DiGangi and Stephen Orgel imply that in texts like Riche or *Haec Vir* men "become" like women in order to be more appealing to them, that this kind of "effeminacy" is both "a consequence of heteroerotic desire" and "literally homoerotic," since women want "versions of themselves."[46] Is this also why *Venus and*

Adonis was supposedly so popular for women readers? And yet it is not only that a male wooer has "crossed over" into some sort of emasculated subject position, men's desire for women being seen as itself effeminating in the period (the term "womanize" meant to become *like* women rather than merely to show interest in them, just as the term "effeminate" was a verb as well as an adjective).[47] For what kind of a female figure is Venus herself if not a Hic Mulier, a "man-woman" who tries to cross the bounds of feminine modesty through aggressive wooing but whose "real" nature as a woman renders her only "*like* a bold fac'd suitor" (*Venus,* 6; my emphasis)? Venus, as DiGangi so penetratingly remarks, not the woman herself but "the disorderly passion that afflicts unruly women and womanish men," really becomes the source of *all* the confusion.[48] Hic Mulier is seen to have crossed lines of gender "first"; men don't just "become" women but female wooers like Venus: the male wooer in Riche or in *Haec Vir,* or in the *Venus* parodies, is not only an effeminate man but in fact a masculine woman. Wooing itself, in other words, is seen as a kind of reversal, a loss of masculine power in pursuit of ("feminine") pleasure. The fact that Venus happens to be a woman is to some degree beside the point; like any wooer, she would be "feminine" whether she were female or not. In this sense, the male speaker of the sonnets is also "feminized," and not simply because he describes himself as being under the control of the young man and the dark lady. Thus, one might argue that Shakespeare's earlier reputation as a gallant and cynical wooer is in a number of interesting ways actually rather similar to the subsequently "gay" author of the 1609 sonnets. For the sake of convenience, we might say that both these reputations are indubitably queer ones.

But the sort of gender "reversibility" we find in Shakespeare's texts also helps to make his literary and/or biographical reputations infinitely adaptable and indeed *usable,* and not least of all with respect to erotic situations. Katherine Duncan-Jones has explored some of the earliest applications of *Venus and Adonis,* concluding that "for the Elizabethans . . . Venus could be identified with . . . anyone engaging in ardent courtship," and that "Adonis, in turn, could stand for . . . anyone's mistress or object of devotion, male or female."[49] The apparent story of the sonnets has had an even more polymorphous fate, and indeed the aftereffects of Shakespearean biographical reconstructions are similarly protean. As in the enticing story about the beautiful innkeeper's wife, everything and anything that is known or is possible to infer about Shakespeare—life records, legends, rumors, allusions, plays, poems—has lured readers to imagine for themselves, and naturally enough with very different results, the bard's most intimate relationships. It is notable, however, that nearly all of these edifices also include sexual "reversals" of one form or another: the men wooed by women, the love poems addressed to a man, the dominant dark ladies, boys in women's clothes, heroines dressed "back" as boys, the poet's early marriage to an older woman, the patronage of Southampton (which, as we saw in the introduction, Rowe claimed to be "almost equal to that profuse Generosity the present Age has shewn to *French* Dancers and *Italian* Eunuchs" [*WS*, 2:267]), the mysterious "only begetter" Mr. W. H., and many others.[50]

The problem is to absorb all of these details into one master narrative, whether a "straight," "gay," or "bisexual" one, especially since the modern idea of a sexual Shakespeare pulls readers in two (or perhaps three) seemingly contradictory directions: the "homosexual" Shakespeare of the young man sonnets or the transvestite theater; the "heterosexual" one of the comedies, Manningham's tale, the dark lady poems, *Willobie His Avisa*, or *The Passionate Pilgrim*; or both. The bawdy bard did on occasion stir up indignation or moral outrage from all sides. In the mid-nineteenth-century *Cabinet Cyclopaedia*, he is accused of being "not wholly untainted by the vices of the period," "not averse to the bottle, or to pursuits still more criminal," but according to Schoenbaum's summary this refers only to Shakespeare's presumed associations with women.[51] At the same time, however, one is reminded of the "criminal" suspicions at the bottom of same-sex disputes as well, as in the disagreement between Steevens and Malone over sonnet 20, mentioned in chapter 1, wherein Malone defended Shakespeare by arguing that "such addresses to men, however indelicate, were customary in our author's time, and neither imported criminality, nor were esteemed indecorous."[52]

Ingenious readers sought to combine these two Shakespeares together into one glorification of the supreme artist who could be both "masculine" and "feminine" at the same time. The best example is Frank Harris's tandem volumes, *The Man Shakespeare* (1909) and *The Women in Shakespeare* (1912).[53] Schoenbaum reasonably suggests that Harris's model may have been his friend and contemporary Oscar Wilde, and yet for Harris any suggestion of Wildean "unnatural passion" is "a contradiction in terms" when it comes to the Swan of Avon.[54] Even the young man sonnets are patterned after those to the dark lady rather than the other way around: "Shakespeare makes use of the passion he has felt for a woman to give reality to the expression of his affection for the youth"; "the sonnets . . . addressed to the young man which have any warmth of desire in them, are one and all copied from the lyrics to the 'dark lady.' "[55] Within such a narrative framework, the Davenant story fits like a glove. "No doubt Shakespeare made up to her from the first," Harris imagines, even if the whole thing was just a reaction against being enslaved by his unresponsive "gypsy-mistress" Mary Fitton, the "wilful-wanton" dark lady herself. In sum, "from eighteen to forty-five [Shakespeare] was as inconstant as the wind, and gave himself to all the 'subtle games' of love with absolute abandonment, till his health broke under the strain."[56]

The godfather legend could thus be said to be "already" a queer one in a number of ways. We might conclude by examining the story's most triumphant return, in the convoluted theories of Arthur Acheson, where Mrs. Davenant of the Crown tavern becomes equated not only with the dark lady of the sonnets but with A. D. of *Willobie His Avisa*. A connection between *Willobie* and the dark lady had been argued as early as 1886,[57] and perhaps a woman with whom Shakespeare was rumored to have fathered a child might seem a predictable enough guess for the femme fatale characterized in the final twenty-eight poems. But there were also a number of problems to overcome: the resolutely chaste A. D. we meet in *Willobie* hardly seems to resemble the dark lady; it is not at all clear that W. S. had ever been in love with A. D. rather than with some other woman or women; the inn in *Willobie* appears to be a St. George rather than a Crown; and most of all A. D., or rather Mrs. Davenant, was unfortunately named Jane. Hardly deterred by all of this, in the finest bardolatrous tradition, Acheson musters up a vast bulk of evidence from which he can simply fashion a first wife for John Davenant out of thin air, happily by the name of Anne, and in the meantime show that before the Crown tavern Davenant owned a St. George in the early 1590s. But if Sir William wasn't even born until ten years later? Acheson concludes that the scandals described in *Willobie* and in the dark lady sonnets had simply been confused by later readers such as Aubrey and Wood—with a little help from Sir William himself, whose mother was in fact the second Mrs. Davenant, and "whose literary vanity led him, when in his cups, to forward . . . distorted gossip . . . to his bibulous cronies."[58] The godfather story, it seems, has come full circle; perhaps Shakespeare was not the father of William Davenant after all, but the sexual scandals were still firmly in place. Indeed, our continued interest in them has saved poets and playwrights like Davenant from fading completely away into the shadows of early modern culture, just as the godfather story, and others like it, have ironically saved many worthy and often brilliant texts, even if they are just "Shakespeare allusions," from being totally forgotten.

The most recent manifestation of a godfather Shakespeare is probably Clemence Dane's sentimentalized version in *The Godson: A Fantasy*, a fitting if rather pathetic end to our idea of Shakespeare the gallant. Shakespeare, now an old man, learns from Mrs. Davenant herself, on one of his last trips through Oxford, that little Will Davenant is really his child:

> "He is mine, eh?"
>
> She did not answer, but still opposed him, half smiling, while a man might count five heart-beats; then she pulled her cloak about her, took the lantern from him and led the sleepy, stumbling boy away with her down the primrose path.

> Mr. Shakespeare of New Place followed them, but slowly. Presently, because the night air struck chill, he flung about his shoulders, after the fashion of a player-king, the coverlet of the second-best bed [which, we are told, contains pictures of Venus and Adonis].[59]

Shakespeare as father, Shakespeare as god. His offspring include not only plays and poems and sonnets but other (god)children like *Willobie His Avisa* and *The Passionate Pilgrim*. And one can only imagine the generations of others besides Davenant who might have "seemed contented enough to be thought his Son." Shakespeare himself uses curiously similar terms when addressing Southampton in the dedication to *Venus and Adonis*: "I account my selfe highly praised, and vowe to take advantage of all idle houres, till I have honoured you with some graver labour. But if the first heire of my invention prove deformed, I shall be sorie it had so noble a god-father: and never after eare so barren a land, for feare it yeeld me still so bad a harvest." If *Venus* or *Lucrece* are "deformed" children, however, it is mainly because one idea of a bawdy author of erotic works has been consistently overshadowed, since the eighteenth century, by the scandal of another kind of sodomy in the young man poems. Perhaps it is this "later" reputation, more than any other, that has had to be desexualized. But sexual Shakespeare should remain a resolutely *multivalent* idea, in order to combat the tendency for squeezing him into any one-dimensional erotic narrative—featuring, for instance, Southampton alone. A vast variety of Shakespearean wooers and wooing scenes would then wither away into a group of "gay" love sonnets addressed to another man.

CHAPTER 3

Sexual "Shakespeare": Sexuality and the Authorship Controversy

IN THE first two chapters of this study, we have seen some of the ways in which, by the end of the eighteenth century, cumulative attempts to establish Shakespeare as a cultural icon had to make way for a "new" realization that he was also responsible for a large group of love poems addressed to another man. But I have also tried to show that a sexualized Shakespeare, author of the sonnets in particular, cannot really be reduced to a question of chronology, or to a simple before-and-after scenario in which bardolators were suddenly forced to incorporate the poems' disreputable stories (about the young man or the dark lady). It may be that the sexual Shakespeare suggested by the sonnets came as something of a shock to late-eighteenth-century readers, but it was also an idea or a reputation that had displaced a different (but equally "sodomitical") one already in place for two hundred years—one that had grown out of his earliest fame as the author of eroticized, Ovidian narrative poems. Even from the very beginning, one might say, some notion of a sexual Shakespeare had been there all along. And to some degree, it had always gotten in the way.

Similarly, sexual problems were surely exacerbated once the eighteenth century had canonized him as the national poet (with a series of apostolic multivolume editions, a life-sized statue in Poets' Corner at Westminster Abbey, and an ostentatious Shakespeare Jubilee organized by David Garrick), for an already fantasized biography now had to live up to the glories of English literature in general. But as early as the First Folio of 1623, readers had been presented with an individualizing engraving of the author's face on the title page of the volume, which sought not only to canonize Shakespeare but to fix him as both exemplary author and all-inclusive literary authority.[1] The contradictory forces of Shakespearean (de)sexualization, in other words, had been set into motion long before the bardolatrous 1700s. Ben Jonson's contributions to the Folio encapsulate this incongruity very succinctly, for on the one hand he praises the engraver as having "had a strife / with Nature, to out-doo the life," and on the other hand he clearly tries to ennoble Shakespeare as "not of an age, but for all time."[2] Later readers have stood similarly united in their glorification of the works as infinite and immortal, despite having been written by a man whose all-too-human face (as we will see in chapter 4) stares out at us from the very first page. This adulation has gone by many names and served many different critical purposes: the bard's large and comprehensive soul (Dryden), his just representation of general nature (Johnson), myriad-mindedness (Coleridge), negative capability (Keats), civilized humanity (Sidney Lee), impersonality (T. S. Eliot), contemporaneity (Jan Kott), and so on ad infinitum. Hazlitt found in the plays "the germs of every faculty and feeling," and most recently, Shakespeare is nothing less than the inventor of the human (Harold Bloom). Each of these conceptions, however, is a particular kind of response to the meager and lackluster list of facts that we do in fact possess, and thus Shakespeare's fabled "invisibility" is really a product of his biography rather than simply the cause of—in this case—no biography at all. How could such a high-culture hero bear to be sexualized at all? How could he ever stand up to the impossible universal history that he is supposed to represent and even personify?

In this chapter, we will examine one of most complex responses to this ongoing problem of bardolatrous ambivalence, namely, that William Shakespeare isn't William Shakespeare at all but merely someone else in disguise. We will see, however, that even if the *Life of Shakespeare* is not the life of the real author, sexual problems do not thereby disappear; moreover, the very refusal to accept Shakespeare of Stratford as the author of his own plays and poems is to some degree a logical outgrowth of a much more extensive and long-standing desire to desexualize him: to place the works and the "man himself" above and beyond the troublesome categories of the personal, the individual, and the physical. Even in the recent *Norton Shakespeare,* yet one more attempt to standardize the bard for general audiences, a long introduction by Stephen Greenblatt only perpetuates the confusion by trying to compensate for the facts (which are, Greenblatt admits, "a bit dull") with three "biographical daydreams," hoping thereby to fill some of the gaps between Shakespeare's enigmatic life and "the particular shape of the theatrical imagination associated with his name." Greenblatt is appropriately self-conscious about the conjectural nature of these fantasies, unlike so many of his predecessors, but one is left wondering precisely what he is endeavoring to explain. Why aren't the facts enough? Or, put another way, what kind of Shakespeare do we really want or require? If we should turn to the first-person sonnets instead, we encounter not additional facts but only cultural and personal anxieties of a different sort, and the author regularly disappears once

Martin Droeshout, portrait engraving of Shakespeare, detail from the title page of the First Folio (1623). By permission of the Folger Shakespeare Library.

again. A case in point is Greenblatt's brief treatment of homoeroticism in Jacobean court life ("including, most famously, the majority of Shakespeare's sonnets"), which, like the absent life of Shakespeare himself, is simply cast away as "opaque."[3] Is the anachronistic question of sexuality, then, just one more item in a long list of new-historical features belonging to what the introduction calls "Shakespeare's world," along with pageantry, life expectancy, religious ritual, xenophobia, censorship, and sumptuary laws?

And Shakespeare's life? How does it fit into this mélange of extra-biographical particulars, which in any case come first in Greenblatt's treatment? The seemingly secondary "traces of a life" produce only discomfort and dissatisfaction; we require a biography, a person, an authentic portrait, but at the same time we must have Shakespeare, or, rather, Shakespearean daydreams. To say, then, that William Shakespeare was not William Shakespeare at all might seem to be the neatest and indeed simplest solution to the ongoing problem of the absence (or is it presence?) of biographical fact, for according to this sort of reading, the lack of information is both intentional and necessary, since Shakespeare is only a pseudonym or a ruse. One should hardly be surprised if such readings were fraught with the very same anxieties, sexual and otherwise, that plague more traditional bardolators, but readers may well be surprised to learn just how strongly anti-Stratfordian solutions have taken hold in the popular imagination.

In fact, those who find themselves interested in the debate must immediately come to grips with the fact that it has produced a mass of material greater than any other single subject in Shakespeare studies—if not literary studies in general. One compiler, Joseph Galland, treated the subject as his life's work, and in 1949 the result was an immense annotated bibliography of more than four thousand entries, which evidently was just too expensive to publish.[4] Fifty years later, one can only guess how much space an updated version might require. In 1944, Hyder Rollins had also managed to surface from this cave of despair with a two-volume variorum edition of the sonnets; he fearlessly catalogued and summarized centuries of Stratfordian as well as anti-Stratfordian readings of these supposedly autobiographical poems. The result is one of the great monuments of literary criticism from any age. Two useful updates appeared in 1958, and there has also been no shortage of journalistic reviews, with or without a Stratfordian bias, with such titles as *Who Wrote Shakespeare?* and *The Shakespeare Controversy*.[5] The most important recent exploration, however, is Schoenbaum's *Shakespeare's Lives*, written very much in the spirit of Rollins, which takes up the arduous task of reviewing, century by century, life stories for the bard (which uncannily seem to resemble their authors' own).[6]

Which "Shakespeare" would not fit into such a scheme? Practically every well-known early modern figure (not to mention obscure and even imagined ones) eventually turns up as a candidate, and one gets the feeling that readers are simply shuffling a finite number of people, places, and circumstances in order to come up with their own version of the solution to the crime. The resulting combinations are surprising and often amusing, and the degree to which they resort to "illicit" sexual acts is indeed remarkable: Mr. W. H. is Southampton, the illegitimate son of Queen Elizabeth and the earl of Oxford, alias Shakespeare; the young man of the sonnets is the earl of Oxford's illegitimate son (by the queen) and *he* became an actor called William Shakespeare; Shakespeare, or rather Francis Bacon, is the illegitimate son of Queen Elizabeth and the earl of Leicester; and so on. Some readers try to sidestep sexual questions by arguing that Shakespeare is really a woman, as we have also examined in chapter 1. Others attempt to escape the sexual altogether by arguing that Shakespeare isn't even a person; the works were composed by a coterie of playwrights such as Bacon, Oxford, Marlowe, Raleigh, and the countess of Pembroke.[7] Personally, I'm most partial to the proposal that a group of Jesuits wrote the plays, and I also have a soft spot for explanations like *Jesus' Teachings by Shakespeare's Spirit*.[8]

There is a point, however, at which one ceases to be amused, and the thrill of watching these high-wire acts inevitably becomes surfeited. Rollins began his preface by hoping that the "wearisome task" of reading "the 'literature' under which Shakespeare's sonnets are submerged . . . should not have to be repeated."[9] And one can only sympathize with Schoenbaum's concluding confession that "this has been the cruelest endeavor I have ever confronted."[10] Part of the problem is the inordinate length of many of the anti-Stratfordian tomes. In 1857, Delia Bacon, first in a long line of published "heretics," set an unfortunate precedent with six hundred practically unreadable pages.[11] Her troubled life has understandably attracted far more attention than her tortuously written remarks. One might simply try to avoid this sort of material altogether, but the debate certainly shows no sign of subsiding, and looked at as a whole the phenomenon itself still has much to teach us.

The most recent development has been a host of Stratfordian and anti-Stratfordian Internet web sites and personal home pages. When I first began to contemplate my own foray into this literary-critical minefield, I was encouraged by a colleague, to whom I owe many valuable suggestions, to look into some of these web pages and on-line discussion groups, academic or otherwise.[12] Had the Internet changed the face of the debate, he wondered? I certainly had no trouble finding grist for the mill, beginning with the home page of the Shakespeare Oxford Society (www.shakespeare-oxford.com). Yet what was immediately apparent was precisely the seamlessness of this new transfer to a hypertext format. For if any literary debate positively demanded on-line exchanges, chat rooms, and cybertalk, this was surely it. Hasn't this particular debate *always* been a "globalized" free- for-all in the guise of open-minded discussion, a total democratization of undifferentiated viewpoints and surmises connected by links to other, often nameless or uninformed authorities? The byword of the anti-Stratfordian revolution has always been freedom—from the Shakespeare industry, from the professors, from British conservatism—and it has often been noted how many of the participants in this cacophony of voices, in print or on-line, are American.[13] One might even claim that it is not merely that the Shakespeare authorship controversy has been brought on-line, but that the majority of on-line discussions themselves seem to have adopted the tenor of the Shakespeare authorship controversy.[14]

To be fair, however, the Shakespeare Oxford Society's web site does have the virtue of more or less dispassionate orderliness, and it reads rather like a shadow of innumerable other mainstream literary societies, with their formal journals and annual conferences in Hilton hotels. We are invited to "stay a few moments and look into what is undoubtedly one of the world's greatest mystery stories," and the uninitiated are first directed to a separate "Beginner's Guide to the Shakespeare Authorship Problem." Here are thumbnail sketches of the various suspects. There are also useful links to downloading recent "major stories" in *Harper's* and *The Chronicle of Higher Education,* both of which I was pleased to receive. If, however, our main objective is "talking about Shakespeare or the Shakespeare authorship," and one suspects that this applies to a great many people, we are given necessary links to newsgroups, discussion pages, and the like. I imagine that this web site is a little too academic for many hard-line chatters and conspiracy theorists, but it is still a logical place to begin one's own criminal investigation. There is also an "Honor Roll of Skeptics," a list of doubters including celebrities and Shakespeare actors—particularly convincing witnesses, one must assume.

In a word, the very perseverance and the breadth of the debate are extraordinary; Marjorie Garber aptly remarks that nobody really wants to find a solution to the Shakespeare problem, since "we prefer the problem to any answer."[15] My own discomfort does not really stem from a worry that "our" English national poet and high-culture hero might have to be dethroned, or that my own personal academic and institutional investments in teaching, reading, and studying the bard might become endangered. For even if Shakespeare were "only" a pseudonym, would it really help to explain anything? In an earlier essay, Garber observes that the debate has become "an exemplary literary event in its own right,"[16] and it is at this point that we begin our own inquiry. Specifically, what happens to the problematic and anxiety-ridden idea of a sexual Shakespeare if the bard were really someone else? We have seen that the very thought of his sexuality is at once both foregrounded and routinely marginalized in traditional Shakespeare criticism, and of the sonnets in particular. But the very same issues have to be confronted, ignored, or explained away in anti-Stratfordian polemics. In his 1952 treatment of the sonnets, Edward Hubler included an appendix on two Shakespearean "misconceptions," the bard's alleged homosexuality and the equally inflammatory authorship question. But are these two connected? Hubler's text is actually rather open-minded for its time, for it implies that the sonnets have *produced* anti-Stratfordian as well as "homosexual" interpretations, even as the very idea is both papered over and relegated to an appendix.[17]

It is indeed no accident that two of the major candidates for the real William Shakespeare, Francis Bacon and Christopher Marlowe, are "documented" sodomites (in the sense of their erotic relationships to other men), although any whiff of homoeroticism is just as often used against them. In Shakespeare biographies of the A. L. Rowse stamp, for instance, the bard's "highly heterosexual nature" is used to elevate him above his sodomitical inferiors: "make no mistake about this, Shakespeare's interest in the youth [of the sonnets] is not at all sexual—as Marlowe's or Bacon's might well have been."[18] Indeed the sodomitical "interest" of any of the candidates has traditionally been avoided; the sexual "orientation" of a Bacon or a Marlowe or an earl of Rutland is no more conspicuous than the Swan of Avon's. The ultimate proving ground has always been the sonnets, which began causing anxiety as soon as they were recovered by Malone in 1780. Yet if these really represent the confessions of someone else, wouldn't the young man and the dark lady need to be included in some alternative and equally disreputable story? If the poems appear to suggest a sexual relationship between the man from Stratford and a younger addressee, W. H. or someone else, what do they suggest about the author as Cardinal Wolsey or Sir Walter Raleigh?

Indeed, the sonnets are the stumbling block of Shakespearean and anti-Shakespearean readers alike, except that the dissenters are ostensibly more concerned with the presumed social status and learning of their author than with his romantic predilections. The greatness of the Shakespeare canon, so we are told, proves that it was produced by a nobleman, a lawyer, and a university graduate, not a beggarly player and country bumpkin from Stratford. Such biographical requirements were in fact the source of the very first doubters' cautious hypotheses. But is a *sodomite* also required?

A certain Rev. James Wilmot started the ball rolling when, in the last twenty years of the eighteenth century (exactly the time of Malone), he scoured the countryside around Stratford for traces of the bard, especially for books that must have belonged to his surely vast personal library.[19] Finding nothing, he decided that Francis Bacon was the true author. Though Wilmot destroyed his notes before he died, a summary of his findings was preserved for posterity in an 1805 report to a local philosophical society, by one James Corton Cowell, who in the very repetition of such heresy declared himself "a Pervert, nay a renegade to the Faith I have proclaimed and avowed before you all."[20] This is long before Freud, of course, but by the end of the nineteenth century "perverted" readings were being recited ad infinitum, even if very few of them openly dared to address sexual matters. Delia Bacon is predictably coy or uninterested in this area, and just as predictably focuses her analysis on *King Lear, Coriolanus,* and *Julius Caesar* instead. Her Francis Bacon, who seems to have served as the head of a group of authors, is much more interested in high Roman and ancient English ideals, or in philosophical questions of statesmanship and commonwealth, than in a liaison with the likes of the fair young man. So far as I can determine, the sonnets, although occasionally quoted, are not even mentioned in her book.

In fact, later Baconians who explicitly take up sexual questions are few and far between. Typical for its period is Edward George Harman's *The "Impersonality" of Shakespeare* (1925), which includes only one short paragraph on the poems. He espouses the familiar view that "there are many things about the Sonnets which seem quite irreconcilable with their authorship by an actor of humble origin." But then the subject is dropped: "It would take too much space however in this book—already over-long—to deal with the Sonnets and I must leave them with this brief note."[21] Indeed, brevity has never been a Baconian strong point, but one might have wished that this particular area had been pursued in greater detail. For unlike the seemingly "impersonal" quality of the life of William Shakespeare, we have no shortage of biographical particulars relating to Sir Francis Bacon—Lord Chancellor, Baron Verulam, Viscount St. Albans—including some rather notorious assertions about his sexual preferences. In the nineteenth century, this information was played down in James Spedding's standard edition of Bacon's works, but the gossip was well enough known even in Bacon's time. Most conspicuous today is John Aubrey's remark that Bacon "was a *paiderastes*," and that "his Ganimeds and Favourites tooke Bribes."[22] Recent biographers have dwelled at greater length on these and other charges, from Sir Simonds D'Ewes and Bacon's mother among others,[23] and indeed Bacon has become one of the key figures in English Renaissance queer studies in general. There are in fact few figures from the period who have so readily been characterized as "gay" in the modern sense of the term.[24]

But Baconianism as a whole was largely sidetracked by its furious search for anagrams, acrostics, and secret ciphers, presumably because Bacon himself was so interested in them.[25] A recent biographer has even suggested a possible connection between Bacon's secretiveness and his sodomitical inclinations with other men.[26] But in the late nineteenth and early twentieth centuries, a stunning variety of hidden messages and directives for reading the plays was slowly uncovered, once again demonstrating the lengths to which people were willing to go to make their candidate as cerebral as possible. Decoders looked for veiled pronouncements in Thorpe's dedication, or in *Love's Labour's Lost*'s famous "honorificabilitudinitatibus," instead of reading the texts themselves. The long word, especially, gave amateur cryptographers a real run for their money, since there are just too many *i*'s and only one *c* if one wanted to produce the name Francis Bacon, in English or in Latin. One clever participant proposed, "But thus I told Franiiiiii Bacon." Hardly a joke, its inventor solemnly declared that Fran plus six *i*'s equals Fran-six or Francis.[27] This is a game any number can play. Why not "I, I built Fran. Bacon shit, I'd i.o.u. it"?

But the occasional incautious reader who actually broached the subject of Bacon's sodomy was, at the very least, ignored. An excellent example is (the Rev.) Walter Begley's *Is It Shakespeare?*, which was discreetly published as "by a Cambridge graduate" in 1903.[28] The book argues that the sodomitical evidence found in Aubrey and elsewhere (Aubrey's notebooks had just been published for the first time in 1898) are in fact corroborated by Bacon's works as Shakespeare, and by the sonnets in particular. The poems, however, lead us to believe that Bacon was really innocent of these charges, despite being "a born lover of youthful semi-feminine beauty" as well as "at bottom a bit of a misogynist." William Shakespeare of Stratford, on the other hand, was "a virile married man and the father of twins," and "was most distinctly *not* the kind of man for a scandal of this nature." "Not much sexual inversion about *him*." Who else but Bacon could have been responsible, Begley wonders? Even his women were boy players.[29] Although Begley himself ultimately refused to believe the very scandals he so bravely rehearsed (Bacon, he concludes, was simply "given to unusual intimacy with loose and unprincipled people"), clearly *this* kind of "Shakespeare" was a figure that Begley's fellow Baconians didn't want either, and the book was effectively silenced by his partners in heresy.[30] Other Baconians could avoid the issue altogether simply by arguing that although the poems are autobiographical, the young man and dark lady are just allegorical figures. "It is plain enough," writes Roderick Eagle, that "he [Bacon] is reasoning with himself as to whether he should marry and beget a son in whom his name and memory would survive." Otherwise, one would have to "saddle their author with immorality, sexually and homosexually."[31] Again, the historical William Shakespeare was already married so he couldn't be the real author. The only problem, of course, is that history has saddled Francis Bacon with an even more "homosexual" reputation than the man from Stratford.

In any event, Baconian theories were eventually superseded by others, once the somewhat unluckily named J. Thomas Looney unveiled his new candidate in 1920: Edward de Vere, seventeenth earl of Oxford. Perhaps Bacon seemed too far-fetched anyway, especially since he is the author of so many other works, and moreover because there seems to be such a distance between his philosophical works and those in the Shakespeare canon. One reader remarked that a Shakespeare play and a Bacon essay "have nothing in common except the use of the English language," and Spedding himself sardonically commented that "whoever wrote the Plays of Shakespeare it was certainly not Bacon."[32] Indeed, Oxford is by far the leading candidate even today, and long monographs from reputable presses are still pouring out.[33] His adherents have always had the unenviable task of trying to dissociate themselves from the mad Delia Bacon and company, but the main problem with this candidate is that Oxford died in 1604, a date rather too early for a number of late Shakespeare plays. So there were obstacles still to be overcome; Looney himself decided that *The Tempest* was apocryphal, for example.[34]

He began by making a list of eighteen necessary "features" for the true author (this is Shakespearean impersonality with a vengeance), and then proceeded to look for a suspect who could fit such objective, commonsense reasoning—in other words "an actual person who merely lacks a name."[35]

The result is a Shakespeare who must have been "a member of the higher aristocracy," "unconventional," "of superior education," "a lover of music," and so on. We also learn that he was "doubtful and somewhat conflicting in his attitude to woman," perhaps a euphemism for other sexual attitudes left unmentioned.[36] A crucial "discovery" was a rather cliché poem by Oxford on the subject of women, which Looney found in a nineteenth-century anthology when he set out to look for poems written in the same stanzaic pattern as *Venus and Adonis.* The number of contestants "turned out to be much fewer than I had anticipated," which is natural enough, since several other poems are rejected for unexplained reasons "as being unsuitable."[37] And there is a delicious irony in the fact that the other of two finalists was discarded because it was anonymous.

It is notable, moreover, that the current Shakespeare Oxford Society home page has whittled down Looney's original list of character traits to ten, and that the earl's "attitude" toward either sex has been removed altogether. Looney himself had a problem with the sexual suggestiveness of the sonnets, despite the fact that Oxford's presumed attitude toward "woman"—often with a capital w—"may indeed afford an explanation for the very existence of the Shakespeare mystery." These hazards are left largely for his followers to deal with. Regarding the dark lady, for instance, Looney admitted that she "presents a problem not yet solved." But as for the young man? The first seventeen poems are much more easily accounted for, since they were directed to Southampton, who was at the time engaged to marry Oxford's daughter. But one is left in the dark about this future son-in-law and the rest of the young man group. "It is not in the nature of things for such a man," Looney concludes, "to pass away and leave no insoluble mysteries."[38]

One of his key points is that Thomas Thorpe refers to "our ever-living poet" in his dedication, and this term, we are told, was never used to refer to an author who was still alive. Remarkably, in other words, one of the chief pieces of evidence for Oxford's authorship of the poems (not overlooking a convenient pun on "ever-living" and E. Vere), is that he was the only major candidate who was *dead* in 1609 (the equally dead Christopher Marlowe being discounted). We also learn that Oxford's "final or Shakespearean period," between 1591 and his death in 1604, "is almost a complete blank."[39] Therefore, much like the case with that other William Shakespeare, we have a convenient vacuum fittingly called the poet's "lost years." If Bacon's works had been too extensive, Oxford's are practically nonexistent—but this was exactly his attraction. A number of poems still exist, and in 1598 Francis Meres noted that he was proficient at playwriting, although none of his efforts in this medium have survived.[40] Indeed, Shakespeare's absent life and these absent works are said to "dovetail" perfectly, and this has always been proof enough as far as the anti-Stratfordian mind is concerned.

But Oxford, too, is not free from the scandal of sodomy with another man, although this aspect of his life is much less familiar than similar allegations against Bacon or Marlowe. Looney, for one, refuses to recount these "murderous charges."[41] Charlton Ogburn's massive Oxfordian tome twice refers to accusations of sodomy between men, but the charges are discounted at once and no details are provided, save referring the reader to a "prurient" piece in the London *Times,* "replete with lurid details of an alleged episode."[42] Sidney Lee's *Dictionary of National Biography* entry for Oxford also mentions that his father-in-law, Lord Burghley, attacked him over an apparent alienation from his wife after he returned from an Italian tour in the 1570s.[43] This period is only briefly surveyed by Looney, but analyzed at great length by Ogburn. The latter, however, argues that far from bringing back the influence of Italian vices, an index of evils that stereotypically included sodomy, Oxford's triumphant return was accompanied by nothing less than "the spirit of the Renaissance."[44] (We will pass over the fact that this spirit is hardly at odds with the very vices so often anathematized.)

Oxfordians predictably tend to avoid these sorts of rumors if they can; otherwise, huge passages of prose are required to be rid of them. The accusation of "buggering," which Ogburn refuses to name, is twice mentioned in the recent roundtable discussion appearing in *Harper's* in April 1999, but this detail is clearly being recited rather than pursued.[45] There is also an embarrassing piece of tattle that appears in Aubrey, in which the earl is said to have farted when bowing before the queen,[46] but this tiny crumb never even disgraces Ogburn's 892 pages (or the *Harper's* story). The sodomitical scandals, once again, are not really used to *support* the idea of love sonnets addressed to another man. Instead, as Ogburn so confidently puts it, "if de Vere ever had homosexual interests, they were surely subordinate"; rather, this is a man of "excessive heterosexual zeal." Similarly, Ogburn's description of sonnet 20 must rank as one of the most confusing and anxiety-ridden explanations ever offered. As I understand it, W. H. is Southampton, the illegitimate son of Oxford and his dark lady Anne Vavasor, and since "the love . . . expressed in the *Sonnets* could have only one of two bases"—homosexual or paternal—the author came up with the idea to create a "paradox" in which love for a woman was mingled with love for a son. And all because Oxford couldn't publicly acknowledge Southampton as his child.[47]

I recommend that one refrain from thinking about this theory (such as it is) too hard; instead, one should simply note how it stems from a fundamental impasse in many readers' minds over what to make of a poem that Ogburn predictably calls "quite gratuitous." Indeed, such a tortured explanation *needs* a paradox, and Ogburn's "solution" is only one of the most recent, and in some ways most egregious, examples of a more general dismay (and not merely among Oxfordians) over the poems' sexual implications. One might also be interested to learn that Ogburn rejects Marlowe as Shakespeare for precisely the opposite reason, since Marlowe "would hardly have had so obsessive an affair with the dark lady of the *Sonnets.*"[48] While sodomitical gossip against Oxford is never considered (and not even enumerated), the equally unproven charges against Marlowe are simply taken at face value. Queer Shakespeare is turned on his head; Marlowe cannot be the bard because Marlowe *is* homosexual.

But not all Oxford supporters were so adamant and even panicky in their outright rejection of homoeroticism. One of the most interesting examples comes from the pen of Gerald Rendall, a retired professor of Greek at Liverpool who, at the age of eighty, became a fervent and prolific Oxford convert. In a 1930 volume on the sonnets, Rendall refers to the earl's Italian travels as "a Byronic vein of extravagance and braggadocio, which the designing would find it only too easy to exploit." A discreet footnote adds: "It would be easy to elaborate the Byron parallel in detail, but such parallels are apt to become misleading." Misleading how? We also read that Oxford "sat loose to family ties and affections, and preferred the society of men, with occasional interludes of fashionable excitement, to the quieter routines of domestic intercourse." Moreover, "the evidence points to relaxation of moral sanctions, and to the heightened sexuality, which Italian surroundings were so apt to induce."[49]

But of course this sort of "heightened sexuality" is precisely the problem, however easy it may be to blame it all on Italy. When the sonnets are discussed in detail, in fact, these difficulties only intensify. The majority of Rendall's book consists of a running commentary on each of the sonnets, with some telling omissions. The dark lady poems are completely "disassociated" from the first group and barely analyzed, although special praise is offered for 129—written not, as Rendall remarks, for publication or for the friend, "but rather, as has so often been the case, for relief of an intolerable strain." Indeed, "sexual strain" is a favorite (albeit confused) category here, since it is also applied to sonnets 40–42 (in which another woman appears), which are skipped entirely because they are "parenthetical, and not of special interest." "Canons of sexual morality" are always in flux, we are told, and "no leading representative [of Elizabethan court society] escapes, or would even have disclaimed, charges of sexual irregularities."[50]

And referring to sonnet 20, which Rendall titles "The Charmer,"

> there is no need to waste trouble upon details in a Sonnet so unpleasing to our taste. It is enough to notice the emphasis laid upon the brightness of the eyes, . . . and the feminine types of beauty, which characterized Southampton in his youth. . . . On the question of taste, it is essential to bear in mind not

> only relative standards of propriety, but also that among Sonnets written for personal intercourse, we may look for many neither intended, nor approved, for publication. And smoke-room pleasantries are not answerable to the rules of the public censor. That any one can seriously suppose that William Shakspere, Actor, could address the Earl of Southampton in this strain, seems almost a record in literary credulity![51]

Despite the hesitancy of all this, Rendall's "answer" to the sonnets seems to be that a meticulously implied, but yet unnamed sodomy between men is admissible for noblemen like Oxford and Southampton, but not for the likes of Shakespeare—at least not with a member of the aristocracy. Even in 1999, Joseph Sobran has claimed that such an affair between Southampton and "William of Stratford . . . would be bizarre, if not insane."[52] It is no accident, of course, that in Rendall's discussion sonnets 40–42 are disregarded. Many readers have been troubled by the "sudden" appearance of a woman in these poems, but in order to understand this dilemma more completely, we must digress briefly to another "homosexual" interpretation from the other side of the Stratfordian fence, Samuel Butler's 1899 rearrangement of the poems in *Shakespeare's Sonnets Reconsidered.*

Butler's influence in Shakespeare studies has always been somewhat underrated, and his text is regularly cast off along with the many other editions that have attempted to find a more pleasing order for the 154 poems printed by Thorpe. Yet Butler's treatment of sexuality is particularly unequivocal for its day, and we should not be surprised if this aspect of his work was also overlooked by readers on both sides of the debate. He begins with a glance at George Chalmers's follies of exactly a century before, the subject of our chapter 1, but Butler also notes that his precursor was the first to argue that W. H. was the "onlie begetter" of the poems in the sense that he *inspired* them. The floodgates had thus long been open, and Butler's own identification of W. H. as a navy steward turned sea cook—decidedly not a nobleman, in other words—is hardly less fabulous than Chalmers's insistence that the sonnets were really addressed to the queen. The only difference, says Butler, is that his own reading looks at the poems unflinchingly as "unguarded letters in verse," which cannot and should not be excused simply by trying to change the gender of the addressee (this from the author of a book that had argued that the *Odyssey* was written by a woman).[53]

No doubt he had also read Wilde's essay on Willie Hughes, though it is never mentioned, but Butler's amazingly detailed and "squalid" story goes much further: a young and cynical W. H. sexually "trapping" the poet; a practical joke played on Shakespeare by W. H.'s friends, who burst in on the two during their lovemaking, beating and temporarily laming the poet; and so on.[54] Despite the rather startlingly detailed nature of this reading (and Schoenbaum points out a number of possible parallels with Butler's own sexual history), it is one of those rare entries in the debate that is actually able to take the idea of a same-sex relationship seriously—although, as Schoenbaum also notes, "the word *sexuality,* or any variant, appears not once in his essay."[55]

In fact, Butler takes everything to the opposite extreme—and this is where he most resembles Rendall—by arguing not only that the dark lady poems are out of place, but also that most of them aren't even addressed to a woman. Like Rendall, Butler was troubled by the abrupt reference to a woman in sonnets 40–42, as well as by the fact that any sort of traceable "story" seems to fall away once the dark lady is introduced ("a medley of disjointed sonnets," judges Rendall).[56] Butler's solution is simply to move most of the dark lady poems into that section of the young man group, but a complicated wrinkle in Shakespeare's love story is also required: "unable to induce his friend to marry, and indignant that he should continue to be so unappreciative of the charms of woman, [Shakespeare] resolved to bring his own mistress and his friend together—believing this (for the age was lax) to be the greatest service that he could render him." Indeed the *entire* sequence has now become a story of "Greek love," or "the love that passeth the love of women" (terms that are mentioned only on the very last page), just as a number of other dark lady poems, including sonnet 129, are quietly disposed of in an "appendix."[57] As in Rendall's more circumspect rendering thirty years later, in which the dark lady group is also said to have "not much in common" with the young man poems, the sonnets have, but only for the most fleeting of moments, become thoroughly "homosexual" poetry.[58]

Rendall has earned his place in the history of Shakespeare studies for being an influence on Freud's notorious advocacy of the Oxford cause,[59] even though Butler's more forthright rendering might have seemed more attractive from a psychoanalytic point of view. Rendall was also cited by later Oxfordians with great regularity, but they seemed largely to steer clear of the details of his sonnets argument and concentrate on his other books. Butler, on the other hand, was both ridiculed and attacked from the start, but more for his sea cook theory than his sexual daydreams. As Rollins so nicely puts it, this W. H. "aroused considerable and not undeserved mirth."[60] To be sure, a few readers also responded by coming to Shakespeare's defense in matters sexual: "the man capable of writing the sonnets to the dark woman was not a pervert," one of them fumes.[61] But most objectors tried to protect the sonnets from sodomy between men in slightly less direct (or less public) ways. One example appears in a letter from future poet laureate Robert Bridges in 1899, which espoused the familiar defense that the sonnets' "ideal love could be heightened by dissociation from sex." "I think it was the absence of sexual feeling which enabled him to use the sexual imagery," Bridges continues, since this imagery "is of universal application in metaphor, and could only be excluded from a treatment of ideal love by secondary considerations of propriety and the fear of a misunderstanding which S[hakespeare] did not fear."[62] It is not merely that the sonnets are not "homosexual," therefore, whether the term is ever mentioned or not, but that if the poems are sexual at all it is only by virtue of "secondary considerations" that must be kept at bay. Typically, the poems are either "Greek" or desexualized altogether.

Most Looney followers, on the other hand, retreated to other corners, as well as to other characteristics in their master's original eighteen-point list. A good example is Hilda Amphlett's *Who Was Shakespeare?* (the use of self-inflicted question marks in anti-Stratfordian titles deserves a chapter in its own right). She briefly reiterates Looney's idea of the real Shakespeare's attitude toward women ("is it not a little cynical?" she wonders), and although the sonnets display a "constitutional capacity for deep and enduring affection" (but for which gender?), the speaker "yet shows a continual doubt and distrust of women's constancy." Homoeroticism is almost invisible in this discussion as well, not to mention the fact that men played women's roles on the stage: "These women are vital personages . . . they have minds of their own." And as for the fact that the poems to the young man continue well after the marriage theme has dropped away, Amphlett suggests: "Had it become a habit and a solace, as diary-writing always is?" Some habits die hard, and we are politely asked to consult Rendall for further details.[63]

Like so many other Oxfordian treatments of the sonnets, Amphlett's concentrates instead on the speaker's presumed attitude toward money, yet one more argument for his status as a nobleman. Looney's list requires that the real author was "loose and improvident in money matters," and Amphlett concurs: "Is it not evident that Shakespeare regarded money as trash in every sense?"[64] I have always found this reading of the poems particularly puzzling, for it seems to me that the speaker of the sonnets is positively obsessed with husbanding riches from expense, with the expense of spirit in any form, with saving, spending, harvesting, increase, loss, and absence. Far from being the kind of aristocratic poems that nearly all anti-Stratfordians so ardently crave (Looney's earl of Oxford is simply addressing the earl of Southampton), the sonnets seem to me the most bourgeois poems imaginable. Similarly, when Amphlett concludes that the sonnets were "too self-revealing and never intended for publication," we are never told why. Because they were *financially* profligate? In any case, *Hamlet*, as always, is considered the poet's true autobiography.[65]

Finally, let us turn our attention to one last candidate, Christopher Marlowe. Even more than Francis Bacon (or the earl of Oxford), Marlowe has become a standard and indeed central figure in surveys of Renaissance homoeroticism: not merely because of contemporary accusations about his sodomitical inclinations with men (a biographical feature of many other sixteenth-century figures), but also because he has left a body of work that is thought to contain particularly noticeable "queer" passages. The list includes a striking and highly unusual dramatization of Edward II's "homosexual" reign; the opening scene of *Dido, Queen of Carthage,* in which Jupiter is seen dandling Ganymede on his knee; and Neptune's arousal over the naked Leander swimming in his waters. Accounting for such moments is never anxiety-free, and the range of defense mechanisms evident in Marlowe criticism parallels and indeed rivals that of Shakespeare. But here too there is a problem with dates: Marlowe died in 1593. On the contrary, the conspiracy theorists' eyes light up at the strange "coincidence" between this date and the appearance of Shakespeare's *Venus and Adonis,* "the first heir of [his] invention." Thus the solution, which has taken a surprisingly tenacious hold in the anti-Stratfordian imagination, is that Marlowe must have faked his death for political reasons, and gone off to live in exile somewhere in France or Italy or the English countryside (more "lost years"!), whiling away his time lamenting his fate and writing the plays and poems of Shakespeare.[66] And the sonnets, according to this reading, fit like the glove on the hand for which it was made.

The Marlowe theory wasn't new when Calvin Hoffman published *The Murder of the Man Who Was "Shakespeare"* in 1955, but Hoffman's exotic story of lifelong love between Marlowe and his patron, Thomas Walsingham (Walsing-ham is W. H.), written in a suitably sensational journalistic prose, caused quite a stir in its day. The fact that the book runs out of steam halfway through its 250 pages hardly seems to have mattered for "the weirdest cloak-and-dagger tale ever conceived." The coincidence of dates, as well as numerous "parallelisms" found between Marlowe's and Shakespeare's plays, leads Hoffman to conclude that "no one *but* Christopher Marlowe could have written the works of Shakespeare." "But" because of sodomy? Marlowe's "tie" with Walsingham "was unnaturally strong," and the plays usually ascribed to him are full of "implied sexual inversion," "erotic perversion," and "open homosexual love." Marlowe was also mixed up with Raleigh's School of Night circle, some of whom "turned to their own sex for virile outlet" (although "these men were males at all times," and "while they could, and did, indulge in unsanctioned practices, they were soldiers, duelists, poets, normal lovers [*sic*], and adventurers"). Hoffman wonders whether this brotherhood might have "demanded more as an admittance fee than brilliancy and wit; and the possibility that they were all, from Sir Walter Raleigh on down, prone to sexual inversion must be considered." And finally, "it is significant that, up to his reported assassination in 1593, Marlowe is never identified with the opposite sex."[67]

But why is he *Shakespeare*? The answer, not surprisingly, lies in the sonnets, which "take on fresh meaning" if one reads them as expressing "the anguish of a pleading soul, suffocating under forced anonymity." Despite some wonderfully imaginative passages, printed on the best dime-novel paper, Hoffman's discussion of the sonnets themselves is allotted only ten pages, and here he seems to back down, oddly, from the homosexual hypothesis he had so gleefully set up. The emphasis, rather, is on lonely exile, and the fact that the sonnets have led many scholars "to admit that Shakespeare might have been homosexual" is barely mentioned.[68] One has to assume that for Hoffman the Marlovian sonnet story speaks for itself, and indeed there has been no shortage of people willing to step in where Hoffman left off, construing the sonnets as the autobiography of this shoemaker's son (but Cambridge graduate) with the same tireless industry awarded to the sonnets as by Oxford or Bacon.

But that some of these readers should also object to Hoffman's conclusions is hardly surprising. A recent example is A. D. Wraight's *The Story That the Sonnets Tell,* also far from brief, which complains that theories like Hoffman's "have proved scandalous to Marlowe's reputation." "It falls to my hand," Wraight believes, "to exonerate him from the plethora of cruel and unjust calumny that he has borne for so long." The key here is that W. H. and the poet's patron are not the same person, that the sonnets are addressed primarily to Walsingham (for whom "love" and "lover" are merely terms of friendship), while poems to the young man are interspersed throughout the young man group in order to obscure the story. Why, one wonders? In any case, "the one form of love they do *not* celebrate is homosexual love. . . . The sexual love of the *Sonnets* is heterosexual throughout. Any other reading derives from the reader, not from the Poet, *who must be judged essentially as an Elizabethan.*" The proof? Bawdy language was common at the time, "but this was all heterosexual jesting."[69]

Moreover, "Marlowe demonstrably did not commend [homosexuality], as quotations from his works clearly show," and a section titled "Evidence of Marlowe's Heterosexuality" follows. *Edward II* has always been the main obstruction here, and in Wraight's reading, the fact that the king is murdered by being anally penetrated with a red-hot spit "is sufficient evidence that this is not the dramatist's self-identification with the practice of homosexuality. . . . I do not believe that anyone who was himself a homosexual could have written this play." Other scenes with Jove and Neptune are merely mythological, and regarding the sonnet speaker's love for the dark lady, "if he had a sexual problem, it was not a homosexual aberration, but the venereal disease he contracted through his passionate love for a beautiful harlot." Sonnet 20's sexual innuendo was written merely to entertain the young law students of Gray's Inn, but we are never told precisely what, in the final couplet in particular, would have "delighted" them. "Heterosexual jesting"? "Without forcing the sense of a single word or phrase," Wraight concludes, "these autobiographical poems fall naturally into place in the story that has been unfolded, giving the whole that intrinsic quality of an autobiographical tale which has the ring of truth." Such rings may peal less loudly for some, just as the "cries of dismay and disbelief" Wraight expects may well be of another sort.[70]

Have we had enough? We might end by examining a Marlovian groupie who has simply taken the "homosexual" argument to its logical extreme, by claiming that Marlowe/Shakespeare was nothing more nor less than an "out" gay man who unapologetically represented homosexual love over and over again in his plays and poems. This is one of my candidates for the worst Shakespeare authorship book of all time, although I realize these things are a matter of personal taste. It is William Honey's self-published, 1,414-page, single-spaced typescript titled *The Life, Loves and Achievements of Christopher Marlowe, Alias Shakespeare* (1982). Most menacing of all is that according to the title page this is only volume one. I was eternally grateful for the presence of an index, and even a brief perusal of a few of these pages rewards the reader with a taste of the surprising details that lie within. Marlowe poisons the actor William Shakespeare in 1593 and takes his place, since they happen to resemble each other; there are two young men in the sonnets, Southampton and Shakespeare's younger actor-brother Edmund, also Marlowe/Shakespeare's lover and rival for the black prostitute Dark Lady; and so on.[71]

This Christopher Marlowe is a wondrous combination of literary God and vice-ridden superman (murderer, atheist, plagiarist, syphilitic, alcoholic, "defiant homosexual"), who "recklessly 'came out,' as it is called to-day, and everywhere flaunted his homosexuality." "Throughout his works he portrays himself, under a mask of allegory and allusion, as the brilliantly endowed homosexual, scorning the inferior intellects . . . and bewailing the hypocrisy and arrogance of heterosexual society." Lest one try to read into these pages an impassioned, gay pride stance of Honey's own, he also "grudgingly acknowledge[s]" that "homosexual love is as powerful a motivating force as heterosexual," and that there are some poor souls who might "waywardly" desire to "mutate" into homosexuals. I do not care enough to wonder how Honey himself (another W. H.) fits into all of this. Much more important is the fact that "nearly all the plays, and certainly all the poems, of both Marlowe and 'Shakespeare' are exclusively founded upon homosexual love," a stance reminiscent of Butler and Rendall; and that Southampton "reaped the doubtful benefits of friendship with the world's greatest poet and dramatist, being idolatrously revered in the Sonnets and devotedly lauded in the plays, in most of which he appears, sometimes in male guise, sometimes in female, and sometimes in both." We are presented with a body of works in which gay love is expressed by changing the gender of the characters from men to women à la Tennessee Williams (Portia is Southampton; the author is "camping it up" as Constance in *King John*; Cleopatra is in reality a male vamp, and so on), and all because, early on, Marlowe saw "the horror evoked by his too uninhibited portrayal of the homosexual Edward II." The "grotesque liaison with the Black Woman" is necessarily separated from the all-male affair of the sonnets, and the poet eventually overcomes his disgust with her in order to "sacrifice" himself for the sake of Edmund Shakespeare, although the result is that both men end up with syphilis.[72]

I admit that it's unfair to call this particular story "worse" than so many others that have been offered with such astonishing regularity, but I would like to harbor my own vain hope that future theorists could, at least, speak more briefly. Our last Marlowe reading fits this bill very well, three pages in a 1998 issue of the *Harvard Gay and Lesbian Review.* Preferring Marlowe to Shakespeare "would help account for the sonnets about separation and gay love," we are told, and a short paragraph follows summarizing the "writings of gay male authors" throughout history.[73] Interestingly, the piece never actually says "Marlowe was gay." Is this because one must assume that the journal's readers will recognize or know it in advance? But since this assumption is also the crowning "proof" for the Marlowe-as-Shakespeare argument, one might have hoped for more. For is *this* view of Renaissance "homosexuality" any more helpful or less anachronistic than outright denials of homoeroticism altogether, or the endless procession of interpretative contortionists focusing on the young man poems?

Finally, we might close with a look back at Joseph Pequigney's now largely discredited "homosexual" sonnet story published in *Such Is My Love.*[74] This reading has been too harshly ruled out, to be sure, but at the same time one cannot help wondering why the very notion of a sexual Shakespeare, whoever he was, always seems to end up as such an all-or-nothing proposition: a complete identification with the author as some form of protogay man in a homophobic world, or, on the other hand, as a figure in whom sexuality—of any kind—is pushed into the background as much as possible. Shakespeare in a tank top or an angel's robes—it seems as if there are now no other choices than these.

There is indeed something about sexual Shakespeare that readers cannot seem to abide, since even a bisexual bard isn't enough to explain or complete his works' perceived universality, or a Shakespeare that must be "for all time." In a long book on bisexuality Garber refers to the category as "the radically *discontinuous* possibility of a sexual 'identity' that confounds the very category of identity."[75] A clever insight, but one is hard-pressed to know how to apply these categories to sixteenth-century figures, or even to twentieth-century biographical daydreams about them. Perhaps the real lesson of the authorship debate is that having someone else as William

Shakespeare only reinforces this same impasse—and perhaps the issue is not really with Shakespeare at all. My point is not simply that generations of readers have expended so much energy trying to discover the bard's true identity, whether or not they ever pay heed to the messy questions of an accompanying sexual "orientation," but that the very idea of "our own" identity keeps getting in the way. About whom are we dreaming? For these are biographical daydreams not only about Shakespeare, since the allegory is also our own, and indeed the sodomitical fault, to paraphrase Cassius, seems to lie in ourselves.

CHAPTER 4

The Balding Bard: Sexuality and Shakespeare's Portraits

JUDGING BY his two universally accepted portraits, the engraving by Martin Droeshout on the title page of the First Folio and the sculpted half-length by Gheerart Janssen for the Shakespeare monument in Holy Trinity Church at Stratford-upon-Avon, Shakespeare was a balding bard. Even before Delia Bacon had proposed her namesake as the real author of the plays, thus opening the anti-Stratfordian floodgates once and for all, the number of images purporting to depict Shakespeare's true face had already begun to proliferate. No one knows exactly how many Shakespeares there are, but all of them do have one thing in common: a receding hairline.[1] Moreover, this baldness, often euphemistically referred to as a "perpendicular forehead," has become the single most important test for all pretended likenesses.[2] "There is *one* point," wrote James Boaden in 1824, "in the portraits of our author, on which they are all decidedly agreed—viz. that he was *bald*."[3]

Thus it is hardly surprising that baldness, too, should have become a site for the conflicting forces of Shakespearean (de)sexualization. A "perpendicular forehead," in short, can symbolize a bawdy bard as well as an old or impotent one, a hairless androgyne or a sensual libertine (with respect to men or women). The possibilities are appropriately infinite, not to mention the fact that Shakespeare's hair, like his fantasized "sexually active" youth, can always be restored (a recent example is *Shakespeare in Love*). In the end, however, there is a familiar and even more powerful tendency in which these images are supposed to exhibit nothing sexual at all, for that broad expanse of scalp, like embodiments of Shakespeare in general, becomes little more than the marker of the comprehensive and universal brain that lies within. For Washington Irving, Shakespeare's "finely arched forehead" showed "clear indications of that cheerful, social disposition, by which he was as much characterized among his contemporaries as by the vastness of his genius"; for A. L. Rowse, "that magnificent bald cranium [is] like another dome of

St. Paul's—plenty of room there for the most lively (and living), the most universal brain among the Elizabethans."[4]

It is no accident that the whole question of Shakespeare's baldness should have come to a head (so to speak) only at the end of the eighteenth century, just at the time when Edmond Malone had almost single-handedly invented the idea of the authentic Shakespeare. Debates over the portraits began early (Boaden's treatise was the first), but the totality of portrait criticism is thankfully much less extensive than in the parallel debates about authorship or textual accuracy.[5] Readings of the portraits, however, shy away from questions of sexuality in a much more noticeable manner, a surprising fact given that some of the most familiar representations (especially the Chandos portrait, now in the National Portrait Gallery in London) appear to show us a much more romantic and sensuous countenance than the notoriously "wooden" faces of the print and the bust. This relative lack of sexual commentary is also very telling, for in the sixteenth and seventeenth centuries, baldness could be associated not only with old age, infirmity, or impotence, but also with sexual disease.

Indeed, when men's hair was discussed at all, for instance in Shakespeare's own works, it was either with some (satiric) reference to sexual

Martin Droeshout, portrait engraving of Shakespeare appearing opposite the title page of the Fourth Folio (1685). Note that repeated retouching of the engraving has led to the bald forehead appearing more pronounced than ever. By permission of the Folger Shakespeare Library.

Gheerart Janssen, half-length bust of Shakespeare, the Shakespeare monument, Holy Trinity Church, Stratford-upon-Avon. Photo from M. H. Spielmann, *The Title-Page of the First Folio of Shakespeare's Plays: A Comparative Study of the Droeshout Portrait and the Stratford Monument* (London: Humphrey Milford, 1924). By permission of the British Library (11761,dd 17).

potency[6] or to syphilis.[7] Little wonder that viewers have been reluctant to hypothesize a syphilitic forehead for Shakespeare, although such a reading would by no means be beyond the pale of the anything-goes nature of Shakespeare studies as a whole. Biographers make only the most roundabout references to the bard's own lack of hair, if they mention it at all. "He had evidently grown bald early," writes A. L. Rowse, "as early as *The Comedy of Errors* there is a touch of self-consciousness about it." Park Honan concurs: "losing his hair perhaps at about 30, Shakespeare finds baldness a sign of wit, or syphilis, or both."[8] Or was his head shaved?[9] In any case, only the very exceptional reader actually hinted at the possibility of a sexual disease, especially in connection with the dark lady of the sonnets—who is, after all, suspected of having "fire[d] . . . out" the speaker's "better angel" in 144.[10] Presumably one also has to worry about the final two poems, in which the speaker admits that "sick withal, the help of bath desired," a "healthful remedy / For men diseased." Yet the sonnets are almost never linked to Shakespearean portraiture in this way, and to that "perpendicular forehead" in particular.

We are, on the contrary, relentlessly sidetracked by a drastically over-simplified and indeed anachronistic question of whether any of the overflow of Shakespeare portraits really resemble him. Critics usually contend that the print and the bust are the only "verifiable" representations, despite the fact that Jacobean frontispiece engravings and funerary sculptures were not likenesses in the modern sense. These are not Polaroid snapshots and do not try to be (and even a photograph would be a misrepresentation); the print and the bust serve particular functions and represent the artist as an author in very formal and indeed quite stereotypical ways. One regularly reads how these images must in some way show us Shakespeare's true face because they were produced during or shortly after his own lifetime, and that they must have been accepted or at least approved by his family and acquaintances (Jonson praises the Droeshout engraving in an accompanying poem for having "hit" the face of the bard; Shakespeare's wife and other family members were still living at the time of the construction of the monument).[11] Yet Jonson's verse is an utterly hackneyed statement that has no necessary connection to the engraving at all, and indeed there is no reason to assume that he had even seen the print. Moreover, worrying about whether a Jacobean tomb statue actually looked like the recently departed is ludicrous from an art historical perspective. But what else do we have to go on? Surely, it is argued, these two portraits embody some small semblance of verisimilitude, and indeed looked at together, do they not at the very least show us the same person?

What bothers critics most of all, in fact, is that the print and the bust are so unsatisfying on purely artistic grounds.[12] How does one decide on a face for Shakespeare? Or more to the point, how can the bard be embodied? Once again, this discontent seems to have begun only in the eighteenth century. George Steevens described Droeshout's faces as being "as hard as if hewn out of rock."[13] "It is said that when Gainsborough accepted a commission to paint a portrait of Shakespeare he refused to bother with the engraving: 'Damn the original picture,' he exclaimed; 'I think a stupider face I never beheld.'"[14] And if the print is a "pudding-faced effigy," the bust shows us a "self-satisfied pork-butcher." Indeed the sculpture is also regularly criticized for its "unintellectual expression," its "curious, and at first sight stupid, aspect," or its "stupidly hard, coarsely-shaped half-moon eyebrows . . . set too high on the frontal bone." "What are we to make of [this] well-fed gentleman with his short neck, plump sensual cheeks, and vast forehead, who stares at us—rather stupidly, it must be granted—from his station?"[15]

In the seventeenth century, however, the Droeshout engraving had been used for each of the four folio editions, and the plate consequently became more and more worn and needed periodic retouching. By the Fourth Folio of 1685, the latest round of additional cross-hatching had darkened the face so much that the highlight in the center of the forehead was more pronounced than ever, prompting one modern viewer to decry its "horrible

The Chandos portrait of Shakespeare. By courtesy of the National Portrait Gallery, London.

hydrocephalus development." "The face, now swarthy, gleams with oily highlights . . . . Thus did the attempt to freshen the plate demean the subject."[16] Rather than having the portrait entirely reengraved and reinterpreted, as had already occurred at least three times during the seventeenth century,[17] the Chandos portrait was substituted instead. Beginning with Rowe's edition of 1709, engravings of the Chandos face, in a variety of versions and reworkings, began to grace a series of eighteenth-century editions produced by the Tonson publishing house, which both took the portrait as its trademark and owned exclusive rights to reprint the plays.[18] Only in 1773 did the Johnson-Steevens edition return to the Droeshout image. An exception is Pope's edition of 1723, which "in a monumental lapse" used a miniature that probably depicts James I instead (how appropriate for the bard to become king!), but this edition also included an engraving of the Stratford monument that replaced the original head with a version of the Chandos one.[19] Indeed, the question of which image to use had already become a surprisingly important and much-argued topic of discussion for each successive editor. During the last decade of the eighteenth century alone, more than fifteen new editions appeared,[20] each of them requiring a (different) frontispiece portrait of the national poet.

But while the Chandos head was the most popular Shakespeare likeness throughout the eighteenth century, Margreta de Grazia has demonstrated that before Malone's thoroughly "modern" obsessions, editors and engravers showed little interest in actually copying the Chandos head. We see, rather, a series of distinctly classicized interpretations of the image without regard to replicating the painting as it really existed. The exact details of the face, in other words, were not of primary importance for a coronation portrait.[21] A similar "apathy" is traceable in early engravings of the Droeshout print and Stratford monument, which are also at some distance from their originals. This has led to rather pointless controversies about the monument in particular, since it was hypothesized that it had actually been altered in the eighteenth century. The earliest engraving, in William Dugdale's *Antiquities of Warwickshire* of 1656, seems to diverge in radical ways from what we now see. But Dugdale, too, was uninterested in the particulars of Shakespeare's face, not to mention the particulars of the monument itself. His focus, rather, is on the coat of arms, which is meticulously described, and later engravers routinely worked from the Dugdale version without feeling any need to make a trip to Stratford. In fact, they often introduced inventions of their own, such as placing the now-favored Chandos face on the body of the original statue (as in Pope's edition). In the Dugdale version, Janssen's plump-faced, well-to-do figure is made over into what appears to be an "emaciated," "sickly, decrepit old gentleman," or "a decrepit elderly tailor."[22] And the monument's stiff, formal pose, in which the figure is shown with pen and paper writing on a surface resembling a cushion, becomes in Dugdale a pillow pressed against the poet's stomach as if he were "suffering from abdominal pains."[23] One might note that anti-Stratfordians have gotten a lot of mileage out of these "problems," since elaborate theories of a Shakespeare conspiracy are only enhanced by the idea that wholesale changes had been carried out as some sort of cover-up, and a variety of secret messages have been found in the accompanying inscriptions to support such claims.[24] Malone's mistaken attempt to "restore" the sculpture in 1793 by having it painted white also contributed to the confusion; colors were not reapplied until 1861, just at the start of the next wave of advanced bardolatry.

Malone, then, changed everything by preferring the Chandos image as the *authentic* Shakespeare.[25] But what else did he see? As his most recent biographer puts it, summarizing Malone's own manuscript notes on the painting, its appeal lay in its "'poetic' informality: the gold earring in the left ear, a long moustache and a short beard, long and rather untidy hair, open collar, and intelligent eyes."[26] Despite its "perpendicular forehead," in other words, this is a long-haired, romantic Shakespeare rather than a bald

George Vertue, engraving of the Shakespeare monument using the Chandos head, from Pope's edition of Shakespeare, 1723–25. By permission of the Folger Shakespeare Library.

one, and the painting certainly offers a more "human" face compared to the Droeshout print and the Janssen bust. The fact that it is a painting also added to its allure, but criticism remains divided as to its authenticity. Is it Shakespeare? It certainly dates from the (early) seventeenth century; the first recorded copy was presented to Dryden in 1694, and another early imitation apparently dates from the 1660s.[27] But its early provenance remains unclear. By the middle of the eighteenth century, it was hypothesized both that Richard Burbage had painted it and that William Davenant had been one of its former owners.[28] Positing a fellow player as the artist is a nice touch, since it adds new flavor to the appealing notion of a (theatrical?) portrait made by a close friend. As for Davenant, our first bardolator, it is hardly surprising that his name should have become associated with the Chandos as well. In their famous dispute over the picture, Malone and Steevens argued over whether Davenant might have been given the painting since he was the bard's (god)son.[29] However, as we have seen in chapter 2, Davenant was also responsible for perpetuating the poet's early reputation as bawdy gallant, inveterate wooer, and cynical womanizer. Might he have seen *this* kind of Shakespeare in the Chandos face, if he had ever owned it at all?[30] Or did Malone perceive something of the ("heterosexual") libertine that he found in the sonnets?

Certainly, from one perspective, the Chandos seems much closer to showing us a sexual Shakespeare, or, at the very least, a more embodied one. It is, as David Piper has noted, "borne on the main stream of Shakespearean theatrical tradition."[31] In this sense, it has always represented something of an "alternative" Shakespeare image, and if the posthumous Droeshout and Janssen presentments have been considered stiff and masklike, the adjectives chosen to describe the Chandos form a long and telling history of their own: swarthy, romantic, wanton, bohemian, informal, coarse, poetic, untidy, lubricious, ironic, melancholy, foreign, Italian, alien. The most extreme reaction came from Steevens, Malone's archenemy, who referred to it as "exhibit[ing] the complexion of a Jew, or rather . . . a chimney-sweeper in the jaundice." This cannot be a portrait of our (English) Shakespeare, he reasoned, even in the role of Shylock. Like Peter Scheemakers's misleadingly "cavalier" and "gallant" statue in Poets' Corner at Westminster Abbey (erected in 1741), the face of which is heavily based on the Chandos, such images of Shakespeare can "provide no just resemblance of the sober and chastised countenances predominating in the age of Elizabeth." The real Shakespeare, rather, is "modest and unassuming."[32] Part of Steevens's malice is due to the fact that he had found a rival candidate of his own, which he touted with equal fervor as "the only genuine portrait of [the public's] favourite Shakspeare." He is referring to the Felton portrait, discovered in 1792 and also said to be by a player. The tousled Chandos or the lofty fantasy in Poets' Corner

Ozias Humphry, crayon drawing after the Chandos portrait. By permission of the Folger Shakespeare Library.

(which Horace Walpole had called "preposterous") were perhaps just a little too human; the Felton, on the other hand, presented an appropriately "less spritely and confident assemblage of features," "a *quiet* and *gentle* bard of the *Elizabethan* age."[33]

The most remarkable thing about the Felton portrait, however, is that the already extensive Shakespearean forehead has grown to absolutely astonishing proportions—being called, among other things, a "sugar-loaf skull" and an "elongated goose-egg of a head."[34] Indeed Shakespeare's scalp has overtaken the entire image, bolstering, to be sure, Steevens's renewed emphasis on the poet's mildness and sobriety. And while the Chandos was said to have been the property of Davenant, the Felton was assumed to be the earl of Southampton's, an even more impressive prospect. Another dubious candidate discovered in 1770, the Janssen portrait (not to be confused with the Janssen sculpture), was also supposed to have been made for Southampton, and other doubtful Shakespeares appearing by the end of the eighteenth century (the Soest, the Zuccaro, the Hilliard and James I miniatures) all elevated the status of the bard from lowly player to the highest levels of society and fashion. In this sense, perhaps, the Chandos was also an early

The Felton portrait of Shakespeare. The "perpendicular forehead" is here gargantuan. By permission of the Folger Shakespeare Library.

exception, since its open drawstrings, slightly parted lips, unkempt hair, expressive eyes, and gleaming earring might seem more the iconography of a melancholy lover than a man of property (although perhaps both at once).

We should note that not all of these portraits were outright forgeries. Some had simply been mistaken for the bard in the rush to fill the Shakespearean biographical void. Other images might have been passed off as Shakespeare with or without a little retouching (and practically any balding, dark-haired image might do).[35] Still others might be "memorial portraits" made in imitation of Droeshout or Janssen but without any intention to deceive.[36] Malone cites an anecdote in James Granger's *Biographical History of England* (originally published in 1769), in which an admirer "caused a portrait to be drawn for him from a person who nearly resembled" Shakespeare. David Piper has suggested the Soest portrait falls into the same category.[37] And yet it is startling how many of the "revised" pictures had their original hair painted over to make it conform more closely to the requisite Shakespearean forehead. The Janssen painting (not the bust) was originally a

The Janssen portrait of Shakespeare (after restoration). The hairline had been painted out in order to make it resemble Shakespeare's "perpendicular forehead" more closely. By permission of the Folger Shakespeare Library.

portrait of Thomas Overbury, without receding hairline.[38] Another example is the life-sized, three-quarter-length painting known as the Ashbourne, which had one of its ears removed as well. One of the most imposing of all in terms of its presentation of the social status of its sitter, it also caused considerable sensation for anti-Stratfordians when it was proposed that the portrait "beneath" was really that of the earl of Oxford.[39] And the Flower painting, which surfaced in 1892,[40] also seems to have had a doctored scalp at some point in its history.[41]

It is clear, in other words, that a bald bard was already the marker of Shakespearean authenticity, and that in spite of its potential unattractiveness, or even more worrisome connotations, it must have had a certain appeal as well. The earliest treatise on Shakespeare's portraits, Boaden's *Inquiry into the Authenticity of Various Pictures and Prints* (1824), praises the Janssen painting for precisely this feature: "It is extremely handsome; the forehead elevated and ample; the eyes clear, mild, and benignant, . . . the hair receding from the forehead, as of one who would become bald."[42] One of the most curious early fakes deceived Charles Lamb for similar reasons: a Shakespeare

The Ashbourne portrait of Shakespeare. A number of anti-Stratfordian readers have argued that this is actually a portrait of the earl of Oxford, the "real" William Shakespeare. By permission of the Folger Shakespeare Library.

portrait painted on a pair of bellows said to have belonged to the queen herself. The Bellows portrait, as it is now known, shows an exaggerated forehead surpassed only by the Felton, but Lamb described it as "a lovely picture, corresponding with the Folio head": "The countenance smiling, sweet, and intellectual beyond measure, even as He was immeasurable."[43] For Steevens, Shakespeare's "unusually high" forehead suggested a similarly "mild and benevolent character," and a "placid and amiable disposition."[44]

In fact, the Janssen painting stands out as the only likeness that really seemed to inspire Boaden ("nothing can more distinctly embody our conceptions of Shakspeare"),[45] and it is significant that Shakespeare's baldness isn't even mentioned until this painting comes under discussion. An engraving of the Janssen also served as Boaden's frontispiece. We might note that this is the same James Boaden who had been involved in the exposure of William Henry Ireland's Shakespeare forgeries some thirty years earlier. Once a believer himself, he became one of the first to condemn the papers in print, and, as we have seen in chapter 1, he never forgave Ireland for having committed such an "enormous crime . . . against the divinity of Shakespeare."[46] Boaden's *Inquiry* actually begins with a glance at those "outrageous liberties which in the year 1796 were taken with [the bard's] name,"[47] and the preface commences with a very interesting admission: "in spite of the recommendation of Jonson, . . . I sometimes allowed myself to be drawn from [Shakespeare's] works to their writer; the plays sent me back to the portrait before them, and the portrait seldom failed to return me to a more ardent perusal of the plays."[48] In his verses facing the Droeshout print, Jonson had indeed warned Shakespeare's readers to "looke / Not on his Picture, but his Booke," but this sort of back-and-forth movement between picture and text was by Boaden's time a reciprocal reinforcement of the authentic Shakespeare himself, and a similar gesture can be traced in Ireland's own imaginary version of the bard. Thus it might be profitable for us to return to the Ireland case in order to understand the invention of the true Shakespeare (likeness) in greater detail, since this audacious teenager provided not only letters, plays, documents, receipts, annotated books, and a will for the bard, but also several portraits.

Shortly after the imposture came to light, Ireland's *Authentic Account* listed three forged likenesses, all of them based on the bald Droeshout print. The first was a rather childlike drawing of the Droeshout surrounded by a frame, nonsense symbols, the coat of arms, and Shakespeare's initials and signature. The elder Ireland, himself an engraver, was predictably unimpressed by this new find, so his son duly produced a letter from Shakespeare to one Richard Cowley (a player), which presented the drawing as a "whymsycalle conceyte whiche I doe suppose thou wilt easylye discoverre."[49] "I wrote the letter," Ireland later admitted, "thereby wishing to prove *Shakspear* as a perfect good natured man; nothing was meant by the pen and ink drawing, however[;] the world said it was certainly some witty *conundrum,* [and] as to their not being able to explain it, there is nothing surpising [*sic*] in that, for I myself do not know its meaning."[50] The mystery was never unraveled, and this (bald) head was engraved by the elder Ireland and included as the frontispiece for the octavo edition of facsimiles he published in 1796, pompously titled *Miscellaneous Papers and Legal Instruments under the Hand and Seal of William Shakspeare . . . in the Possession of Samuel Ireland, of Norfolk Street.*[51]

One of the most remarkable aspects of this story was the question of how the Droeshout image could have been available at such an early date (even if, as it is still supposed, the engraver worked from an earlier image now lost).[52] This fact did not escape Malone. In his scathing attack on the documents as a whole, and this "miserable drawing" in particular, he sarcastically wondered how Shakespeare, "in addition to all his other great powers, [could] delineate himself after he was dead."[53] In a well-known satirical print from 1796, moreover, "The Oaken Chest, or the Gold Mines

William Henry Ireland, drawing of Shakespeare after the Droeshout engraving, surrounded by nonsense symbols. Samuel Ireland, *Miscellaneous Papers and Legal Instruments under the Hand and Seal of William Shakspeare . . .* (London, 1796). By permission of the Folger Shakespeare Library.

of Ireland," Samuel Ireland is shown pulling various treasures out of a trunk stamped with the initials W. S., while his family are busily creating more forgeries around him. A Shakespeare head graces the wall behind them, inscribed as, "My Own Portrait Drawn by my own Hand from that rare Print by M Droeshout."

We must remember here, as with so many other Shakespeare heads before and since, that much of the attraction for such an admittedly ungainly drawing lay in the idea that it was a portrait *from life,* unlike the dough-faced, posthumous likenesses by Droeshout or Janssen. The Chandos and the Felton, among others, had been similarly venerated. But even better, the letter to Cowley had transformed the "whymsycalle conceyte" into a self-portrait! No wonder that despite its crudeness, Samuel Ireland had selected it as a towering new frontispiece. But William Henry had learned a lesson about artistic merit, so his next attempt was an alteration of the head of someone else. This new portrait, which he says he found one day in a broker's shop, started out as a small two-sided colored drawing with a young English gallant on one side and an elderly Dutchman on the other. "It suddenly struck me," he writes, "that the limning might be of utility to me

"The Oaken Chest, or the Gold Mines of Ireland" (1796). The entire Ireland family is shown busily producing Shakespeare forgeries, with Samuel Ireland at the center, pulling "A Lock of my Dear Williams Hair" several feet long out of a trunk filled with documents, letters, and lost plays. William Henry is shown at left. By permission of the Folger Shakespeare Library.

in my Shaksperian employment." Beside the Dutch figure he added a pair of scales and a knife, transforming him into Shylock, and the English head was enhanced by adding the poet's coat of arms (unfortunately reversed), initials, and a few play titles. Moreover, "having before me a copy of Droeshout's print, I altered the lineaments of the face of the figure represented, giving it as much as possible a resemblance to the print before me."[54]

Bardolators immediately pronounced the drawing as Shakespeare in the role of Bassanio (another new discovery: Shakespeare the player), and "it was gravely stated that the drawing had in all probability graced the green-room of the Globe theatre."[55] Ireland commented that it "was deemed rather extraordinary" that Shylock "should have been arrayed in the *costume* of a

William Henry Ireland, colored drawing of Shakespeare as Bassanio. Samuel Ireland, *Miscellaneous Papers and Legal Instruments under the Hand and Seal of William Shakspeare . . .* (London, 1796), folio ed. only. By permission of the Folger Shakespeare Library.

North-Hollander," but this detail, along with so many others, was easily overlooked. With the aid of a magnifying glass, one expert was even able to find the signature of a well-known Jacobean artist; no one else, including an amazed William Henry himself, was able to see it—although it is clearly visible in the (colored) plates included in the *Miscellaneous Papers*. The elder Ireland added the following rather cautious note: "The figure, there is some reason to believe, although a feeble effort of art, was intended as a portrait of Shakspeare."[56] We cannot determine how the gallant's face had actually been modified, and a hat covers that famous receding hairline. Perhaps the mouth is supposed to suggest the "cupid's bow" shape found in Droeshout, as well as the small moustache and beard; Samuel Ireland noted that the ruff is similar to the print (and also that a stage curtain might be represented in the background), but in any case the two images seem to resemble each other in only the most general way. Malone admitted that he hadn't seen the drawings, and that he was "not entitled, by any knowledge of the art, to decide upon their merit or authenticity" (a somewhat contradictory statement from a man who so often extolled the virtues of the Chandos portrait), yet he quickly

William Henry Ireland, colored drawing of Shylock, on reverse side of the Bassanio drawing. Samuel Ireland, *Miscellaneous Papers and Legal Instruments under the Hand and Seal of William Shakspeare . . .* (London, 1796), folio ed. only. By permission of the Folger Shakespeare Library.

dismissed them as "washed" and "of a recent date," discolored "by tobacco-water" and "fumigation by smoke and brimstone." "The Dutch Shylock," he concludes, "with his blue night-cap, and his hands in his trowsers, will, I am told, be easily recognized by any one who has either visited Holland, or seen any representation of the natives of that country."[57]

William Henry gleefully replied that the drawings did in fact date from the Jacobean period.[58] But a question remains: why Shakespeare and Shylock? Was it dictated merely by the chance of his having found this particular double-sided drawing? In his *Authentic Account,* Ireland claims that he "conceive[d] the design originally to have represented . . . the contrast of a money getting old father, to a son squandering his property in gay apparel and dissipation." A slightly embellished version of the same defense appears in the *Confessions,* but either one might seem a rather odd explanation, especially since the story sounds much more like William Henry's relationship to his own father than anything in *The Merchant of Venice.*[59] Indeed, Shakespeare as Bassanio doesn't even appear to be part of the original plan. Shakespeare as prodigal son? In addition to the recurring romantic daydream in which the bard is very like Ireland himself, perhaps the young man is attempting to reflect (if not quite counteract) numerous other legends that surrounded

Shakespeare by the end of the eighteenth century: deer stealer, horse holder, and so on. Thus, both the creation and the reception of this ironically two-faced image, as is the case with so many other Ireland forgeries, reveals what was really important to a late-eighteenth-century audience: Shakespeare himself, often by his own hand, in all his well-rounded and complex glory. "These papers bear not only the Signature of his hand; but the Stamp of his Soul, & the traits of his Genius," writes one enraptured believer: "his Mind is as manifest, as his hand. . . . They exhibit him full of Friendship, Benevolence, Pity, Gratitude, & Love. The milk of human kindness flows as readily from his Pen, as do his bold & sublime descriptions. Here we see the Man, as well as the Poet."[60] Or, as Samuel Ireland triumphantly states in his preface, "these Papers can be no other than the production of Shakspeare himself."[61]

There was also a third portrait, rarely mentioned and not illustrated in the *Miscellaneous Papers,* which Ireland describes as a "coloured head . . . on parchment [presumably based on Droeshout as well], round which I affixed the names of several players of the day," also gleaned from a copy of the First Folio. The *Confessions* adds that the drawing included Shakespeare's coat of arms as well as his name and age (once again, this is a life-portrait). Ireland reports that "this performance, I know not why, was supposed to be from the hand of the facetious master Cowley, the player; and was gravely stated to have formerly adorned the green-room of the Globe theatre, in all probability as a companion to the Shylock and Bassanio drawing which has been before mentioned."[62] So many grave statements remind us once again of a finite number of persons and places being used to explain everything and anything, but there is also a convenient allusion to the competing legend that Burbage had painted Malone's favored Chandos. Furthermore, below the drawing Ireland had originally included a manuscript poem praising the bard's face signed by Jonson (yet another one!), but he removed it before presenting the picture to his father. Always one to advertise his own literary talents, Ireland included the original poem in the *Confessions*, along with many other examples of the brilliant young man's occasional verses, imitations, and acrostics, as well as long extracts from *Vortigern, Henry II,* and other "Shakespeare" plays.[63]

For the Irelands and their believers, then, the Droeshout image remained the fountainhead of all representations of Shakespeare's likeness.[64] And yet something of the (sexual?) Chandos was clearly also in the young man's mind. For one of his more audacious early creations was an effusive love letter and poem to "Anna Hatherrewaye" from her "Willy Shakspeare," which included a lock of the poet's own hair knotted with silk. One has to assume this is from the pre-bald head of the young bard, who married at the age of eighteen. A (colored) facsimile of the lock was also included in the

Miscellaneous Papers, and according to both Ireland and Malone, an unnamed inner circle of bardolators actually had bits of the holy relic set into rings.[65] "The letter to . . . his wife," William Henry explains, "was to shew his love for her, and that was also meant by the lines addressed to her; as for the lock of hair, it was more a childish frolic than any ways done to strengthen the authenticity of the papers." The *Confessions,* as usual, provides a fuller and somewhat "improved" story, and once again points to the importance of the Droeshout print: "As the engraving of Shakspeare prefixed to the folio edition of his plays, and executed by Droeshout, represents our bard as having short, straight, and wiry hair, I selected a lock of a similar kind, then in my possession (which in my boyish days had been given me as a *gage d'amour*), conceiving it very appropriate to my purpose."[66]

In a certain sense this is a fantasy not only of being able to restore Shakespeare's hair, and thus ridding him of that unsightly "perpendicular forehead," but also a way of supplying a piece of sexual Shakespeare himself—not, however, Malone's "swarthy" sodomite but an ardent young lover in the purest romantic tradition. And yet the Shakespearean lock is also one of our earliest examples of a recurring theme, to which we will return, in which Shakespeare's face is connected to ideas of femininity, since that "short, straight, and wiry" braid is actually a girl's (assuming that it was a female admirer).[67] In any event, the seemingly endless supply of the sacred tress was parodied in "The Gold Mines of Ireland" as well: Samuel Ireland is shown holding "A Lock of my Dear Williams Hair" several feet long.[68] Malone also had a field day attacking the letter and its accompanying hair (the poem, he avers, isn't even worth our attention); taken together, he caustically notes, this is our chance to "behold our bard in circumstances in which he has never before been viewed."[69] The sexual insinuations are apparent. And in his long-winded apology for Ireland's forged Shakespeare papers, George Chalmers wondered why Malone could not accept a young man of eighteen having written such an effusive letter and enclosing such a token, "which, indeed, cool reason can scarcely comprehend."[70] It is notable, however, that this kind of passion is acceptable for Chalmers, even as (as we have seen in chapter 1) he must rule out the possibility of "amatory" sonnets being addressed to another man.

We are beginning to see a familiar conflicting tendency in visualizations of Shakespeare's face, in which his embodiment must be safeguarded from more undesirable sexual implications. Whatever likeness one imagines or indeed finds—and the possibilities are limitless—there seems to be an even more powerful temptation to desexualize him altogether. Something of these contradictory impulses can be traced in the most important Ireland portrait of all, which, however, never actually surfaced. According to his own account, this nonexistent portrait plagued him throughout the months

William Henry Ireland, forged letter from Shakespeare to Anne Hathaway, including a lock of his hair. Samuel Ireland, *Miscellaneous Papers and Legal Instruments under the Hand and Seal of William Shakspeare* . . . (London, 1796). By permission of the Folger Shakespeare Library.

in which he fabricated Shakespearean artifacts. It is not referred to in the *Authentic Account*, but in the *Confessions* we are introduced to the following unhappy slip of the tongue:

> One day being seated at Mr. Samuel Ireland's after dinner [William Henry commonly refers to his father in the third person], during the exhiliration [*sic*] of the moment I was so bereft of my senses as to inform Mr. Ireland that a whole-length portrait, as large as life, and painted on board, would be forthcoming among the various other documents. I had soon sufficient cause to rue this effervescence of the moment; for scarcely a day transpired but I was hourly importuned respecting the whole-length portrait; the production of which, it was stated, would infallibly stamp the validity of the manuscripts.[71]

Not surprisingly, this particular enticement could hardly be fulfilled, since young William Henry's amateurish dabblings in pen and ink or in watercolor were hardly up to the task of such a grand panel portrait, and a full-length one at that. It seems we can take this particular confession at face value, judging by a letter from the elder Ireland in which he boasts of soon being able to procure "a whole length Portrait of him in oil as large as life."[72] The phrase "as large as life" is quite telling, both here and in William Henry's own account, since the bits and pieces of Shakespeare that had thus far been acquired, including even a lock of his hair, pale in comparison to such a prodigious image. The portrait would have been considered the greatest find of all, far outdistancing (and indeed silencing) the enemy Malone and his competing claims regarding the preeminence of the Chandos canvas. Moreover, it seems crucial that such a portrait would, as the *Confessions* so clearly puts it, "infallibly stamp the validity of the manuscripts" as a whole. A full-length life-portrait of Shakespeare, in other words, would not be just one among many important new discoveries, including even two uncut copies of the First Folio that William Henry promised his father at the same time.[73] Sexual or not, this life-sized life-image would also, and even more compellingly, be the monumental representation of the national poet that had been wanting for so long, and that the new age of the authentic Shakespeare now demanded more insistently than ever.

Duped as always, the elder Ireland began to write to his son's fictive benefactor, Mr. H., begging him to remember his promise that "a number of Documents should be brought forth, not only papers, but pictures, drawings etc." "The latter articles," he once again concludes, "would be particularly interesting and might, as being a new specimen of evidence, tend in a great measure to give authenticity to the Papers."[74] At a later point in the imposture, young Ireland presented his father with a schedule of Shakespearean artifacts still in the possession of his Mr. H., but the items were now divided between things that William Henry claims to have seen and those he has only heard about. Various plays and parts of plays in manuscript; verses addressed to Elizabeth, Raleigh, and others; two drawings of the Globe theater; a catalogue of the poet's library in his own hand; even a "Miniature of Shakspeare set in silver" were all confirmed treasures. But the "whole length portrait, said to be of him in oil," is significantly no longer vouched for.[75] For a young self-described genius like Ireland, drawing the Globe, imitating Renaissance penmanship, or even composing a Shakespeare play were easy enough to accomplish, but how on earth would he be able to procure Shakespeare himself in all his full-length glory?

"The Gold Mines of Ireland" shows a miniaturized copy of a such a portrait, barely discernible as it lies on the ground in front of W. S.'s trunk: "My Own Figure at Length 6 Foot," it is inscribed. And as a further indication of the overwhelming import of this sort of find, even Malone, in the concluding remarks of his *Inquiry,* addresses the rumors that such a painting might exist:

> Several months ago we were informed by the believers in these fictions, that the *unknown gentleman* to whom we are indebted for all these fooleries, was possessed of a whole-length portrait of Shakspeare, painted in oil colours; that he there appeared a most goodly personage, of no ordinary stature; that he had been long concealed from the vulgar ken by having been consigned to a garret[;] . . . that Mr. *Ignoto* never thought of washing the poet's face till he was prompted to it by the discovery of other treasures which he has so liberally poured forth; but that this invaluable portrait being at length perfectly cleaned and varnished, it would by the very first opportunity be conveyed to the Metropolis. Week after week, however, has passed away, and month succeeded to month, without the amateur's being gratified with the most curious sight. In the same repository also, we are told (about the same time) two copies of the first folio edition of his plays had been found, with the edges of the leaves uncut, which had been the actual copies that had belonged to Messrs. Heminges and Condell, . . . and added such authenticity to all the rest of the discoveries, as must flash conviction into the most incredulous, and strike all opponents dumb.

But, as he tellingly concludes, we must "acknowledge that whenever these folios and this portrait (the latter of which I do not yet despair of seeing) shall be *brought forward,* they will add considerable support and credit to the manuscripts in question."[76] Even in Malone's eyes, then, such an authentic picture ("of no ordinary stature") might actually validate everything. And yet this is also a rather unguarded moment in his attack as a whole, since a portrait of the bard—which he "do[es] not yet despair of seeing"—was perhaps the one area of Shakespeare studies where the great editor was not so impartial or detached, and where decisions about authenticity could be taken for granted or based more on personal "conviction" than anything else. His obsession with the Chandos painting is legendary; he had it copied at least three times, the most famous version being a crayon drawing commissioned from Ozias Humphry.[77] If the Chandos image was preferable to the other "stupid" representations by Droeshout or Janssen, it was a verdict based on very little concrete evidence. The fact that Davenant's name is mixed up with its shadowy history was seen to authenticate it,[78] but at the same time why should other Davenant interventions (that he was the bard's bastard son, that he possessed a letter from King James addressed to the poet) be discounted while the Chandos fantasy was believed so readily and so completely? Here is Malone's most glaring blind spot, which also prompted him, at exactly the same time, to have the colors on the Stratford bust eliminated to conform more closely to contemporary (or rather his own) taste.

Moreover, the *Inquiry* concludes with a very peculiar daydream of its own. "While I was employed in this investigation," it begins, "I sometimes fancied that I was pleading the cause of our great dramatick poet before the ever-blooming God of melody and song. Possessed with this idea, having after a very restless night closed my eyes at an early hour of the morning, I imagined myself transported to Parnassus, where Apollo and his nine female assessors were trying this question, and were pleased to call on me to deliver my sentiments, as Counsel for Shakspeare, before they should proceed further in the cause." He continues:

> The various poets of all times and countries were amusing themselves with their lyres on the celebrated hill. . . . I immediately knew our author by his strong resemblance to the only authentick portrait of him, which belonged to the late Duke of Chandos, and of which I have three copies by eminent masters. He appeared to be a very handsome man, above the middle size, and extremely well made. The upper part of his head was almost entirely denuded of hair; his eyes were uncommonly vivid, and his countenance was strongly marked by that frankness of air, and gentle benignity, which all his contemporaries have attributed to him.[79]

Here is a full-length portrait all his own. Malone's many enemies were delighted to have such an easy target for ridicule ("a farrago of nonsense," scoffs Ireland in the *Confessions*),[80] and they derided him most of all for using the dream as yet one more opportunity to advertise his beloved Chandos, "denuded of hair," as "the only authentick portrait." Even Samuel Ireland's otherwise feeble response to the *Inquiry* cleverly notes a certain irony in Malone's claim of having three copies of the "only authentick" image.[81]

For Malone, the Chandos embodied a familiar combination of intellectualism and "frankness," handsomeness and "gentle benignity," but it had also become, more than anything else, Davenant's Shakespeare: Shakespeare the wooer, with enticing open collar, earring, and sensual, "swarthy" features.

This is even more conspicuous in the continuation of Malone's dream narrative:

> At the top of the hill [Shakespeare] had found out a pleasant even lawn, where he was playing at bowls with Spencer [*sic*], Sir John Suckling, little John Hales, and two other friends. . . . He had been hunting at an early hour of the morning . . . in the adjoining plains of Phocis, with Diana . . . and a bevy of her nymphs. . . . Recollecting the numerous proofs which his writing (corroborated by the testimony of his contemporaries) exhibit, of the tenderness of his heart and his passionate admiration of the fairer part of the creation, whose innumerable graces add a zest to all the pleasures, and sooth [*sic*] and alleviate all the cares of life, I was not surprised to hear him tell one of his female associates in the chase, that his sport that day had far exceeded any amusement of the same kind he had ever partaken of in his sublunary state.[82]

This bard is plainly interested in other, more amatory sports besides bowls. Might this be the same Shakespeare who had fathered an illegitimate son by Jane Davenant?

Such a bizarre vision (and visualization) is certainly one of the most unexpected fantasies about the Swan of Avon in all his "tenderness of . . . heart" and "passionate admiration of the fairer part of the creation." Yet even Malone's sexualized fantasy figure is bald, by now a convenient (if inadvertent) combination of a gentle and benign Shakespeare and a potentially syphilitic one, a distinctly bawdy bard chasing after nymphs in his paradisiacal afterlife. The irony is that such a "denuded" forehead can be suggestive of so many other things, some of which might be rather unwelcome. I also can't refrain from thinking of an even deeper irony in William Chetwood's *General History of the Stage* (1749), which was the first text actually to print the rumor that Davenant was something more than Shakespeare's godson. For Chetwood goes on to compare the features of the two poets as shown in their folio portraits, and concludes that Davenant's features "seem to resemble the open Countenance of *Shakespear,* but the want of a Nose gives an odd Cast to the Face."[83] The irony is that Davenant *had* lost his nose to syphilis.

As the centuries passed, tastes and requirements changed; we might waver between benign sympathetic Shakespeares and bawdy ones, between earthy middle-class Shakespeares and those of distinctly noble bearing, yet baldness has remained our only constant. And yet this is not an impotent or diseased "perpendicular forehead." It is, rather, an expanse large enough to encompass the brain responsible for the crowning achievements of English literature. And, evidently, the larger the better. This is Shakespeare's comprehensive, universal, and myriad-minded brain, which is somehow degraded by Droeshout and Janssen, despite the admittedly extra-large skulls they both portray. It is also inevitable that there have been numerous "returns" to the primacy of the Droeshout print (if not the Janssen bust) as well, and perhaps precisely because its famed masklike qualities are just the right mirror or inkblot for a wide variety of cultural preoccupations. Not all viewers have maligned the image. Boaden was impressed by its "aspect of calm benevolence and tender thought; great comprehension, and a kind of mixt feeling, as when melancholy yields to the suggestions of fancy." One mid-eighteenth-century viewer preferred the "nobility" of its forehead over "romanticized" versions like the Chandos, and William Blake made a beautiful grisaille after the print.[84] But these deadpan features have also signified that curious and recurring mixture of masculine and feminine qualities embodied by the universal bard, with which I would like to conclude.

One of the clearest examples appears in a 1963 biography by the ubiquitous A. L. Rowse:

> We can tell very well from the Droeshout portrait, which [Janssen's] bust corroborates, what [Shakespeare] looked like. The whole impression is dominated by the magnificent domed forehead and bald cranium—very convincing, plenty of room for that capacious brain. . . . The eyes, under the well-arched brows, are all one could hope for: luminous, full of intelligence, observation, sympathy, but with puffy pouches under them. The face is of a rounded oval shape, cheeks full, prominent nose, fleshy and sensual, with refinement in the nostril. The lips confirm this impression, sensitive and mobile, as became an actor, rather voluptuous, almost a Cupid's bow. Where the upper part of the head is all intelligence, the lower is all sensibility and gives something of a feminine impression, not weak but readily responsive. For we can see under the mask-like expression of an inferior painter that the molded features, in their pallor, are very mobile, could easily come alive with a smile that would communicate itself to laughing, kindly eyes. The hair was worn moderately long over the ears, with a little moustache and goatee beard on the chin; rather a hairless face. What indication we have of the figure beneath the high starched ruff is of a rather slight, sprightly, neatly made man. But, above all, one can never forget the splendid dome of the head, candid and serene, yet retaining what secrets![85]

One could hardly ask for a more legible fantasy of the masculine and feminine combined: the "bald cranium" and the "hairless face"—a bard of intelligence and sympathy, observation and sensitivity, sensuousness and refinement. Above is all "capacious brain," below is that "voluptuous . . . Cupid's bow" of a mouth; a "magnificent domed forehead" atop "a rather slight, sprightly, neatly made man." So much for the customary complaint that the Droeshout head is too large for its body. And all of this also has to be integrated with Rowse's equally vociferous characterization of the bard, in another biography published ten years later, as "excessively heterosexual."[86]

Rowse's praise is not really praise of Droeshout's print, however; rather, he appears to be speaking about the Flower painting, commonly referred to as "the Droeshout portrait" (note, too, that he derides the "inferior painter" and not engraver). This distinction is not very clearly made in the text, perhaps indicative of the fact that such a rhapsody on Droeshout's engraved likeness presents just too much of a challenge—although anything is possible, and even Dugdale's distortion of the Stratford monument has found its admirers.[87] The Flower painting, in fact, makes numerous corrections to Droeshout's quirky performance.[88] Rowse's book also uses the Flower picture as its frontispiece, but it is now a grotesque hybrid of a visibly retouched photograph of the Flower face and collar superimposed on a drawn body and background.[89] Hardly the first time Shakespeare heads have been placed on different bodies, for whatever reason, this is also a premonition of innumerable computer-enhanced and virtual Shakespeare images yet to come.[90]

Yet one does not have to look very far to find parallel examples of visual and/or rhetorical retouching, both popular and scholarly, usually tucked away at the end of Shakespeare biographies and general introductions. Robert Speaight's *Shakespeare: The Man and His Achievement* also comments on the masculine/feminine Flower painting (although once again not mentioned by name), as "not a very lively portrait, but it tempts one to exclaim with Hamlet: 'See what a grace was seated on this brow . . . the front of Jove himself / An eye like Mars to threaten and command,' balanced by the sensitivity of the nose and mouth." Peter Quennell finds in the Droeshout lips a "faint ironic smile" worthy of the Mona Lisa, but only "if we examine them very closely"; in sum, "a worldly face, sensual, skeptical, alert; Shakespeare was no visionary artist, who shrank from distracting mundane pressures, but a man of the world who grasped the chances it offered and, shrewdly, perhaps a trifle cynically, made them serve his own creative ends." Park Honan's long biography, published in 1998, has hardly improved matters. The preface begins by claiming that "the factual truth as we piece it together is more exciting, suggestive, and tantalizing than anything so far dreamed up about him."[91] Hardly, since Honan's own dreams frequently go so much further. The Droeshout print, for example, "suggests a different side of him" from his early reputation as a womanizer, "for which there is plenty of evidence." Rather,

> Droeshout's engraving portrays a thoughtful man with delicate if not fastidious features, an observer who, though "of an open and free nature," is most unlikely to have impressed anyone as a flamboyant extrovert. If the portrait lacks the "sparkle" of a witty poet, it suggests the inwardness of a writer of great intelligence [versus the usual complaint of the "stupid" face of the print], an independent man who is not insensitive to the pain of others, and who could have written *Timon of Athens*, *Macbeth*, or *King Lear* [and the sonnets?].[92]

This passage is typical of Honan's presentation as a whole, in which random bits of "factual truth" are simply "pieced together" by purely imaginary—and indeed highly romantic—leaps of logic and inference. What is so "exciting, suggestive, and tantalizing" about this reading of the Droeshout print, or about illustrating a side view of the Stratford bust alongside facsimiles of Shakespeare's signature?

In *The Art and Life of William Shakespeare,* Hazelton Spencer justly laments that "there is no more to be gained by waxing eloquent against the stolid features of the two earliest portraits than by rhapsodizing over the noble forehead both exhibit."[93] But what does this baldness signify? Weakness, debility, old age? Passion, or perhaps even a certain feminized hairlessness? Is this a syphilitic forehead or a fecund, creative, and even motherly one, whose more than ample size is simply an indicator of the poet's amazing breadth of mind? Baldness, in short, paradoxically covers up rather than reveals, for the "perpendicular forehead" indicates an emotional, feeling, and above all "gentle" Shakespeare, who, precisely by virtue of his universality and all-encompassing nature, is capable of swallowing up any unsavory suggestiveness (sexual disease, profligacy, sonnets to a young man).[94] We might call it the Shakespeare of the Tribe of Edmond: an authentic Shakespeare who might, according to early modern definitions, be a sodomite with women or with men; who might have mastered the rhetoric of wooing or theatrical gender disguise or the witty "reversal" of gender roles; but who, ultimately, could just as easily be divested of sexuality of any kind. And like the appreciably more "human" Chandos image, or the bawdy poet of Malone's dream, or even Ireland's never-to-be-uncovered full-length portrait, each likeness, in its own way, seems tailor-made for just this sort of appropriation. It is certainly much easier to see an androgynous, hairless face than a syphilitic one, but it is even more obligatory—this is "Shakespeare" after all—to find the awesome, sage brow of the "impersonal" national symbol.

Fortunately, Shakespeare's (lack of) hair has never spawned its own industry of critical commentary, despite occasional commotions surrounding such finds as traces of auburn-colored hair (although only of the eyebrows and beard) in the famous Kesselstadt death mask, discovered in 1849.[95] Painstaking measurements were taken to authenticate it, bolstered by the fact that Janssen's bust once showed hair of a similar color (it had not yet been restored from Malone's whitewashing), as well as a long tradition, perpetuated by Malone himself, that the bust itself was made from just such a mask.[96] Once again we find a fantasized restoration of Shakespeare's hair, and as at many other points in history the whole process might have been carried much further were it not for a convenient curse inscribed on the poet's tomb, successfully guarding its remains from being disturbed.

There have been a number of crusades to exhume the bard's body, beginning around the time of the death mask, and one imagines that finding the poet's skull would, to many, seem the final means of authenticating the portraits.[97] We could then move into a new and exciting period of DNA-Shakespeare research,[98] proving that the bard was Queen Elizabeth after all, and although it might also prove beyond a shadow of a doubt that the forehead was distinctly "perpendicular" in shape, we would still be left with the question of whether—and why—it was "denuded of hair."

We might close by wondering why there seem to be so few explicitly "homosexual" readings of Shakespeare's portraits, and especially the Chandos, since a balding man with an earring was, at least at one time in the late twentieth century, a stereotyped image for gay men. Certainly such readings exist, but one can safely say, I think, that the general trend in Shakespeare portrait criticism has always been in precisely the opposite direction: to embody the bard even as he is desexualized, thereby steering him away from all varieties of sexual suggestiveness, which the (authentically "perpendicular") bald forehead might also signify. If Shakespeare's biography is tormented by these issues, one can only expect to find similar conflicts in discussions of the poet's likeness. And both areas are really "lost years" characterized by a profound lack of reliable evidence.[99] As Steevens so aptly put it in 1793, just as Shakespeare "was careless of the future state of his works, his solicitude might not have extended to the perpetuation of his looks."[100]

Surveying the commentary on Shakespeare's baldness is made easier only insofar as there is so much less of it. At least we are free from the kind of relentless onslaught that surrounds the authorship controversies, but wading through art-historical pronouncements by traditional Shakespeare scholars, offering distinctly unscholarly comment on what the "authentic" Shakespeare must have looked like, is not necessarily less painful or less misleading. Favored candidates are accepted without any proof, and, on occasion, even with the awareness that the image isn't authentic at all.[101] As in Malone's *Inquiry,* the whole discussion usually remains something of a blind spot—or rather bald spot—that can always be covered over. Yet what kind of likeness could possibly satisfy us? As Marjorie Garber has written, "Shakespeare as an author is the person who, were he more completely known, would not be the Shakespeare we know."[102] If he has to be embodied, and indeed it seems that he *has* to be embodied, then any portrait, like any version of the life, will never be authentic enough.

EPILOGUE

Shakespeare in Love: An Idiot's Guide

SHAKESPEARE MAY not be the universal high-culture icon he once was, but he continues to be a very marketable commodity. Witness the extraordinary artistic and commercial success of John Madden's 1998 film, *Shakespeare in Love,* which stands at the center of a vogue for Shakespeare-related representations in late-1990s popular culture. The film's popularity is certainly due to its extremely conventional story of star-crossed heterosexual love, based on an equally conventional reading of *Romeo and Juliet.* But since Shakespeare himself is a rather academic subject for most audiences, it is surprising to see the film capturing the public's imagination to such a degree. Making Shakespeare look like a young pop star has certainly helped, not to mention a convenient fashion for beards of all shapes and sizes, but at the same time the film goes to great lengths to create an authentic "Elizabethan" setting, filled with names, places, and dates otherwise encountered only in an undergraduate lecture course. Screenwriters Marc Norman and Tom Stoppard have clearly done their homework, whether it consisted of reviewing old school notes or reading new ones from "Dr. Stephen Greenblatt," respectfully thanked in the film's closing credits.[1] The film is set in 1593, conveniently enough in the bard's "lost years," just before the death of Christopher Marlowe, an integral part of the film's story, too. Future tragedian John Webster also plays a key role, and luckily enough we know even less about his early life than about Shakespeare's. The Master of the Revels, Queen Elizabeth, the Admiral's Men, Ned Alleyn, the Rose theater, Philip Henslowe: all the names are there. Yet many other aspects of the film—sadly or refreshingly, depending on one's point of view—are hardly Elizabethan at all.

One can always come to the film's defense—as my students invariably do when I begin to rant and rave in Shakespeare seminars—that the story is after all "only fiction." We have seen that the Shakespeare biography is indeed something of an open field, but what we should like to know is precisely what kind of fiction the film is, and moreover what has been done to render Shakespeare not only palatable but apparently irresistible to a contemporary mass-market audience? It is not my aim to offer an in-depth reading of the film and its place in contemporary mass culture, a task that has been very capably begun elsewhere,[2] but only to point out that one of the film's most tellingly ambivalent aspects is precisely its depiction of a sexual Shakespeare. Not only do we see an expressly "heterosexual" bard, and barely even the licentious womanizer found in pre-Malone biographical reconstructions, but even the boys-as-women theatrical convention, which once again the film is careful to depict in a purportedly accurate fashion, is distinctly devoid of sexual connotation or erotic innuendo. When we first meet boy player Sam Gosse, "female star of the Admiral's Men," a worried Will Shakespeare "thrusts a hand between Sam's legs" since the latter's voice seems to have broken. "Have they dropped?" Will asks (*SIL*, 52). Later on when the company has been accused of using a woman in its production of *Romeo and Juliet,* Tilney proceeds to pull up Sam's dress in order to unmask "her." While the camera focuses on Sam's face, everyone else looks on in silence as, we assume, the boy player's male anatomy is revealed. The screenplay is more explicit: "Tilney pulls up his [Sam's] skirt, ignoring Sam's rather guttural yells of protest and pulls down Sam's drawers" (*SIL*, 122). Whatever sort of sexual connotations the film may be trying to suggest in these two examples, and the answer seems to me far from clear, everything is soon overshadowed by the film's "trick" of a woman in disguise as a boy rather than the other way around (although these two crossings are hardly symmetrical).[3] Just after Sam's skirt is lifted up, in fact, Viola reveals herself by screaming at a mouse and frantically removing her wig (*SIL*, 122). "Her hair is pinned up," says the screenplay, "but there is no question about her gender" (*SIL*, 122). Could the same ever be said for the gender of an Elizabethan boy player, whether or not his wig were pulled off like Jonson's Epicoene, or whether or not, as in *Shakespeare in Love,* his (undeveloped) sexual organs were the constant object of bawdy jokes?

The center of the film, rather, as well as the chief interest of this sexual Shakespeare, is Viola. Since she is still wearing a man's clothes in many of her love scenes with Will, one might argue that the film does contain moments that could be called homoerotic. But in two instances when they kiss with others looking on, once while rehearsing and once in a boat crossing the Thames, any suggestion of homoeroticism is just as quickly papered over. In the first example, a completely undeceived boatman immediately addresses Viola as "my lady," countering and indeed saving Will from his "stunned" surprise at having been kissed by a young man (*SIL*, 67). In the second example, during the company's rehearsal of the first act of *Romeo and Juliet* ("the moment when 'Romeo' and 'Juliet' kiss for the first time," the screenplay reminds us [*SIL*, 73]), Will steps in to show Viola as Romeo how s/he should kiss the boy Juliet. But instead of kissing Juliet, Will kisses Romeo, and Ned Alleyn's sarcastic reaction is garbled and cut off a little too early. The screenplay is once again much more suggestive: "Well! It was lucky you were here! Why do not I write the rest of your play while you—" (*SIL*, 75). The idea seems to be that Alleyn, and by extension all those present, sees Will passionately kissing a male player and getting carried away ("they lose themselves for a fraction of a moment," the screenplay notes [*SIL*, 75]), but the film immediately moves away from the sexual implications of this indeed very Elizabethan moment, and instead focuses on the low comedy of Juliet's nurse played by Ralph Bashford, a burly adult male player who, like the boy playing Juliet, is seen wearing a dress but no wig or makeup. (Never mind that there is absolutely no historical evidence that older female speaking roles would have been played by adult rather than juvenile actors.) Much like the earlier moment in the boat, Will (or rather the viewer) is again conveniently rescued from the boy-actor convention's potentially disruptive sexual suggestiveness, which the film only seems willing to depict when there is a woman beneath the clothes rather than a boy. We are like the young John Webster spying on the lovers through a hole in the wall: "I saw her bubbies!" (*SIL*, 121)—and so do we, in more than one scene.

The film is also careful to show us male actors simply wearing dresses rather than men in drag, even if this happens to accord quite well with contemporary Elizabethan practice, where boy players were hardly supposed to fool the audience into thinking that they were "really women." The same rules do not apply, however, to Viola's disguise as Thomas Kent (how does she get all that hair under her boy's wig anyway?), and the film's novelty of having Viola play Romeo rather than a Romeo play Viola serves in effect as a reassurance for mass-market audiences that what we see, despite all appearances to the contrary, is just a man and a woman embracing. We can have our Shakespeare in love but at the same time remain free from the necessarily homoerotic remainder of boys who play women.

Similarly, despite the film's clear attempt to depict a historically accurate theatrical setting, the performance of *Romeo and Juliet* we see at the film's climax is made to mark a kind of theatrical "revolution" that brings us firmly into an anachronistic world where only women play women. Everyone seems to forget that in 1593 boys were actually *preferable.* The moment when Viola steps on the stage in her own wedding dress as Juliet is perhaps the film at its most fantastic: "There is a collective gasp. Nobody has ever seen a boy player like this" (*SIL*, 137). Indeed. Viola herself mouths the "correct" criticism of boy performers as far as the film is concerned: "Stage love will never be true love while the law of the land has our heroines played by pipsqueak boys in petticoats!" (*SIL*, 20). "True love" is only viable when boys remain boys, and the acting style itself must be emphatically "natural." This is Marlon Brando, not Richard Burbage. The film marks this overthrow even with Viola's first audition: "Where did you learn how to do that?" a shocked Will involuntarily asks (*SIL,* 34). Or as the screenplay puts it, during the duel between Mercutio and Tybalt, "the tone of the playing is unlike anything we have seen before: without bombast, intense and real" (*SIL,* 139). A lengthy and important sequence in the middle of the film, which rapidly crosscuts between the company rehearsing the play and the lovers themselves acting out a version of it in Viola's bed (*SIL,* 80–85), is another clear statement of the film's conviction regarding a necessary intermingling of art and life, or rather between the development of Shakespeare's genius and his own intimate, true-love experience. Just as in countless biographical fantasies, from Thomas Tyler's Mary Fitton to A. L. Rowse's Emilia Lanier (not to mention Wilde's W. H.), Viola is even the direct inspiration for all of Shakespeare's early work, including the sonnets and *Twelfth Night* ("Write me well" is her valediction to Will [*SIL,* 153]). "Shall I compare thee to a summer's day" is quite literally addressed to her as a "letter-poem" (*SIL,* 61). There is no hint here of poems to a fair young man, or for that matter even a dark lady, although there is at least some suggestion of the latter in the figure of Rosaline, "big breasted, dark-eyed, dark-haired, sexual" (*SIL,* 14), who had asked early on: "When will you write me a sonnet, Will?" (*SIL,* 17). But she too ultimately must be overcome in the name of "true love," just as, even more urgently, genders must be straightened out (sexualities don't really come into play at all), and acting must become "believable" even to the extent where one is asked to equate actors and their roles, before this purportedly Elizabethan performance—and by extension the film we are watching—is able to succeed. During the balcony scene, "we cannot tell whether this is the play or their life. The audience, and the rest of the world, might as well not exist" (*SIL,* 141). A similar reminder, which oddly does not actually appear in the film, occurs when Romeo kisses Juliet in the death scene: "Viola's eyes flicker open . . . and the lovers look at each other for a moment as Will and Viola rather than as 'Romeo' and 'Juliet.' Their eyes are wet with tears." The film seems more interested in the fact that the spectators "are weeping openly" (*SIL,* 143). True love, true theater. And at the play's conclusion, after a long moment of silence, "the audience goes mad with applause" (*SIL,* 145); one almost expects them to be holding programs.

It is also true, however, that the film is quite self-conscious about many of its fictions, and indeed that it is also meant to be a parody of the (lack of) Shakespearean biography and the theatrical milieu in which his plays were written and performed. Elements of satire are once again more explicit in the screenplay. It's a pity that it has become just another tie-in for the film ("Now a Major Motion Picture," the front cover boasts), having been reduced to the level of a volume like *Shakespeare in Love: The Love Poetry of William Shakespeare,* also published by Miramax, a very slender collection of poems and songs from the plays along with a few sonnets, all presented in a specifically heterosexual context and accompanied by still photographs from the film (the screenplay unfortunately includes this last feature as well).[4] The screenplay's stage directions, however, often provide clues as to how lines should be read, or to the tongue-in-cheek nature of many of the characters' actions. While waiting in the wings, for instance, Will Kempe "has one foot on the box [of props]. He finds a skull . . . in other words he reminds us of Hamlet" (*SIL,* 13; ellipsis in original). During a gathering at Viola's home, "the guests form up to begin a changing-partners dance (the very same one you get in every *Romeo and Juliet*)" (*SIL,* 42). The fight with Wessex "becomes a parody of the Hamlet duel" (*SIL,* 119), and so on. Most of these moments also come across in the film, especially for viewers in the know, and there are also some nice in-jokes regarding long-standing Shakespearean controversies, such as our first glimpse of Will practicing his signature in a variety of different spellings (*SIL,* 5), or Viola's clever anti-Stratfordian joke before she and Will make love for the first time: "Answer me only this: are you the author of the plays of William Shakespeare?" (*SIL,* 68). Norman and Stoppard have also made clever use of the popularity of Marlovian tragedy constantly plaguing the aspiring Shakespeare; of future blood-and-guts playwright John Webster gleefully feeding mice to a cat; and of first-draft names for plays such as *One Gentleman of Verona* or *Romeo and Ethel.* We are also clearly meant to think of Shakespeare's own cross-dressed heroines (Portia, Rosalind, Viola) when Viola de Lesseps masquerades as Thomas Kent. She seems most closely modeled on Rosalind, even if the film's sexual complexity pales in comparison to *As You Like It*: the film bears little trace of a Rosalind pretending to flirt with a deceived Orlando while she is disguised as a boy, and no trace at all of a Phoebe who falls in love with Rosalind, too. Perhaps Hymen also comes to mind during the film's own deus ex machina resolution, in which the queen herself, however historically ridiculous it may be, descends upon a public theater to rescue the play and its true-love lovers. It's a nice touch to provide her with a reminder that like a boy player she too is passing in a man's world (*SIL,* 148), but I'm not certain that there is irony intended in her remarkably chatty invitation to "Master Shakespeare," future god and national poet, to call on her at Greenwich. In chapter 1 we examined William Henry Ireland's ludicrous letter from Elizabeth to "goode Masterre William," and we might also be reminded of an equally preposterous story, published in 1825, in which the queen herself "used frequently . . . to sit delighted behind the scenes when the plays of our bard were performed."[5] *Shakespeare in Love,* in so many ways, is an equally romantic document.

Or, rather, the film represents a late-twentieth-century version of romantic caricature, in which exceedingly conservative notions are simply reintroduced with a new pretense of "ironic" self-awareness. In this sense the film is certainly no different from other recent attempts to make the bard more accessible and indeed masterable for general audiences. I am thinking particularly of a new series of guides to Shakespeare and his theater now found in shopping mall bookstores, shelved in a special Shakespeare section (he is the only "classical" author still accorded this privilege) alongside a myriad of new editions (there's clearly a lot of money to be made here as well) and an arbitrary selection of "serious" Shakespeare criticism. These guides are not simply a result of the overwhelming commercial success of *Shakespeare in Love,* for the film itself has simply grown out of a larger and far more complex cultural impulse to "dumb down" Shakespeare, in Richard Burt's felicitous phrase.[6] Like the film, the overall tone of these volumes can be described as a peculiar combination of outspokenness and prurience, for while they claim to bring Shakespeare to the general reader with a fashionable in-your-face frankness, the resulting analysis, when it is historically accurate at all, can espouse surprisingly outdated and even repressive views of "Renaissance" sexuality. Indeed these are "idiot's guides" in the truest sense of the word, and one may well wonder whether they are meant to appeal to a self-described idiot or whether they just make you into one. Popular introductions are hardly new to the Shakespeare industry, but these newest how-to volumes are different. At the risk of sounding overly simplistic, it seems to me that instead of encouraging readers to break out of their own everyday experience for the sake of a new level of understanding, these volumes are intent only on reducing Shakespeare to pop culture norms and idioms and buzzwords, enabling us to "understand" the works by bringing them to a level that we already know, as if one should never want to get beyond the world of the chat room or the strip mall.

The most egregious example of this tendency may be *The Complete Idiot's Guide to Shakespeare* (1999), advertised on the cover as by "Laurie Rozakis, Ph.D." While this certification supposedly ensures that the material is factual and professionally validated, the constant onslaught of slang terms and idioms to follow (American only, please), especially in chapter and section titles, obscures whatever argument might also be present. Surprisingly, this self-aware, postmodern guide barely even mentions women's roles being played by boys, but then again what kind of idiom could one find to account for something so far removed from modern gender prejudice? "What a Drag," the section is called. The text proceeds to inform us that Shakespeare couldn't really portray physical manifestations of sexuality in his plays precisely because everyone was male! "Now you know the main reason why there's so little hanky-panky touchy-feely in Shakespeare's plays." "But what's a boffo play without a little nooky?" this Ph.D. concludes; "walking that fine line between class and trash, Shakespeare peppered his plays with bawdy puns and sexual allusions."[7] These few turns of phrase tell us nothing, and we have to wait a very long time before the text broaches such sexual questions again. It is only in the very last chapter, in fact, on the sonnets, in a section called "I've Looked at Love from Both Sides Now." The issue of male homoeroticism can no longer be avoided, it would seem, but here the book rather startlingly asserts that *all* the poems were addressed to a man. "We're pretty certain that the sonnets were addressed to a man (yes, even the 'Dark Lady' ones). This suggests to many that Shakespeare was gay or bisexual." At this point we are referred to Joseph Pequigney's *Such is My Love,* the only scholarly reference in the entire book, despite the fact that Pequigney makes no such argument about the dark lady poems, so far as I know. "Dr. Pequigney . . . was one of my professors," the author ultimately reveals. But what has she (or we) really learned? Simply that "no one knows whom Shakespeare addressed in the sonnets. It appears to have been a man, which raises the issue of Shakespeare's sexual orientation."[8] Hardly. One would be hard-pressed to identify any issue that this book has actually "raised," least of all having to do with "sexual orientation," a term that has no meaning at all in an early modern context.

Shakespeare for Dummies (1999) is an ostensibly more serious presentation, and it is markedly more "English" than the *Idiot's Guide* (there's even a foreword by Judi Dench). But the text repeats the same old party line that boys were used for female roles simply because actresses weren't available. Consequently, "Shakespeare made life a little easier for boy actors by writing parts in which the female characters dress up as males."[9] Why should it be easier for a boy to dress as a girl dressed as a boy? Remarkably, there is no mention at all of the potential eroticism in this convention, and perhaps even more astonishingly, there isn't even any mention of homoeroticism in the book's chapter on the sonnets. One is relieved to see far fewer slangy puns here, and the volume does have the virtue of explicitly encouraging us to read and watch Shakespeare, but what sort of information is being fed to—or rather withheld from—the "dummies" addressed on the title page?

A third example is *Shakespeare for Beginners* (1997), part of a well-known series of comic books with similar titles, but here the accompanying texts are of an equally cardboard nature. We are told for example that "the women's parts were played by [adult] men. Ingenues (young girls) were usually played by boys."[10] What is the source for this amazing piece of inaccuracy? A summary of the sonnets informs us that "many of the poems in the group 1–126 seem to be addressed to a young man, a friend of the poet's; numbers 127–154, on the other hand, feature poems directed to a darkly featured woman, addressed as the poet's difficult lover."[11] We might as well be in the eighteenth century, when critics also carefully distinguished between the absolute categories of friend and lover, young man and dark lady. And like Malone, Coleridge, and Boswell before him, our modern author also dares not even speak the name of sodomy.

Last and perhaps least, we have *Naughty Shakespeare* (1997). The purpose of this volume is to expose "the seamier side of Shakespeare," to convince us "that when the Bard was bad, he was *really* bad."[12] A British edition published the following year includes a similarly colloquial subtitle: "The Lascivious Lines, Offensive Oaths, and Politically Incorrect Notions of the Baddest Bard of Them All." Yet even in this volume the boy player convention goes unmentioned until the last chapter, disturbingly called "A Note on Unnatural Acts." The discussion begins by reminding us that "friendship and love weren't as sharply distinguished in Shakespeare's day as they are now," and thus one can "find romantic terms in surprising places, such as the *Sonnets*." "Despite the florid poetry, Shakespeare really only toys with the youth; he's flattering him, not making a pass at him," even if today "the sexual overtones of the platonic sonnets have come to seem less innocent." Malone lives! But it gets worse: "Tempting as it is to psychoanalyze the Bard, we must take into account the Elizabethans' less squeamish attitude toward intense male bonding. So long as the bonding didn't cross the line into actual sexual activity [!], they were content to allow men to *talk* like lovers." "That boys played female parts was unremarkable at the time, though it did cause the Puritan fits. Elizabethans were quite capable of suspending disbelief and they had to be [!]. . . . A boy who dressed and talked like a girl functioned in everyone's mind as a girl." One senses that the possibility of Shakespeare himself "making a pass" at a man must be kept at bay at all costs, even if "in the text of his plays, Shakespeare imagines a whole range of possibilities for same-sex affection." The examples chosen are telling indeed. The relationship between Antonio and Bassanio in *The Merchant of Venice* "is only the strong bond between an older relative and a younger [!]. Antonio *is* hurt and jealous when Bassanio marries; but that doesn't mean he's *sexually* jealous." Need we go on? Some plays are "a bit more curious," for example *As You Like It* and *Twelfth Night,* which are summarized but not analyzed, and the boy brides in *Merry Wives* are "also interesting." But "all this is within the bounds of 'natural' emotional folly." The appeal to "nature" is always a last resort. "A few other cases, however, call for more serious attention. Hostess Quickly obviously refers to unnatural acts when she says that Falstaff 'will foin [thrust] like any devil, he will spare neither man, woman, nor child' (*2 Henry IV* 2.1.16–17). But she doesn't even realize she's equivocating lewdly. . . . There's no way to avoid the obvious meaning, though, in two plays that deal with Greeks and Romans, whose sexual tolerance was notorious [to say nothing of the English]. Everyone in

Troilus and Cressida knows that the dissolute warrior Achilles has a thing going on with Patroclus," and regarding *Coriolanus*, "we can only imagine what Aufidius's passion would have led to, since before it gets much farther he kills Coriolanus. Talk about tough love."[13] End of chapter, end of discussion.

My apologies for having quoted this blithely homophobic, "naughty" text at such length, but its selection of "curious" or "interesting" references to homoeroticism, as opposed to "obvious" examples that can easily be explained away, seems to me indicative of a larger tendency to underwrite a postmodern sexual Shakespeare that is willing to go only so far and then stop dead in its tracks. A depressing but familiar mixture of candor and exclusion, our Shakespeare in love hardly seems to have advanced in the last two hundred years, even though his ghostly presence is stronger than ever. Hardly an example or a spokesman of a heightened sense of the reality and variety of human sexualities, including queer ones, this is a sexual Shakespeare who, in short, continues to be thoroughly desexualized.

Notes

Introduction

1. Including, for example, a never-ending spate of new editions and facsimile reprints, with their variant readings, glosses, introductions, and critical commentary; occasional scandals caused by renewed attempts to absorb previously excluded works or versions of works into the true Shakespeare canon; and (despite its anti- or postauthorial claims to the contrary) the study of the material conditions under which the works would have been composed, published, or performed (and perhaps best of all, in a newly reconstructed Globe theater). For more on the "authentic Shakespeare," see Stephen Orgel, "The Authentic Shakespeare," *Representations* 21 (1988): 1–25; and Gary Taylor, *Reinventing Shakespeare: A Cultural History from the Restoration to the Present* (Oxford: Oxford University Press, 1989).
2. One can sense a certain drop in the overall value of Shakespearean stock in the contemporary cultural marketplace, where even a basic knowledge of "the bard" no longer seems to be the cultural given it once was. See for example Gary Taylor, "Afterword: The Incredible Shrinking Bard," in *Shakespeare and Appropriation,* ed. Christy Desmet and Robert Sawyer (London: Routledge, 1999), 197–205.
3. S. Schoenbaum, *Shakespeare's Lives,* 2d ed. (Oxford: Oxford University Press, 1991).
4. This list is necessarily highly selective. For example, one might also include versions of Shakespeare in film, video, and popular fiction, none of which are examined here. See Richard Burt, *Unspeakable ShaXXXspeares: Queer Theory and American Kiddie Culture,* rev. ed. (New York: St. Martin's, 1999); Lynda E. Boose and Richard Burt, eds., *Shakespeare, the Movie: Popularizing the Plays on Film, TV, and Video* (London: Routledge, 1997); and Laurie E. Osborne, "Romancing the Bard," in *Shakespeare and Appropriation,* ed. Desmet and Sawyer, 47–64.
5. E. K. Chambers, *William Shakespeare: A Study of Facts and Problems,* 2 vols. (Oxford: Clarendon Press, 1930), 2:264. Edmond Malone is famous for complaining that Rowe's *Life* contained "not more than *eleven* facts . . . ; and of these, on a critical examination, *eight* will be found false" (cited in Margreta de Grazia, *Shakespeare Verbatim: The Reproduction of Authenticity and the 1790 Apparatus* [Oxford: Clarendon Press, 1991], 75).
6. D. Nichol Smith, ed., *Eighteenth Century Essays on Shakespeare,* 2d ed. (Oxford: Clarendon Press, 1963), 5–6.

7. See especially Laura Levine, *Men in Women's Clothing: Anti-Theatricality and Effeminization, 1579–1642* (Cambridge: Cambridge University Press, 1994), 10–25.
8. See Dympna Callaghan, *Shakespeare without Women: Representing Gender and Race on the Renaissance Stage* (London: Routledge, 2000), 73; and Keir Elam, "The Fertile Eunuch: *Twelfth Night*, Early Modern Intercourse, and the Fruits of Castration," *Shakespeare Quarterly* 47 (1996): 34.
9. See Jill Campbell, *Natural Masques: Gender and Identity in Fielding's Plays and Novels* (Stanford: Stanford University Press, 1995), 28–39. Rowe himself also composed a short congratulatory poem on two famous Italian eunuchs of his day: "Upon *Nicolini and Valentini's* First Coming to the House in the *Hay-Market*." See Nicholas Rowe, *Works*, 3 vols. (London, 1728), 1:83.
10. As Campbell notes, "the Italian castrato singers that began to perform in London in 1707 served widely as a cultural text upon which the ambivalences and pressures of the period's sexual ideology could be played out, both in the form of the tremendous popular vogue the castrati enjoyed and in the form of the tireless satiric abuse they sustained" (*Natural Masques*, 29). On the demonization of sodomy in general in the early modern period, see Alan Bray, *Homosexuality in Renaissance England* (London: Gay Men's Press, 1982; New York: Columbia University Press, 1995), 13–32; on sodomy as specifically a product of Catholic France and (especially) Italy, see Cameron McFarlane, *The Sodomite in Fiction and Satire, 1650–1750* (New York: Columbia University Press, 1997), 55–60.
11. Smith, *Eighteenth Century Essays*, 5.
12. For a full account of Pope's alterations, see Smith, *Eighteenth Century Essays*, 284–88, who also notes that for all subsequent editors Pope's text was mistaken for Rowe's. At the other end of the century, Steevens even claimed that the *Life* "had been abridged and altered by [Rowe] himself after its appearance in 1709" (Smith, xxxviii).
13. See Beth Kowaleski-Wallace, "Shunning the Bearded Kiss: Castrati and the Definition of Female Sexuality," *Prose Studies* 15 (1992): 153; and Campbell, *Natural Masques*, 11.
14. When asked why he failed to include the rumor in his edition of Shakespeare, Pope famously replied: "There might be in the garden of mankind such plants as would seem to pride themselves more in a regular production of their own native fruits, than in having the repute of bearing a richer kind by grafting" (cited in Chambers, *William Shakespeare*, 2:277–78). The rumor first appeared in print in 1778; see chapter 2.
15. See Kristina Straub, *Sexual Suspects: Eighteenth-Century Players and Sexual Ideology* (Princeton: Princeton University Press, 1992), esp. 35–36. Campbell has also noted that vast sums of money became an integral part of eighteenth-century stereotypes about castrati, and especially in satires; in 1735 alone, Farinelli was said to have earned £5,000 (*Natural Masques*, 32, 262 n. 34). The most important text on eunuchism in the period, *Eunuchism Display'd*, first appearing in French in 1707 (precisely when Rowe was compiling his

biography) and translated into English in 1718 (just before Rowe's text had been altered by Pope), also begins by noting the "considerable sums of money" and "unexpected favours" offered to Italian eunuchs of the day (cited in Ian McCormick, ed., *Secret Sexualities: A Sourcebook of 17th and 18th Century Writing* [London: Routledge, 1997], 21). On accusations of prostitution in the sixteenth and seventeenth centuries, particularly with respect to boy players, see Stephen Orgel, *Impersonations: The Performance of Gender in Shakespeare's England* (Cambridge: Cambridge University Press, 1996), 37–38.

16. By 1749, in the anonymous *Reasons for the Growth of Sodomy in England,* "catamites" are actually compared to eunuchs since they have no interest in women: "like eunuchs, out of mere madness and disappointment, [they] loathe the dear sex they have no power to please" (cited in McCormick, *Secret Sexualities,* 139). *Eunuchism Display'd* also implies that even those "who were called eunuchs in a figurative sense, inasmuch as they kept themselves entirely chaste, and made no more use of their parts of virility, than as if they really had none," do not escape suggestions of homoeroticism; "figurative" eunuchism, the text concludes, "may be charitably supposed of some of the fellows of both our universities" (cited in McCormick, *Secret Sexualities,* 25). The subtext here is Jesus' reference to three types of eunuchism in Matthew 19:12 ("for there are some eunuchs, which were so born from their mother's womb: and there are some eunuchs, which were made eunuchs of men: and there be eunuchs, which have made themselves eunuchs for the kingdom of heaven's sake"). Translations of the biblical passage, too, also caused a certain amount of anxiety in the sixteenth and seventeenth centuries: see John Astington, "Malvolio and the Eunuchs: Texts and Revels in *Twelfth Night,*" *Shakespeare Survey* 46 (1994): 24–27. Moreover, in the sixteenth century the stage in general had regularly been attacked as the site of diverse forms of licentious behavior, both "homosexual" and "heterosexual" and often involving the players themselves. These terms are necessarily in quotation marks as they are categories that did not exist until the late nineteenth century. I use them here, as throughout this book, as a matter of convenience to indicate that antitheatrical diatribes accused spectators of general disreputable behavior that cannot be reduced, as it sometimes is, to same-sex sexual activity. Sodomy, similarly, was a term used to encompass any form of non-normative sexual act, from nonvaginal intercourse to masturbation, adultery, bestiality, rape, and sex between men or between women. The related literature on this subject is now enormous; the most useful studies include John Boswell, *Christianity, Social Tolerance, and Homosexuality: Gay People in Western Europe from the Beginning of the Christian Era to the Fourteenth Century* (Chicago: University of Chicago Press, 1980); Bray, *Homosexuality in Renaissance England;* Gregory W. Bredbeck, *Sodomy and Interpretation: Marlowe to Milton* (Ithaca: Cornell University Press, 1991); Jonathan Goldberg, *Sodometries: Renaissance Texts, Modern Sexualities* (Stanford: Stanford University Press, 1992); and Mark D. Jordan, *The Invention of Sodomy in Christian Theology* (Chicago: University of Chicago Press, 1997).

17. By the eighteenth century, although famous for their liaisons with women, actors were also becoming increasingly "feminized" or symbolically castrated objects of spectacle upon which various "suspect" forms of sexuality could be projected. See Straub, *Sexual Suspects,* 36–38. *Reasons for the Growth of Sodomy in England* also decries singers of Italian operas making Englishmen more "effeminate": "whereas they used to go from a good *comedy* warm'd with the fire of love; and from a good *tragedy,* fir'd with a spirit of glory; they sit indolently and supine at an OPERA, and suffer their souls to be sung away by the voices of the *Italian Syrens* [male or female?]" (cited in McCormick, *Secret Sexualities,* 141).
18. See Todd S. Gilman, "The Italian (Castrato) in London," in *The Work of Opera: Genre, Nationhood, and Sexual Difference,* ed. Richard Dellamora and Daniel Fischlin (New York: Columbia University Press, 1997), 49–70. On the castrati vogue and its importance for female sexuality, see Campbell, *Natural Masques,* 30; and Kowaleski-Wallace, "Shunning the Bearded Kiss," 153–70. Note also that one of the main focuses of *Eunuchism Display'd* is the social and legal ramifications of whether eunuchs should be permitted to marry; the full title of the English version even adds that the translation was "Occasion'd by a young Lady's falling in love with *Nicolini,* who sung in the Opera at the *Hay-Market,* and to whom she had like to have been Married."
19. There is, however, a wonderful discussion of Shakespearean castration in modern pornographic representations of him: see Burt, *Unspeakable ShaXXXs-peares,* 103–11.
20. The term is Michel Foucault's, from *The History of Sexuality,* 3 vols., trans. Robert Hurley (New York: Pantheon, 1978–86), 1:101.
21. See James P. Carson, "Commodification and the Figure of the Castrato in Smollett's *Humphry Clinker,*" *Eighteenth Century* 33 (1992): 27. In *Eunuchism Display'd,* eunuchs are called "a third sort of men; *Tertia Hominum Species,*" and "neither male nor female, but a prodigy in nature" (cited in McCormick, *Secret Sexualities,* 22–23). The most common worry about eunuchs, however, was whether they were really impotent; a 1766 publication, for example, speaks out against anyone who argues "that their state is not so deplorable as we imagine, for that they are capable of love." The truth is that castrati "can but affect a passion, because [they are] deprived of that procreant *stimulus* by which we are goaded on to love" (cited in McCormick, *Secret Sexualities,* 174).
22. There are a number of other references to eunuchs in the Shakespeare corpus (the most famous being Mardian in *Antony and Cleopatra*), always foreigners and usually linked to singing (e.g., *A Midsummer Night's Dream* 5.1.44–45; *Coriolanus* 3.2.114–15; and *Cymbeline* 2.3.27–31).
23. The best treatment of Viola's (and Rosalind's) apparently pansexual appeal is Valerie Traub's discussion of "circulations of sexuality" in *Desire and Anxiety: Circulations of Sexuality in Shakespearean Drama* (London: Routledge, 1992), 117–44. Callaghan has expertly argued that a key element in the appeal of Renaissance English boy players in general was their unbroken *voices,* and thus once again the idea of Viola as a eunuch is in some sense exemplary (if not

redundant); as Callaghan concludes, "economic and sexual practices molded the boys, aesthetically, if not surgically, into the shape of eunuchs" (*Shakespeare without Women,* 67). Interestingly, John Philip Kemble's eighteenth-century rewriting of *Twelfth Night* has Viola claim she will dress as a page and not a eunuch (cited in Elam, "Fertile Eunuch," 30 n. 91).

24. Giles Jacob, *Poetical Register; or, The Lives and Characters of the English Dramatick Poets* (London, 1719), cited in Schoenbaum, *Shakespeare's Lives,* 90.
25. See Schoenbaum, *Shakespeare's Lives,* 177; and de Grazia, *Shakespeare Verbatim,* 138.
26. Chambers, *William Shakespeare,* 1:62. In his *Outlines of the Life of Shakespeare,* 7th ed., 2 vols. (London: Longmans, 1887), J. O. Halliwell-Phillipps notes a competing legend in which the gift was used to buy New Place in 1597. How else could Shakespeare have afforded to buy such a grand piece of property? "The largest emoluments that could have been derived from his professional avocations would hardly have sufficed to have accomplished such a result" (1:147). There is still another legend mentioned in a mid-seventeenth-century diary, to the effect that Shakespeare "frequented ye plays all his younger time, but in his elder days lived at Stratford: and supplied ye stage with 2 plays every year, and for it had an allowance so large, it hee spent att ye Rate of a 1,000.*l* a year, as I have heard" (cited in Chambers, *William Shakespeare,* 2:249–50).
27. Cited in *Poems,* variorum ed., ed. Hyder Edward Rollins (Philadelphia: J. B. Lippincott, 1938), 114.
28. Cited in Schoenbaum, *Shakespeare's Lives,* 375.
29. Edmond Malone, *Supplement to the Edition of Shakespeare's Plays Published in 1778 by Samuel Johnson and George Steevens,* 2 vols. (London, 1780), vol. 1. The text was fully canonized in *Plays and Poems,* ed. Malone, 10 vols. (London, 1790), vol. 10. On Malone's role in the invention of the authentic Shakespeare in general, see especially de Grazia, *Shakespeare Verbatim,* a book to which my own discussions are much indebted.
30. *Poems,* ed. John Benson (London, 1640). The best account of Benson's arrangement is in Rollins's variorum edition of the *Sonnets* (Philadelphia: J. B. Lippincott, 1944), 2:18–28.
31. Cited in George Chalmers, *A Supplemental Apology for the Believers in the Shakspeare-Papers* (London, 1799; New York: Kelley, 1971), 73.
32. See Peter Stallybrass, "Editing as Cultural Formation: The Sexing of Shakespeare's Sonnets," *Modern Language Quarterly* 54 (1993): 91–103. For a fuller history of the sonnets' reception in this regard, see Joseph Pequigney, *Such Is My Love: A Study of Shakespeare's Sonnets* (Chicago: University of Chicago Press, 1985).
33. Renaissance (adult) players, not unlike eunuchs, were also sometimes stereotyped as the obsessive object of women's attraction. One thinks of a ribald story in John Manningham's diary from 1602, which we will discuss in chapter 2, in which Shakespeare is said to steal an enamored female spectator away from Richard Burbage. A satirical character sketch of a player from 1628 quips that "waiting women Spectators are over-eares in love with him, and Ladies

send for him to act in their Chambers" (John Earle, *Micro-cosmographie; or, A Peece of the World Discovered; in Essayes and Characters* [London, 1628], sig. E4r).

34. Could even this reputation ironically be linked to eunuchism, not only in the sense that the eighteenth century was obsessed with eunuchs' power to procreate and the kinds of sexual pleasure they were physiologically able to enjoy, but also in the sense that castration was occasionally mentioned as a punishment for adultery? *Eunuchism Display'd* gives several examples, as well as the story of a queen making eunuchs of her lovers after they had been "admitted to her bed, . . . lest after having received from her the greatest favours, they should go and have engagements with other women" (cited in McCormick, *Secret Sexualities*, 23).
35. On the appeal of Renaissance English culture for modern gay men in particular, see Alan Stewart, *Close Readers: Humanism and Sodomy in Early Modern England* (Princeton: Princeton University Press, 1997), xv–xlv.
36. E.g., Laurie Rozakis, *The Complete Idiot's Guide to Shakespeare* (New York: Alpha Books, 1999). For a much more scholarly reading, see Marjorie Garber, *Vice Versa: Bisexuality and the Eroticism of Everyday Life* (New York: Simon and Schuster, 1995), 505–15. See also Harold Bloom, *Shakespeare: The Invention of the Human* (New York: Riverhead Books, 1998), where in the opening chapter on "Shakespeare's Universalism" we are told that he "evidently lusted after both genders" (8).
37. The most recent being a 479-page tome by Park Honan, *Shakespeare: A Life* (Oxford: Oxford University Press, 1998).
38. E.g., Jeffrey Masten, *Textual Intercourse: Collaboration, Authorship, and Sexualities in Renaissance Drama* (Cambridge: Cambridge University Press, 1997).

Chapter 1

1. William Henry Ireland, *An Authentic Account of the Shakspearian Mss.* (London, 1796; New York: Kelley, 1971); Ireland, *Confessions* (London, 1805). *Vortigern* was published, along with a spurious *Henry II*, in 1799 (reprint, New York: Kelley, 1971).
2. Ireland, *Confessions*, 45.
3. The basic works on Ireland are Derk Bodde, *Shakspere and the Ireland Forgeries* (Cambridge: Harvard University Press, 1930); John Mair, *The Fourth Forger: William Ireland and the Shakespeare Papers* (London: Cobden-Sanderson, 1938); Bernard Grebanier, *The Great Shakespeare Forgery: A New Look at the Career of William Henry Ireland* (London: Heinemann, 1966); and S. Schoenbaum, *Shakespeare's Lives*, 2d ed. (Oxford: Oxford University Press, 1991), 135–68. These are to be supplemented by Sidney Lee, "Samuel Ireland," in *Dictionary of National Biography*, 22 vols., ed. Leslie Stephen and Sidney Lee (Oxford: Oxford University Press, 1921–22), 10:468–73; Philip W. Sergeant, "Young Ireland: An Unappreciated Jester," in *Liars and Fakers* (London: Hutchinson, 1926), 239–93; Zoltán Haraszti, "Ireland's Shakespeare Forgeries," *More Books: The Bulletin of the Boston Public Library* 9 (1934): 333–50; Schoenbaum,

"The Ireland Forgeries: An Unpublished Contemporary Account," in *Shakespeare and Others* (Washington: Folger Books, 1985), 144–53; and Schoenbaum, *William Shakespeare: Records and Images* (London: Scolar Press, 1981), 117–36. The most recent treatment of the Ireland case concentrates on *Vortigern:* Jeffrey Kahan, *Reforging Shakespeare: The Story of a Theatrical Scandal* (Bethlehem, Pa.: Lehigh University Press, 1998).

4. On Malone and the Chandos portrait, see chapter 4.
5. The remark was made by James Boaden, who later became one of Ireland's fiercest and most relentless critics: "We think it will be clearly proved that all the degrading nonsense, of his holding horses, &c., will be found utterly fictitious, and that this great man was the Garrick of his age, caressed for his powers by every one great and illustrious, that gentle friend of genius, and most excellent in the quality he professed" (cited in Ireland, *Confessions,* 280).
6. This was of course a great age of literary forgery, and one satirist was even prompted to dub (Samuel) Ireland as "the fourth forger," since he followed in the footsteps of William Lauder (who invented evidence relating to *Paradise Lost*), James Macpherson (inventor of Celtic bard Ossian), and Thomas Chatterton (William Henry's idol and inventor of fifteenth-century poet Thomas Rowley). See Schoenbaum, "Ireland Forgeries," 145–46, and Grebanier, *Great Shakespeare Forgery,* 276–77. The difference, however, which supposedly invested Ireland with a "threefold impudence," was that these papers did not relate to some make-believe bard but to The Bard himself, and Ireland actually had the audacity to produce the documents—and even plays!—by himself rather than just transcribing or reporting what he had "found." This also accounts for the famous overstatement of the case made by Boaden, when twenty-five years after the fact he encountered the now-impoverished William Henry in the street: "You must be aware, sir, of the enormous crime you committed against the divinity of Shakespeare. Why, the act, sir, was nothing short of sacrilege; it was precisely the same thing as taking the holy Chalice from the altar and ******* therein!!!" (cited in Mair, *Fourth Forger,* 228). For other contemporary caricatures of Ireland, see Jonathan Bate, *Shakespearean Constitutions: Politics, Theatre, Criticism, 1730–1830* (Oxford: Clarendon Press, 1989), 58–60; and the list of periodicals provided by Robert Witbeck Babcock, *The Genesis of Shakespeare Idolatry, 1766–1799: A Study in English Criticism of the Late Eighteenth Century* (Chapel Hill: University of North Carolina Press, 1931), 26 n. 89.
7. Edmond Malone, *An Inquiry into the Authenticity of Certain Miscellaneous Papers and Legal Instruments . . . Attributed to Shakspeare* (London, 1796; New York: Kelley, 1970), 33. Malone repeats this argument a number of times (e.g., 181, 322, 353), also noting (322–23) that the orthography of all the documents, even though supposedly written by many different persons from different social stations, employs precisely the same techniques.
8. Even Malone brings up this objection, *Inquiry,* 234, 290–91. The clearest summary of this issue is Gerald Eades Bentley, *The Profession of Dramatist in Shakespeare's Time, 1590–1642* (Princeton: Princeton University Press, 1971).

9. See Grebanier, *Great Shakespeare Forgery,* 150–51; and Schoenbaum, *Shakespeare's Lives,* 148. One might also note that Oscar Wilde's "The Portrait of Mr. W. H." also begins with a reference to the Ireland (and other) forgeries. See Wilde, *Complete Works* (New York: Harper and Row, 1989), 1150.
10. Cited in Grebanier, *Great Shakespeare Forgery,* 170. On the subject of Shakespeare's "other" illegitimate offspring, see chapter 2.
11. Malone, *Inquiry,* 352–53.
12. See, for example, Samuel Ireland, *Mr. Ireland's Vindication of His Conduct respecting the Publication of the Supposed Shakspeare Mss.* (London, 1796; New York: Kelley, 1971). See also Grebanier, *Great Shakespeare Forgery,* 273–84. On the elder Ireland's last years see Mair, *Fourth Forger,* 223–27; and Schoenbaum, *Shakespeare's Lives,* 165–66.
13. On the history of eighteenth-century bardolatry, and especially the Shakespeare Jubilee organized by Garrick in 1769, see Grebanier, *Great Shakespeare Forgery,* 3–28; and Schoenbaum, *Shakespeare's Lives,* 104–10. The quotation is from Schoenbaum, *Shakespeare's Lives,* 165.
14. Brian Vickers, *Shakespeare: The Critical Heritage,* 6 vols. (London: Routledge, 1974–81), 6:65.
15. Yet it has also been pointed out many times that precisely because of the ways in which we value him, we know more about Shakespeare than many other Elizabethan writers. See, for instance, Schoenbaum, *Shakespeare: His Life, His Language, His Theater* (New York: Signet, 1990), 15.
16. The most valuable source for these (and other) debates remains *Sonnets,* ed. Rollins. Useful summaries can also be found in Robert Giroux, *The Book Known as Q: A Consideration of Shakespeare's Sonnets* (New York: Atheneum, 1982); and *Sonnets,* ed. W. G. Ingram and Theodore Redpath (New York: Barnes and Noble, 1965); *Sonnets,* ed. John Kerrigan (Harmondsworth: Penguin, 1985), and *Sonnets,* ed. Katherine Duncan-Jones (London: Thomas Nelson, 1997).
17. E. K. Chambers, *William Shakespeare: A Study of Facts and Problems,* 2 vols. (Oxford: Clarendon Press, 1930), 1:561.
18. Cited in Arthur Sherbo, *The Birth of Shakespeare Studies: Commentators from Rowe (1709) to Boswell-Malone (1821)* (East Lansing: Colleagues Press, 1986), 154. See also Schoenbaum, *Shakespeare's Lives,* 140: "[Ireland] created a personal history for the poet, as conceived by a day-dreaming child of the eighteenth century, at that time when the neoclassic temper had already largely yielded to romanticism; a personal history fabricated by a youth regarded as stupid by his elders, but which many mature men of the age would be able to reconcile with the Shakespeare of their sentimental imagination."
19. For a short account of Chalmers, "almost the last of the extinct race of authors who were antiquarians rather than historians," and his "indefatigable industry . . . during the last fifty years of his long life," see Aeneas James George Mackay, "George Chalmers," in *Dictionary of National Biography,* 3:1354–55.

20. Reprinted in Malone, *Inquiry,* 25–26. Facsimiles of many of the forgeries, including Elizabeth's letter, first appeared in Samuel Ireland, *Miscellaneous Papers and Legal Instruments under the Hand and Seal of William Shakspeare: Including the Tragedy of King Lear, and a Small Fragment of Hamlet, from the Original Mss. in the Possession of Samuel Ireland, of Norfolk Street . . .* (London, 1796).
21. As one contemporary put it, "the superscription of queen Elizabeth's letter . . . , written with her own hand, is as carefully worded, as if it were to have been sent by the penny-post; had the office so named been then established" (F. G. Waldron, *Free Reflections on Miscellaneous Papers and Legal Instruments, under the Hand and Seal of William Shakspeare, in the Possession of Samuel Ireland, of Norfolk-Street* [London, 1796], 8).
22. Malone, *Inquiry,* 70–73, 83–84, 88–95, 97–98.
23. Ireland, *Confessions,* 76. On the notion of a personal letter from King James, see Chambers, *William Shakespeare,* 2:270. Malone in fact wonders why the forger didn't just produce a letter from James instead: *Inquiry,* 319–22.
24. George Chalmers, *An Apology for the Believers in the Shakspeare-Papers* (London, 1797; New York: Kelley, 1971), hereafter cited in parentheses as *A.* When citing from Chalmers, I have occasionally repunctuated and removed italics for the sake of clarity.
25. See by way of comparison the theories discussed in *Sonnets,* ed. Rollins; Schoenbaum, *Shakespeare's Lives*; and Frank W. Wadsworth, *The Poacher from Stratford: A Partial Account of the Controversy over the Authorship of Shakespeare's Plays* (Berkeley: University of California Press, 1958).
26. George Elliott Sweet, *Shake-Speare: The Mystery* (Stanford: Stanford University Press, 1956). Sweet's book was also reissued in expanded form in 1963 (London: Neville Spearman). He was, however, not the only reader to posit that Shakespeare was a woman; Rollins cites William Ross, who in 1939 claimed that Shakespeare was really one Anne Whateley (*Sonnets,* 2:46, 227). Ross is discussed more fully in Wadsworth, *Poacher from Stratford,* 144–48. This is also a convenient place to mention the theory espoused in *Famous Impostors* by Bram Stoker (of *Dracula* fame), who argued that Elizabeth was really a man (see Wadsworth, *Poacher from Stratford,* 161; and Joseph S. Galland, *Digesta Anti-Shakespeareana* (unpublished manuscript, 1949; available from UMI Dissertation Service), 1094, 1328.
27. Cf. a contemporary remark from the *Monthly Review* cited in Schoenbaum, *Shakespeare's Lives,* 168: "When a writer has once determined that all Shakspeare's Sonnets must relate to the same subject, and must be addressed to the same person, he will violate every rule of language in order to maintain his position."
28. The most recent discussion of Ireland devotes only one paragraph to Chalmers and mischaracterizes the tone of the latter's position in this regard: "Yes, the papers were frauds, Chalmers argued, but damn fine ones!" (Kahan, *Reforging Shakespeare,* 194). Kahan's discussion is also confused about the titles of Chalmers's books.

29. At the instigation of George Steevens, Chalmers's "Farther Account of the Rise and Progress of the English Stage," as well as his "Addenda to Farther Particulars of the Early English Stage," were included in the Johnson-Steevens-Reed edition of 1803. They also appear in Malone's posthumous edition (*Plays and Poems,* ed. Malone and James Boswell, 20 vols. [London, 1821], 3:410–549), where they immediately follow Malone's own "Historical Account of the Rise and Progress of the English Stage," along with *its* additions and appendix (3:1–409).
30. According to Schoenbaum, when Malone's volume appeared Chalmers had already been planning a book arguing for the authenticity of the papers, and he was "understandably reluctant to lose the fruits of his industry . . . [and] salvaged his demonstration by converting it into a defense of his credulity and an onslaught against the scholar who had embarrassed him" (*Shakespeare's Lives,* 167).
31. For instance, Thomas Caldecott: "For the purpose of exposing that which sufficiently exposed itself, an Answer appeared from Mr Chalmers. . . . He is a very silly Coxcomb, & an execrably bad Writer; but he has not spared his pains, & was possessed of extraordinary sources of Information. Preeminent above his other Follies is the extravagant conceit, that Shakespeare's Sonnets were addressed to a Lady & that Lady, Q. Elizabeth" (cited in Schoenbaum, "Ireland Forgeries," 152–53). George Steevens pithily sums up his view of Chalmers's 600-page admission of error by commenting: "When men confess themselves knaves, there is an end of Detection" (cited in Grebanier, *Great Shakespeare Forgery,* 275).
32. Stallybrass inaccurately remarks that Ireland's letter is "one of the most drastic responses to Malone's edition of the *Sonnets,*" since it proved that the poems "were addressed neither to a male beloved nor to a common woman but to the monarch herself" ("Editing as Cultural Formation: The Sexing of Shakespeare's Sonnets," *Modern Language Quarterly* 54 [1993]: 96). This summary is not correct, since Elizabeth as the poems' addressee is Chalmers's idea and not Ireland's, even if both men were reacting to one and the same cultural anxiety. A similarly faulty summary appears in Margreta de Grazia and Stallybrass, "The Materiality of the Shakespearean Text," *Shakespeare Quarterly* 44 (1993): 271.
33. Cited in *Sonnets,* ed. Rollins, 2:337–38. Rollins also points out here that Steevens is probably referring to all of Shakespeare's poems and not just the sonnets. Taken as a group, the bawdiness of Shakespeare's poetic work, including *A Lover's Complaint, Venus and Adonis, The Rape of Lucrece,* and *The Passionate Pilgrim,* could indeed have been perceived as scandalous. See chapter 2.
34. Stallybrass, "Editing as Cultural Formation," 94–95. On Renaissance sodomy as an "unnamable" vice, see Alan Bray, *Homosexuality in Renaissance England* (London: Gay Men's Press, 1982; New York: Columbia University Press, 1995), 61–62.

35. Stallybrass, "Editing as Cultural Formation," 99.
36. There was one edition in 1711 that used Thorpe's text, without explanatory notes, but its title page identifies the poems as "One Hundred and Fifty Four Sonnets, all of them in Praise of his Mistress" (cited in *Sonnets,* ed. Rollins, 2:36–37; emphasis removed). De Grazia points out, in "The Scandal of Shakespeare's Sonnets," *Shakespeare Survey* 46 (1994): 35–36, that Benson did not change every reference to another man, as is sometimes implied in the criticism. The notorious sonnet 20, for example, remains intact, with the exception of a new title: "The Exchange." Gender changes occur only in sonnets 101, 108, and 113 (and perhaps 104). Sonnets 122 and 125 are given titles identifying a female addressee, and poem 126 (beginning "O thou, my lovely boy") is missing altogether. Other missing poems include 18, 19, 43, 56, 75, 76, and 96. It is difficult to ascertain why most of these should have been omitted. For a full account of these changes see *Sonnets*, ed. Rollins, 2:20–21.
37. Malone, *Inquiry,* 3–4; *Plays and Poems,* ed. Malone. See also de Grazia, *Shakespeare Verbatim: The Reproduction of Authenticity and the 1790 Apparatus* (Oxford: Clarendon Press, 1991), 152–62.
38. A useful facsimile of the 1609 text is included in Stephen Booth's edition (New Haven: Yale University Press, 1977), as well as in Helen Vendler, *The Art of Shakespeare's Sonnets* (Cambridge: Harvard University Press, 1997).
39. *Plays and Poems,* ed. Malone, 10:207, and cited in *Sonnets,* ed. Rollins, 1:55n.
40. Compare Coleridge's remark that Shakespeare's gender confusion (particularly in sonnet 20) must have been "a purposed blind" (cited in Stallybrass, "Editing as Cultural Formation," 99), and Sweet's idea that the dark lady poems were written "as part of his [i.e., Elizabeth's] disguise" (*Shake-Speare: The Mystery,* 62).
41. See *Sonnets,* ed. Rollins, 2:248; Schoenbaum, *Shakespeare's Lives,* 168; and de Grazia, *Shakespeare Verbatim,* 173.
42. Cited in Schoenbaum, *Shakespeare's Lives,* 182, 186.
43. Chalmers, *A Supplemental Apology for the Believers in the Shakspeare-Papers* (London, 1799; New York: Kelley, 1971), hereafter cited in parentheses as *SA.* According to his entry in the *DNB* (3:1355), Chalmers returned to the controversy yet once more with *An Appendix to the "Supplemental Apology" for the Believers in the Supposititious Shakspeare-Papers* (London, 1800), but in fact this text no longer has any connection with the Ireland forgeries at all. According to H. H. Furness, Chalmers's "attack was so sudden and so sharp, and the *Apology* revealed such an intimate acquaintance with Elizabethan literature, wherein Malone and Steevens had been wont to consider themselves the chiefest authorities among men, that apparently Malone's breath was taken away, and although it was frequently reported, I believe, that he was preparing an answer to Chalmers, no answer ever appeared" (*The Tempest,* variorum ed., ed. Furness [Philadelphia: J. B. Lippincott, 1892], 277). I am indebted to Arthur Freeman's (unpaged) preface to the facsimile reprint of Chalmers's *Apology* for this reference.

44. In fact Chalmers's account of this poem tellingly omits the final four lines (*SA,* 70). One also thinks of the end of sonnet 94: "Lilies that fester smell far worse than weeds."
45. On the asymmetry of Shakespeare's gender designations, see Eve Kosofsky Sedgwick, *Between Men: English Literature and Male Homosocial Desire* (New York: Columbia University Press, 1985), 28–48, as well as chapter 2.
46. See *Sonnets,* ed. Rollins, 2:239; Schoenbaum, *Shakespeare's Lives,* 168; and Joseph Pequigney, *Such Is My Love: A Study of Shakespeare's Sonnets* (Chicago: University of Chicago Press, 1985), 40: "This poem seems a curiously inappropriate one for annotators and critics to single out as the principal prop of their contention that the friendship treated in the Sonnets is innocent of erotic content. But . . . [the poem] confronts so openly the question of eroticism in the relations between the friends that until, or unless, it can somehow be rendered innocuous, their efforts are doomed to failure." Rollins also cites the amusing case of one editor who (probably unwittingly) suggested that "women's pleasure" in line 13 be emended to "all men's pleasure." Rollins jestingly remarks that "one can only shudder at [this] conjecture" (*Sonnets,* 2:59n).
47. "[It] does not perhaps mean *man*-mistress, but *sovereign* mistress," from the 1790 edition, cited in *Sonnets,* ed. Rollins, 1:57n.
48. This is also Steevens's reading, from the 1780 edition, cited in *Sonnets,* ed. Rollins, 1:59n.
49. At this point (*SA,* 60n) Chalmers inexplicably quotes *3 Henry VI*—"That love which virtue begs and virtue grants" (3.2.63)—in order to prove that sonnet 20 describes only an innocent love for the friend (who in this reading is the queen anyway).
50. Schoenbaum, *Records and Images,* 136.
51. See Bray, *Homosexuality in Renaissance England*; Gregory W. Bredbeck, *Sodomy and Interpretation: Marlowe to Milton* (Ithaca: Cornell University Press, 1991); Bruce R. Smith, *Homosexual Desire in Shakespeare's England: A Cultural Poetics* (Chicago: University of Chicago Press, 1991); Jonathan Goldberg, *Sodometries: Renaissance Texts, Modern Sexualities* (Stanford: Stanford University Press, 1992); Alan Stewart, *Close Readers: Humanism and Sodomy in Early Modern England* (Princeton: Princeton University Press, 1997); Mario DiGangi, *The Homoerotics of Early Modern Drama* (Cambridge: Cambridge University Press, 1997); Cameron McFarlane, *The Sodomite in Fiction and Satire, 1650–1750* (New York: Columbia University Press, 1997); and Mark D. Jordan, *The Invention of Sodomy in Christian Theology* (Chicago: University of Chicago Press, 1997).
52. Adultery was also classified as sodomy in the early modern period, and some early readers evidently felt it an even more dangerous and unseemly charge than sodomy between men. See Schoenbaum, *Shakespeare's Lives,* 197.
53. As Stallybrass comments, "the justification of Shakespeare is always subsequent to the charge of deviation—just as the concept of the 'heterosexual' is a belated response to the *prior* concept of the 'homosexual'" ("Editing as Cultural Formation," 102).

54. Sedgwick, *Epistemology of the Closet* (Berkeley: University of California Press, 1990), 1.
55. The homo/hetero distinction has received its most sophisticated analysis in Joel Fineman, *Shakespeare's Perjured Eye: The Invention of Poetic Subjectivity in the Sonnets* (Berkeley: University of California Press, 1986). On the dark lady's "promiscuous womb," see de Grazia, "The Scandal of Shakespeare's Sonnets," 47. On the possible fallacies of simply assuming that the poems fall neatly into two groups, see Heather Dubrow, "'Incertainties Now Crown Themselves Assur'd': The Politics of Plotting Shakespeare's Sonnets," *Shakespeare Quarterly* 47 (1996): 291–305.
56. To be sure, Booth certainly does not rule out questions of sexuality in his prodigious commentary, but his conclusion remains a disappointment: "William Shakespeare was almost certainly homosexual, bisexual, or heterosexual. The sonnets provide no evidence on the matter" (*Sonnets,* 548).
57. Bray, "Homosexuality and the Signs of Male Friendship in Elizabethan England," in *Queering the Renaissance,* ed. Jonathan Goldberg (Durham: Duke University Press, 1994), 40–61.
58. Bray, *Homosexuality in Renaissance England,* 58–80.
59. Pequigney, *Such Is My Love,* 1.
60. Pequigney, *Such Is My Love,* 104–8.
61. I would not, however, subscribe to Rollins's contention that "the subject of homosexuality would never have been discussed in the first place if Shakespeare's readers had not been so eager to prove the friend a real man" (*Sonnets,* 2:239).
62. Indeed, it is perhaps the most vexed question in premodern queer studies. See for example Bray, *Homosexuality in Renaissance England,* 81–114; Randolph Trumbach, "London's Sodomites: Homosexual Behavior and Western Culture in the 18th Century," *Journal of Social History* 11 (1977): 1–33; Trumbach, "Sodomitical Subcultures, Sodomitical Roles, and the Gender Revolution of the Eighteenth Century: The Recent Historiography," in *'Tis Nature's Fault: Unauthorized Sexuality during the Enlightenment,* ed. Robert Purks Maccubbin (Cambridge: Cambridge University Press, 1987), 109–21; Trumbach, "The Birth of the Queen: Sodomy and the Emergence of Gender Equality in Modern Culture, 1660–1750," in *Hidden from History: Reclaiming the Gay and Lesbian Past,* ed. Martin Duberman et al. (New York: Meridian, 1990), 129–40; Trumbach, "London's Sapphists: From Three Sexes to Four Genders in the Making of Modern Culture," in *Body Guards: The Cultural Politics of Gender Ambiguity,* ed. Julia Epstein and Kristina Straub (London: Routledge, 1991), 112–41; Joseph Cady, "'Masculine Love,' Renaissance Writing, and the 'New Invention' of Homosexuality," in *Homosexuality in Renaissance and Enlightenment England: Literary Representations in Historical Context,* ed. Claude J. Summers (New York: Haworth Press, 1992), 9–40; Alan Sinfield, *The Wilde Century: Effeminacy, Oscar Wilde and the Queer Moment* (London: Cassell, 1994), esp. 11–13, 26–33; McFarlane, *Sodomite in Fiction and Satire,* 25–68; and Jordan, *Invention of Sodomy,* 161–63.

Chapter 2

1. *The Oxford Companion to English Literature,* 5th ed., ed. Margaret Drabble (Oxford: Oxford University Press, 1985), 256.
2. Most of the material on Shakespeare's biographical reputation is taken from E. K. Chambers, *William Shakespeare: A Study of Facts and Problems,* 2 vols. (Oxford: Clarendon Press, 1930), and will be cited *WS* in parentheses.
3. S. Schoenbaum, *Shakespeare's Lives,* 2d ed. (Oxford: Oxford University Press, 1991), 62. On Davenant and the Tribe of Ben, see Richard A. Levin, "Shakespeare's Bastard Son," *Notes and Queries* 27 (1980): 177–79.
4. Arthur H. Nethercot, *Sir William D'Avenant: Poet Laureate and Playwright-Manager* (Chicago: University of Chicago Press, 1938), 2, 5. See also Alfred Harbage, *Sir William Davenant* (Philadelphia: University of Pennsylvania Press, 1935).
5. Cited in Schoenbaum, *Shakespeare's Lives,* 62.
6. *Plays and Poems,* ed. Edmond Malone, 10 vols. (London, 1790), 1:158–59. Also included here are the anecdotes of Hearne, Wood, and Taylor (cited below). In the later Boswell-Malone edition, the "antiquated scandal" also makes an appearance in Boswell's prefatory discussion of the authenticity of Malone's beloved Chandos portrait of Shakespeare, another bardolatrous icon once supposedly owned by Davenant, which will be discussed in chapter 4 (*Plays and Poems,* ed. Malone and James Boswell, 20 vols. [London, 1821], 1:xxiv–xxv).
7. Cited in Schoenbaum, *Shakespeare's Lives,* 64.
8. Stephen Orgel, *Impersonations: The Performance of Gender in Shakespeare's England* (Cambridge: Cambridge University Press, 1996), 49.
9. Margreta de Grazia, "The Scandal of Shakespeare's Sonnets," *Shakespeare Survey* 46 (1994): 35–49.
10. Cited in Schoenbaum, *Shakespeare's Lives,* 64.
11. A godson is mentioned in Shakespeare's will, but this is unfortunately one William Walker and not William Davenant (see Chambers, *William Shakespeare,* 2:173).
12. This subject now has an enormous bibliography. See for instance Jonathan Goldberg, *Sodometries: Renaissance Texts, Modern Sexualities* (Stanford: Stanford University Press, 1992), 145–75; Goldberg, "*Romeo and Juliet*'s Open Rs," in *Queering the Renaissance,* ed. Goldberg (Durham: Duke University Press, 1994), 218–35; Gregory W. Bredbeck, *Sodomy and Interpretation: Marlowe to Milton* (Ithaca: Cornell University Press, 1991), 33–48; Michael Shapiro, *Gender in Play on the Shakespearean Stage: Boy Heroines and Female Pages* (Ann Arbor: University of Michigan Press, 1994), 93–117; and Valerie Traub, *Desire and Anxiety: Circulations of Sexuality in Shakespearean Drama* (London: Routledge, 1992), 117–44.
13. See Peter Stallybrass, "Shakespeare, the Individual, and the Text," in *Cultural Studies,* ed. Lawrence Grossberg et al. (London: Routledge, 1992), 593–610, esp. 596–97. On the circumstances of writing and publishing plays in the period, see especially Gerald Eades Bentley, *The Profession of Dramatist in Shakespeare's Time, 1590–1642* (Princeton: Princeton University Press, 1971); and de Grazia

and Stallybrass, "The Materiality of the Shakespearean Text," *Shakespeare Quarterly* 44 (1993): 255–83. On the question of collaborative writing, see Jeffrey Masten, *Textual Intercourse: Collaboration, Authorship, and Sexualities in Renaissance Drama* (Cambridge: Cambridge University Press, 1997).

14. *Poems,* variorum ed., ed. Hyder Edward Rollins (Philadelphia: J. B. Lippincott, 1938), 447.
15. *Poems,* ed. Rollins, 447–75. On editions of *Venus* and *Lucrece,* see also 369–80 and 406–13.
16. Much of the material on Shakespeare's literary reputation is taken from *The Shakspere Allusion-Book: A Collection of Allusions to Shakspere from 1591–1700,* 2 vols., ed. John Munro et al. (London: Humphrey Milford, 1932), and will be cited *AB* in parentheses. I have decided to cite texts from this collection, whatever its problems of inclusion and exclusion may be, for the sake of convenience.
17. E. A. J. Honigmann, *Shakespeare's Impact on His Contemporaries* (London: Macmillan, 1982), 28.
18. Cited in *Poems,* ed. Rollins, 458.
19. John Earle, *Micro-cosmographie; or, A Peece of the World Discovered; in Essayes and Characters* (London, 1628), sig. E4r. Just after the theaters were closed, *The Actors Remonstrance, or Complaint: For the Silencing of Their Profession, and Banishment from Their Severall Play Houses* (London, 1643) mentions "those Buxsome and Bountifull Lasses, that usually were enamoured on the persons of the younger sort of Actors, for the good cloaths they wore upon the stage, beleeving them really to be the persons they did only represent" (6). The text is reprinted in *Critics and Apologists of the English Theatre: A Selection of Seventeenth-Century Pamphlets in Facsimile,* ed. Peter Davison (New York: Johnson Reprint Corp., 1972).
20. Honigmann, *Shakespeare's Impact,* 45–49.
21. Cf. Heather Dubrow, *Captive Victors: Shakespeare's Sonnets and Narrative Poems* (Ithaca: Cornell University Press, 1987).
22. See Honigmann, *Shakespeare's Impact,* 18–19.
23. *Poems,* ed. Rollins, 454.
24. Compare *The Character of a Town Gallant, Exposing the Extravagant Fopperies of Some Vain Self-Conceited Pretenders to Gentility and Good Breeding* (London, 1675), 4–5, which remarks that the gallant's "whole Library consists of the *Academy of Complements, Venus undress'd, Westminster Drollery,* half a dozen *Plays,* and a Bundle of *Bawdy* Songs in *Manuscript.*"
25. Schoenbaum, *Shakespeare's Lives,* 25; Bentley, *Shakespeare and Jonson: Their Reputations in the Seventeenth Century Compared,* 2 vols. (Chicago: University of Chicago Press, 1945), 1:12 n. 9.
26. One might also note the way echoes of Venus and Tarquin recur when Giacomo spies on the sleeping Imogen in *Cymbeline* (2.2.12–16): "Our Tarquin thus / Did softly press the rushes ere he waken'd / The chastity he wounded. Cytherea, / How bravely thou becom'st thy bed! fresh lily, / And whiter than the sheets!" etc.

27. Schoenbaum, *Shakespeare's Lives,* 27.
28. *Willobie His Avisa,* ed. G. B. Harrison (London: Bodley Head, 1926; New York: Barnes and Noble, 1966). Further references to this edition will appear in parentheses. For a general account of *Willobie,* see also *Sonnets,* 2 vols., variorum ed., ed. Rollins (Philadelphia: J. B. Lippincott, 1944), 2:295–313.
29. Cited in *Sonnets,* ed. Rollins, 2:302. I find a recent claim by Johannes Fabricius overstated: "The Oxford students' picture of William Shakespeare is clearly that of a Bohemian and libertine who is the ringleader of an aristocratic jetset specializing in the courtship of beautiful ladies" (*Syphilis in Shakespeare's England* [London: Jessica Kingsley, 1994], 178).
30. See Chambers, *William Shakespeare,* 1:532–37. For more on the initials W. S. in early modern literature, see Donald W. Foster, *Elegy by W. S.: A Study in Attribution* (Newark: University of Delaware Press, 1989).
31. Rollins remarks that even in the case of *Willobie His Avisa* there is a certain ambivalence about whether Shakespeare (of the preface) and W. S. (of the poem) are being praised or satirized (*Poems,* 454).
32. Cited in *Sonnets,* ed. Rollins, 2:310.
33. Respectively, "Gentle thou art, and therefore to be won, / Beauteous thou art, therefore to be assailed"; "She's beautiful; and therefore to be wooed: / She is a woman; therefore to be won"; "She is a woman, therefore may be woo'd, / She is a woman, therefore may be won"; "Was ever woman in this humor woo'd? / Was ever woman in this humor won?"
34. References to *The Passionate Pilgrim* are cited from *Poems,* ed. Rollins. On the 1612 edition, see *Poems,* ed. Rollins, 529.
35. See *Poems,* ed. Rollins, 533–38. Note that it is not Shakespeare himself who protests, and moreover that Heywood's primary concern seems to have been with readers assuming that he had stolen the poems from Shakespeare rather than the other way around. This "manifest injury done me," Heywood says, "may put the world in opinion I might steale them from him; and hee to doe himselfe right, hath since published them in his owne name" (*Poems,* ed. Rollins, 535).
36. See *Poems,* ed. Rollins, 309–11; Gary Taylor, "Some Manuscripts of Shakespeare's Sonnets," *Bulletin of the John Rylands Library* 68 (1985): 225; Stanley Wells and Gary Taylor, *William Shakespeare: A Textual Companion* (Oxford: Clarendon Press, 1987), 456–57; and John Roe, "*Willobie His Avisa* and *The Passionate Pilgrim:* Precedence, Parody, and Development," *Yearbook of English Studies* 23 (1993): 111–25.
37. *Poems,* ed. John Benson (London, 1640), sig. C8r. See also chapter 1.
38. Cited in *Poems,* ed. Rollins, 533.
39. Roe, "*Willobie His Avisa,*" 118–19.
40. Some bardolatrous defenders such as John Jordan (c. 1770) and Samuel Ireland (1795) refer to the deer stealing as "youthful levity," "a juvenile frolic," or "a youthful frolic" (*WS,* 2:293, 295, 297), and the episode was also excused by another defender with the claim that it was only "to celebrate his wedding-day, and for that purpose only" (*WS,* 2:299).

41. See especially Alan Bray, *Homosexuality in Renaissance England* (London: Gay Men's Press, 1982; New York: Columbia University Press, 1995), 33–57.
42. On Shakespeare's sources see *Poems,* ed. Rollins, 390–405.
43. See, for example, *AB,* 2:219; and Katherine Duncan-Jones, "Much Ado with Red and White: The Earliest Readers of Shakespeare's *Venus and Adonis* (1593)," *Review of English Studies* 44 (1993): 497.
44. The two pamphlets are in large part reprinted in Katherine Usher Henderson and Barbara F. McManus, *Half Humankind: Contexts and Texts of the Controversy about Women in England, 1540–1640* (Urbana: University of Illinois Press, 1985), 264–89.
45. Barnabe Riche, *Riche His Farewell to Militarie Profession* (London, 1581), sigs. B2r–B2v.
46. Mario DiGangi, *The Homoerotics of Early Modern Drama* (Cambridge: Cambridge University Press, 1997), 135; Orgel, *Impersonations,* 87.
47. See Gordon Williams, *A Dictionary of Sexual Language and Imagery in Shakespearean and Stuart Literature,* 3 vols. (London: Athlone Press, 1994).
48. DiGangi, *Homoerotics of Early Modern Drama,* 136.
49. Duncan-Jones, "Much Ado with Red and White," 498.
50. As yet one more twist in an ongoing saga, *Sonnets,* ed. Rollins, 2:306, cites an early-twentieth-century reader who argued that Southampton was the real author of *Willobie His Avisa*!
51. Schoenbaum, *Shakespeare's Lives,* 223–24.
52. Cited in *Sonnets,* ed. Rollins, 1:55n.
53. The original title of the latter having been *The Woman Shakespeare,* as we learn from the preface: Frank Harris, *The Women in Shakespeare* (New York: Mitchell Kennerley, 1912), ix.
54. Schoenbaum, *Shakespeare's Lives,* 485; Harris, *Women in Shakespeare,* 276.
55. Harris, *The Man Shakespeare and His Tragic Life-Story* (New York: Mitchell Kennerley, 1909), 233; Harris, *Women in Shakespeare,* 278.
56. Harris, *Man Shakespeare,* 386; *Women in Shakespeare,* 288–89; *Man Shakespeare,* 387.
57. See *Sonnets,* ed. Rollins, 2:269. On Acheson's theories generally, see *Sonnets,* ed. Rollins, 2:269–71, 305–9; and Schenbaum, *Shakespeare's Lives,* 494–96.
58. Arthur Acheson, *Shakespeare's Sonnet Story, 1592–1598* (London: Bernard Quaritch, 1922), 617.
59. Clemence Dane, *The Godson: A Fantasy* (New York: W. W. Norton, 1964), 47–48.

Chapter 3

1. See especially Leah S. Marcus, *Puzzling Shakespeare: Local Reading and Its Discontents* (Berkeley: University of California Press, 1988), 1–50.
2. A number of facsimile editions of the First Folio exist, and photographs of the prefatory pages are also included in *The Riverside Shakespeare,* 2d ed., ed. G. Blakemore Evans et al. (Boston: Houghton Mifflin, 1997), 90–108.

3. *The Norton Shakespeare,* ed. Stephen Greenblatt et al. (New York: Norton, 1997), 26, 46.
4. Joseph S. Galland, *Digesta Anti-Shakespeareana* (unpublished manuscript, 1949; available from UMI Dissertation Service).
5. *Sonnets,* 2 vols., variorum ed., ed. Hyder Edward Rollins (Philadelphia: J. B. Lippincott, 1944); R. C. Churchill, *Shakespeare and His Betters: A History and a Criticism of the Attempts Which Have Been Made to Prove That Shakespeare's Works Were Written by Others* (London: Reinhardt, 1958); Frank W. Wadsworth, *The Poacher from Stratford: A Partial Account of the Controversy over the Authorship of Shakespeare's Plays* (Berkeley: University of California Press, 1958); John Michell, *Who Wrote Shakespeare?* (London: Thames and Hudson, 1996); Warren Hope and Kim Holston. *The Shakespeare Controversy: An Analysis of the Claimants to Authorship, and Their Champions and Detractors* (Jefferson, N.C.: McFarland, 1992).
6. S. Schoenbaum, *Shakespeare's Lives,* 2d ed. (Oxford: Oxford University Press, 1991).
7. See for example Schoenbaum, *Shakespeare's Lives,* 425–30.
8. Cited in *Sonnets,* ed. Rollins, 2:45, 52. Other pleasant escapes include the theory that the dark lady is only a metaphor for the blank ink of the First Folio in its planning stages, and that Kaiser Wilhelm Hohenzollern is the true W. H. (cited in *Sonnets,* ed. Rollins, 2:230, 275). Further highlights abound in Rollins's commentary.
9. *Sonnets,* ed. Rollins, 1:v.
10. Schoenbaum, *Shakespeare's Lives,* 449.
11. Delia Bacon, *The Philosophy of Shakspere's Plays Unfolded* (London: Groombridge, 1857; New York: AMS, 1970).
12. I am grateful to Richard Burt for having led me in this new and fruitful direction.
13. Anti-American sentiment began early: Delia Bacon was disparaged as "a Yankee lady" who "has actually come to England for the purpose of examining" that "the '*Man* Shakespeare' is a *Myth,* and did *not* write those Plays which bear his name" (cited in Schoenbaum, *Shakespeare's Lives,* 387). Georg Brandes echoed the sentiments of many when he cried out against the sudden invasion of "raw Americans and fanatical women" (cited in Marjorie Garber, *Shakespeare's Ghost Writers: Literature as Uncanny Causality* [New York: Methuen, 1987], 8). Ignatius Donnelly, dubious cipher-king (and Minnesota congressman), raised an American battle cry of his own: "Has not the time come for the New World to revise the prejudiced judgments of intolerant and unprogressive England?" (cited in Hope and Holston, *Shakespeare Controversy,* 163).
14. A related example is the amazon.com web site, where search results are automatically accompanied by links to writing or reading on-line reviews, to lists of books that other customers have purchased, etc. Cybershoppers are clearly not only interested in buying. (Or do they need on-line reviews and shopping lists even to know what they're interested in?) Moreover, links are provided for the author and publisher to "comment" on their own books.

This is particularly inviting if one has searched Shakespeare's sonnets, since is this not the ultimate Shakespearean daydream—that a "comment" from Shakespeare (whoever *that* is)—or indeed Thomas Thorpe!—might be just a click away?

15. Marjorie Garber, *Symptoms of Culture* (New York: Routledge, 1998), 207.
16. Garber, *Shakespeare's Ghost Writers,* 3.
17. Edward Hubler, *The Sense of Shakespeare's Sonnets* (Princeton: Princeton University Press, 1952), 136–61.
18. A. L. Rowse, *Shakespeare the Man,* rev. ed. (New York: St. Martin's, 1988), 58. A more recent example is Park Honan's *Shakespeare: A Life* (Oxford: Oxford University Press, 1998), which, despite a now-standard claim in the preface that homosexual or heterosexual identities did not even exist in the early modern period (xiii), goes on to argue that Southampton (rather than Shakespeare) "preferred bisexual or homosexual friends." "Was [Southampton] homosexual?" Honan wonders, since in his portraits the earl is shown as a "slender, lightly built form with delicate fabrics" (176–77). While the sonnets present "puzzles" for readers, (181) the sexuality of the dark lady poems is "perhaps more overt" (191). In any case, "to increase the psychological interest of yearning, the author gives it a homoerotic or, at times, bisexual aspect"; "the effect [in sonnets 20 and 75] is to universalize his feeling without loss of context, and to picture a deep yearning in all human love, both male and female" (186–87). Universalizing the sonnets in this way has, for centuries, been the most convenient means to escape them. And I would like to hold out a fond hope that Honan is only joking when he remarks that the sonnets might not have been published before 1609 because Shakespeare "felt that intimate Sonnets with bawdy wit, carnal imagery, and exposés of lust might have troubled [his mother] Mary Shakespeare, if she, or a literate neighbor at Stratford, saw a volume of them. . . . He had the feelings of others at home to consider" (180). In sum, perhaps "the Sonnets show Shakespeare's understanding of homoerotic feeling" (177), but the poet himself is kept safely outside "the homoerotic world of his patron Southampton and his friends" (xiii).
19. One should note that this same demand was also being met by forgers such as William Henry Ireland, the subject of chapter 1, who also signed Shakespeare's name on a number of sixteenth- and seventeenth-century flyleaves. See, for instance, Sidney Lee, *A Life of William Shakespeare,* 14th ed. (London: Macmillan, 1931), 520–21, and the list of some sixty books forming a "Shakspearian Library, *with Manuscript Notes*" included in the sale of Samuel Ireland's collections after his death: *A Catalogue of the Books, Paintings, Miniatures, Drawings, Prints, and Various Curiosities, the Property of the Late Samuel Ireland, Esq.* (London, 1801), 29–33. This library is also mentioned in Samuel Ireland's preface to *Miscellaneous Papers and Legal Instruments under the Hand and Seal of William Shakspeare: Including the Tragedy of King Lear, and a Small Fragment of Hamlet, from the Original Mss. in the Possession of Samuel Ireland, of Norfolk Street . . . ,* folio ed. (London, 1796), 9.
20. Cited in Schoenbaum, *Shakespeare's Lives,* 399.

21. Edward George Harman, *The "Impersonality" of Shakespeare* (London: Palmer, 1925; New York: Haskell, 1971), 242.
22. John Aubrey, *Brief Lives,* ed. Oliver Lawson Dick (Ann Arbor: University of Michigan Press, 1957), 11.
23. See Perez Zagorin, *Francis Bacon* (Princeton: Princeton University Press, 1998); and Lisa Jardine and Alan Stewart, *Hostage to Fortune: The Troubled Life of Francis Bacon* (London: Gollancz, 1998).
24. As, for example, in a number of essays in Jonathan Goldberg, ed., *Queering the Renaissance* (Durham: Duke University Press, 1994).
25. One of the best and certainly most amusing surveys of the Baconian movement can be found in Wadsworth, *Poacher from Stratford,* 36–93, which also records a few particularly outlandish readers who argued that Bacon was a hermaphrodite, that he journeyed to the Bermudas disguised as a woman in order to hide his Shakespearean manuscripts, and, most interestingly of all, that he was still alive in 1920 (92–93).
26. Zagorin, *Francis Bacon,* 14.
27. Cited in William F. Friedman and Elizabeth S. Friedman, *The Shakespearean Ciphers Examined: An Analysis of Cryptographic Systems Used as Evidence That Some Author Other than William Shakespeare Wrote the Plays Commonly Attributed to Him* (Cambridge: Cambridge University Press, 1957), 106.
28. Walter Begley, *Is It Shakespeare? The Great Question of Elizabethan Literature, Answered in the Light of New Revelations and Important Contemporary Evidence hitherto Unnoticed* (London: Murray, 1903). The copy I have consulted, from the University of Rochester Library, includes a bookplate (and signature) from Henry James, one of the most famous Shakespearean dissenters of his day.
29. Begley, *Is It Shakespeare?* 34, 57, 61, 255.
30. Begley, *Is It Shakespeare?* 52; Michell, *Who Wrote Shakespeare?* 116–119. For a list of reviews of Begley's book, see Galland, *Digesta Anti-Shakespeareana,* 161.
31. Roderick L. Eagle, *The Secrets of the Shakespeare Sonnets* (London: Mitre, 1965), 8, 21; emphasis removed.
32. John Semple Smart, *Shakespeare: Truth and Tradition* (London: Arnold, 1928), 11; Spedding's comment is cited in Michell, *Who Wrote Shakespeare?* 120.
33. E.g., Charlton Ogburn, *The Mysterious William Shakespeare: The Myth and the Reality* (New York: Dodd, Mead, 1984); Richard F. Whalen, *Shakespeare—Who Was He? The Oxford Challenge to the Bard of Avon* (Westport, Conn.: Praeger, 1994); Joseph Sobran, *Alias Shakespeare: Solving the Greatest Literary Mystery of All Time* (New York: Free Press, 1997).
34. J. Thomas Looney, *"Shakespeare" Identified in Edward de Vere, the Seventeenth Earl of Oxford* (London: Palmer, 1920), 503–30.
35. Hope and Holston, *Shakespeare Controversy,* 102.
36. Looney, *"Shakespeare" Identified,* 118–19, 131. "By far the larger and more important set [of sonnets] embracing no less than one hundred and twenty-six out of a total of one hundred and fifty-four, is addressed to a young man, and express a tenderness, which is probably without parallel in the recorded expressions of emotional attachment of one man to another" (129).

37. Looney, *"Shakespeare" Identified,* 137.
38. Looney, *"Shakespeare" Identified,* 149, 449, 452.
39. Looney, *"Shakespeare" Identified,* 367, 419.
40. For Meres's comments, see *The Shakspere Allusion-Book: A Collection of Allusions to Shakspere from 1591–1700,* 2 vols., ed. John Munro et al. (London: Humphrey Milford, 1932), 1:47–48. If Bacon's works seem far removed from those of Shakespeare, the mediocre poems of Oxford are even more problematic. At least Bacon was brilliant. Sobran, *Alias Shakespeare,* reprints Oxford's known poems in an appendix, along with an amusingly long list of "parallels" from Shakespeare (231–70).
41. Looney, *"Shakespeare" Identified,* 219.
42. Ogburn, *Mysterious William Shakespeare,* 342, 645. The reference is to A. L. Rowse, "Shakespeare, the Sexiest Writer in the Language," *The Times,* 24 April 1971, 12. The "lurid details" are, as Rowse cites them, that Oxford was accused by Charles Arundel of being "a buggerer, of a boy that is his cook." Further, Arundel claims, "I have seen this boy many a time in his chamber, doors close-locked, together with him, maybe at Whitehall and at his house in Broad Street. Finding it so, I have gone to the backdoor to satisfy myself, at the which the boy hath come out all in a sweat, and I have gone in and found the beast in the same plight. But to make it more apparent, my Lord Harry [Howard] saw more, and the boy confessed it unto Southwell and himself confirmed it unto Mr. William Cornwallis." (Note the unintended pun on going to the backdoor to satisfy himself.) Looney remarks merely that there is an "evident vulgarity" associated with the very name Charles, which is "insinuated by Oliver into the mind of Charles the wrestler" in *As You Like It* (*"Shakespeare" Identified,* 219). The buggery scandal, one should note, now regularly appears in Oxfordian literature, e.g., Sobran, *Alias Shakespeare,* 125.
43. Sidney Lee, "Edward de Vere," *Dictionary of National Biography,* 22 vols., ed. Leslie Stephen and Sidney Lee (Oxford: Oxford University Press, 1921–22), 20:226.
44. Ogburn, *Mysterious William Shakespeare,* 554.
45. "The Ghost of Shakespeare," *Harper's,* April 1999, 37, 54. See also Sobran, *Alias Shakespeare:* "It appears that the greatest passion of our greatest poet was a furtive homosexual love. Did this forbidden passion lead the poet to adopt the pen name by which we have confusedly known him . . . ? Might this be a key to the identity of Shakespeare?" (100). The book purports to confront "the strong evidence that the poet and his young friend are homosexual lovers" (197), but we don't get much further than the assertion that "Mr. Shakspere of Stratford . . . is not known to have been notorious for anything, let alone sodomy." Oxford, on the other hand, "*was* notorious" (201).
46. Aubrey, *Brief Lives,* 189.
47. Ogburn, *Mysterious William Shakespeare,* 342, 344–45, 645.
48. Ogburn, *Mysterious William Shakespeare,* 141, 345.
49. Gerald H. Rendall, *Shakespeare Sonnets and Edward de Vere* (London: Murray, 1930), 25, 30.

50. Rendall, *Shakespeare Sonnets,* 135, 177, 182, 283.
51. Rendall, *Shakespeare Sonnets,* 161–62.
52. "Ghost of Shakespeare," 55.
53. Samuel Butler, *Shakespeare's Sonnets Reconsidered, and in Part Rearranged, with Introductory Chapters, Notes, and a Reprint of the Original 1609 Edition* (London: Longmans, 1899; New York: AMS, 1971), 44.
54. Butler, *Shakespeare's Sonnets Reconsidered,* 66–87.
55. Schoenbaum, *Shakespeare's Lives,* 326.
56. Rendall, *Shakespeare Sonnets,* 282.
57. Butler, *Shakespeare's Sonnets Reconsidered,* 73, 122.
58. Rendall, *Shakespeare Sonnets,* 285.
59. See, e.g., Schoenbaum, *Shakespeare's Lives,* 440–44.
60. *Sonnets,* ed. Rollins, 2:183.
61. Cited in *Sonnets,* ed. Rollins, 2:234.
62. Donald E. Stanford, "Robert Bridges and Samuel Butler on Shakespeare's Sonnets: An Exchange of Letters," *Shakespeare Quarterly* 22 (1971): 332.
63. Hilda Amphlett, *Who Was Shakespeare? A New Inquiry* (London: Heinemann, 1955; New York: AMS, 1970), 40–41, 161, 167.
64. Looney, *"Shakespeare" Identified,* 131; Amphlett, *Who Was Shakespeare?* 45.
65. Amphlett, *Who Was Shakespeare?* 78, 172. On *Hamlet,* see also Looney, *"Shakespeare" Identified,* 457–86.
66. Interestingly enough, several adherents to Baconian authorship have argued that their hero also faked his death in 1626 (see Wadsworth, *Poacher from Stratford,* 58–59); I have no doubt that somewhere one might find a similar argument advanced for Oxford.
67. Calvin Hoffman, *The Murder of the Man Who Was "Shakespeare"* (1955; New York: Grosset and Dunlap, 1960), xi, xvii, 44, 55–56. As for Raleigh, it is notable that on at least one occasion when he was put forward as the real Shakespeare, it was precisely because of his apparent success with the ladies (Aubrey, once again, being the main authority). Bacon, on the other hand, could never measure up to this requirement: "intrigue with a woman would have been impossible with this slow-witted, calculating politician" (cited in Wadsworth, *Poacher from Stratford,* 137).
68. Hoffman, *Murder of the Man Who Was "Shakespeare,"* 108.
69. A. D. Wraight, *The Story That the Sonnets Tell* (London: Adam Hart, 1994), 65–66, 145–47, 199.
70. Wraight, *Story That the Sonnets Tell,* 199–200, 205, 210, 534–35.
71. William Honey, *The Life, Loves and Achievements of Christopher Marlowe, Alias Shakespeare,* vol. 1. (London: privately printed, 1982). This rare volume has actually turned up in a library in Taiwan, "luckily" for me, a remarkable example of the effects of Shakespeare's supposed universality.
72. Honey, *Life, Loves and Achievements of Christopher Marlowe,* 32–34, 313–14, 329, 462–63, 543, 763, 771, 1350.
73. Carolyn Gage, "The Case for Marlowe as the Bard," *Harvard Gay and Lesbian Review* 5:4 (1998): 34–35.

74. Joseph Pequigney, *Such Is My Love: A Study of Shakespeare's Sonnets* (Chicago: University of Chicago Press, 1985).
75. Garber, *Vice Versa: Bisexuality and the Eroticism of Everyday Life* (New York: Simon and Schuster, 1995), 513.

Chapter 4

1. In 1824, James Boaden referred to "hundreds of copies and pretended originals" of Shakespeare's face: *An Inquiry into the Authenticity of Various Pictures and Prints, Which, from the Decease of the Poet to Our Own Times, Have Been Offered to the Public as Portraits of Shakspeare* (London, 1824; New York: AMS, 1975), 2. Sidney Lee noted more than sixty paintings being offered to the National Portrait Gallery during the first three decades of its existence (i.e., by 1900), as well as more than thirty others that were presented to Lee himself for verification: *A Life of William Shakespeare,* 14th ed. (London: Macmillan, 1931), 533 n. 3. Samuel Schoenbaum reports that even in our own day likenesses are still turning up "with metronomic regularity, being submitted at the rate of one a year to the National Portrait Gallery for authentication": *Shakespeare's Lives,* 2d ed. (Oxford: Oxford University Press, 1991), 477. And these are only the paintings. M. H. Spielmann mentions that 450 engraved portraits were catalogued in 1916, and to this number he can add more than two hundred medals and coins: *The Title-Page of the First Folio of Shakespeare's Plays: A Comparative Study of the Droeshout Portrait and the Stratford Monument* (London: Humphrey Milford, 1924), 1. In addition to reviewing more than thirty painted candidates in detail, Spielmann's still-standard survey in the eleventh edition of the *Encyclopaedia Britannica* alludes to a breathtaking plethora of busts, medals, statues, miniatures, drawings, engravings, stained glass, wood carvings, porcelain, cameos, and wax figures: "The Portraits of Shakespeare," *Encyclopaedia Britannica,* 29 vols., 11th ed. (New York: Encyclopaedia Britannica, 1910–11), 24:787–93.
2. Spielmann, *Title-Page,* 26; Schoenbaum, *William Shakespeare: Records and Images* (London: Scolar Press, 1981), 170.
3. Boaden, *Inquiry,* 129.
4. Both cited in Schoenbaum, *Records and Images,* 161, 170.
5. Modern reviews of major portrait candidates include Lee, *Life of Shakespeare,* 523–43; Lee, "William Shakespeare," *Dictionary of National Biography,* 22 vols., ed. Leslie Stephen and Sidney Lee (Oxford: Oxford University Press, 1921–22), 17:1323–26; Spielmann, "The Portraits of Shakespeare," in *Works of William Shakespeare,* 10 vols., ed. A. H. Bullen et al. (Stratford-on-Avon: Shakespeare Head Press, 1904–7), 10:373–98; Spielmann, "Portraits of Shakespeare," *Encyclopaedia Britannica*; Schoenbaum, *Records and Images,* 155–200; Schoenbaum, "Artists' Images of Shakespeare," in *Images of Shakespeare: Proceedings of the Third Congress of the International Shakespeare Association, 1986,* ed. Werner Habicht et al. (Newark: University of Delaware Press, 1988), 19–39; Schoenbaum, *Shakespeare's Lives,* 202–14, 333–41; David Piper, *O Sweet Mr. Shakespeare, I'll Have His Picture: The Changing Image of Shakespeare's Person, 1600–1800*

(London: National Portrait Gallery, 1964); and Piper, *The Image of the Poet: British Poets and Their Portraits* (Oxford: Clarendon Press, 1982).

6. Gustav Ungerer has examined in impressive detail the case of Sir Andrew Aguecheek's red hair in *Twelfth Night,* arguing that limp hair, like baldness, was considered a sign of sexual impotence. Long hair, which had in earlier periods commonly been stigmatized as "a symbol of female lewdness," had become in Shakespeare's time "a symbol of masculine strength, virile power, sexual maturity, and boundless procreation." One thinks of Palamon's long black mane in *The Two Noble Kinsmen* (4.2.83–84). Curly hair (like the Chandos painting?) was "the ideal mixture of heat and blood" and "a mark of passion, strength, and virility": "Sir Andrew Aguecheek and His Head of Hair," *Shakespeare Studies* 16 (1983): 112–17.
7. As in the lengthy exchange between Antipholus and Dromio of Syracuse in *The Comedy of Errors* (2.2.69–108); in Quince's quip in *A Midsummer Night's Dream* that "[s]ome of your French crowns have no hair at all" (1.2.97) (and cf. *Measure for Measure* 1.2.52); in Timon's remark that syphilis can "[m]ake curl'd-pate ruffians bald" (4.3.159–60); or Bourbon's assurance that his mistress still has her own hair (*Henry V* 3.7.60–61). See also Johannes Fabricius, *Syphilis in Shakespeare's England* (London: Jessica Kingsley, 1994); and Claude Quétel, *History of Syphilis,* trans. Judith Braddock and Brian Pike (London: Polity, 1990), 50–72.
8. A. L. Rowse, *William Shakespeare: A Biography* (New York: Harper and Row, 1963), 454–55; Park Honan, *Shakespeare: A Life* (Oxford: Oxford University Press, 1998), 165.
9. Spielmann wonders, in connection with the Chandos painting, whether "the edge of the hair where it falls away [from the head] is . . . so sharply defined as to suggest a shaving of the head" ("Portraits of Shakespeare," in *Works of Shakespeare,* 10:378).
10. An early-twentieth-century reading to this effect is cited in *Sonnets,* 2 vols., variorum ed., ed. Hyder Edward Rollins (Philadelphia: J. B. Lippincott, 1944), 2:258 n. 1. Frank Wadsworth also cites one Baconian reader who argued that the historical William Shakespeare (but not the author of the plays) died of venereal disease: *The Poacher from Stratford: A Partial Account of the Controversy over the Authorship of Shakespeare's Plays* (Berkeley: University of California Press, 1958), 90–91. But first prize must go to Fabricius's *Syphilis in Shakespeare's England,* which, after an impressively detailed survey of the disease and the myriad of references to it in the early modern period, proceeds to depressingly literal-minded chapters on "Shakespeare and His Circle," "Shakespeare's Unconscious Imagery" (a mixture of Jung and Caroline Spurgeon), and "Shakespeare's Mid-Life Crisis" (175–254), all of which prove by "circumstantial evidence" that "even William Shakespeare may have fallen a victim to syphilis" (273). William Herbert ("identified" as both W. H. and the young man of the sonnets), Robert Greene, Thomas Nashe, George Peele, William Davenant, Sir John Falstaff, Jaques in *As You Like It* ("a self-portrait of the poet" [226]), and perhaps Hamlet all suffered from the disease; and

Willobie His Avisa, the sonnets, and Manningham's diary entry all show us the bard as a "libertine" living "a promiscuous pattern of behavior" (183–84), and "a leading member of literary and dramatic Bohemia during the years he lived in the capital" (a milieu that included Christopher Marlowe, "a known homosexual" who "lived a short and dangerous life"). Moreover, "this particular way of living [i.e., in a "high-risk group"] was not only a consequence of [Shakespeare's] profession and of his separation from his family, but also one that suited certain features of his own personality" (163). It is remarkable that Shakespeare's baldness is not once mentioned, although hair loss is duly included as one of the main visible symptoms of the disease (e.g., 26–27).

11. Even Piper, an eminently qualified art historian, notes that although the print is "incompetently drawn" and the bust is "a vapid icon," "the claim for authenticity of these two images rests in the fact that both are vouched for implicitly in the First Folio, published seven years after Shakespeare's death, in 1623. . . . The editors of the Folio were Shakespeare's colleagues and friends: those responsible for the erection of the bust must likewise have been his friends and his family. Both images were therefore, even if both were made posthumously, vouched for, passed for publication as likenesses of Shakespeare by those who knew him—accepted or, at least, not rejected by them" (*Image of the Poet,* 13–14). A notable exception to this sort of tendency is Marcia Pointon, who rightly emphasizes the "quicksands of portraiture" with respect to Shakespeare in particular: "Shakespeare, Portraiture and National Identity," *Shakespeare Jahrbuch* 133 (1997): 46.
12. The best survey of the "faults" of these two representations appears in Spielmann, *Title-Page,* esp. 9–12 and 31–35.
13. *Plays and Poems,* 20 vols., ed. Edmond Malone and James Boswell (London, 1821), 1:286.
14. Joseph Quincy Adams, *A Life of William Shakespeare* (London: Constable, 1923), 541. Admittedly, it is not entirely clear whether Gainsborough is here referring to the print or to the Chandos painting. See Piper, *Image of the Poet,* 83.
15. Schoenbaum, *Shakespeare's Lives,* 476; Lee, *Life of Shakespeare,* 524; Spielmann, *Title-Page,* 9, 11–12; Schoenbaum, *Records and Images,* 161.
16. Spielmann, *Title-Page,* 32; Schoenbaum, *Records and Images,* 169.
17. In Benson's bowdlerized edition of Shakespeare's poems in 1640; in an edition of *Lucrece* in 1655; and in John Cotgrave's *Witts Interpreter* in 1662 (see Spielmann, *Title-Page,* 44–46).
18. See Margreta de Grazia, *Shakespeare Verbatim: The Reproduction of Authenticity and the 1790 Apparatus* (Oxford: Clarendon Press, 1991), 81–82.
19. Schoenbaum, *Shakespeare's Lives,* 212.
20. See, e.g., Arthur Sherbo, *The Birth of Shakespeare Studies: Commentators from Rowe (1709) to Boswell-Malone (1821)* (East Lansing: Colleagues Press, 1986), 155.
21. de Grazia, *Shakespeare Verbatim,* 83.
22. Lee, *Life of Shakespeare,* 524 n. 1; Spielmann, *Title-Page,* 20; Schoenbaum, *Records and Images,* 162.

23. Spielmann, *Title-Page,* 21.
24. Anti-Stratfordian readers have been attracted to the Droeshout as well, wondering whether it might show us Bacon (or another candidate) in disguise. This is enhanced by the idea that the print's "wooden" face simply depicted someone wearing a mask and wig (but a skinhead wig, like a circus clown?): see, e.g., Joseph S. Galland, *Digesta Anti-Shakespeareana* (unpublished manuscript, 1949; available from UMI Dissertation Service), 208–9. In addition to ubiquitous Baconian ciphers found throughout the First Folio, and even in Jonson's praise of Droeshout, the print's alarmingly unperspectival costume has given rise to the theory (which I myself have never been able to make out) that the intention was to show a body with two left (or is it right?) sleeves. Professional tailors were even called in to offer their expertise (see, e.g., Galland, *Digesta Anti-Shakespeareana,* 1016, 1088). As Edwin Durning-Lawrence so beautifully summed it all up in 1911, "the 'Figure' put upon the title-page of the First Folio of the Plays in 1623 to represent Shakespeare is a doubly left-armed and stuffed dummy, surmounted by a ridiculous putty-faced mask"; this "disposes once and for all of any idea that the mighty plays were written by the drunken, illiterate clown of Stratford-on-Avon, and shows us quite clearly that the name 'Shakespeare' was used as a dummy, a left hand, a pseudonym, behind which the great author, Francis Bacon, wrote securely concealed" (cited in Galland, *Digesta Anti-Shakespeareana,* 449).
25. Piper, *Sweet Mr. Shakespeare,* 34, notes "a general fascination, growing from 1770 on, in historical portraits: a desire now for authentic contemporary likenesses rather than idealized heroic portraits—an antiquarian urge and a very romantic one, the authentic painting taking on the aura of [the] sympathetic magic of a relic."
26. Peter Martin, *Edmond Malone, Shakespearean Scholar: A Literary Biography* (Cambridge: Cambridge University Press, 1995), 92.
27. Schoenbaum, *Records and Images,* 177; Piper, *Image of the Poet,* 42.
28. Cited in Schoenbaum, *Records and Images,* 175–77.
29. *Plays and Poems,* ed. Malone-Boswell, 1:254, 512. As Boswell put it in his own preface, "without giving any credence to this antiquated scandal (for the truth of which I have certainly no wish to contend), Sir William was certainly Shakspear's god-son; [and he] was likely, without any connection of this sort, to have been desirous of obtaining his resemblance, from admiration of his genius; and so nearly his contemporary as to have the means of ascertaining, either by his own recollection, or from others, how far it was correct" (1:xxv).
30. A certain nadir is reached in Fabricius's *Syphilis in Shakespeare's England,* which takes at face value that "Shakespeare's only portrait" was once owned by Davenant, a fact that proves, more than anything else (besides both of them being named William), "that Shakespeare himself might have regarded William Davenant as more than a godson and looked upon him as a son—a substitute for Hamnet, his only son, whom the poet had lost in 1596 at the tender age of eleven" (251).

31. Piper, *Sweet Mr. Shakespeare,* 12. Richard Burt has also pointed out that in a romance novel by Erica Jong, *Shylock's Daughter,* a distinctly sexual Shakespeare is visualized very much after the Chandos portrait: see "*Shakespeare in Love* and the End of the Shakespearean: Academic and Mass Culture Constructions of Literary Authorship," in *Shakespeare, Film, Fin de Siècle,* ed. Mark Burnett and Ramona Wray (London: Macmillan, 2000), 203–31.
32. *Plays and Poems,* ed. Malone-Boswell, 1:286n, 297–98. On other readings of the Chandos as Jewish, see Richard Halpern, *Shakespeare among the Moderns* (Ithaca: Cornell University Press, 1997), 163–66. For more on the Abbey statue, see Michael Dobson, *The Making of the National Poet: Shakespeare, Adaptation, and Authorship, 1660–1769* (Oxford: Clarendon Press, 1992), 134–64.
33. *Plays and Poems,* ed. Malone-Boswell, 1:293, 298.
34. Schoenbaum, *Shakespeare's Lives,* 209; *Records and Images,* 184. According to Boaden, "the ablest artists have assured me, that Nature never produced [a head] of such a form" (*Inquiry,* 95).
35. As Boaden notes: "Every thing . . . that had a high forehead, little or no hair, and the slightest look of the known prints of him" was claimed to be Shakespeare (*Inquiry,* 99). Boaden also rejects the Hilliard miniature because of its "strong tuft of hair growing in front of the forehead, [which] is indeed very unusual with persons who yet are exceedingly bald toward the temples" (*Inquiry,* 130).
36. Spielmann, "Portraits of Shakespeare," *Encyclopaedia Britannica,* 787.
37. *Plays and Poems,* ed. Malone-Boswell, 2:509; Piper, *Image of the Poet,* 41–42.
38. See Piper, *Image of the Poet,* 105.
39. William L. Pressly, "The Ashbourne Portrait of Shakespeare: Through the Looking Glass," *Shakespeare Quarterly* 44 (1993): 63. J. Thomas Looney, famed originator of the Oxfordian hypothesis, perceived Oxford's face in this portrait as well as in the Grafton, now in the John Rylands Library at the University of Manchester: *"Shakespeare" Identified in Edward de Vere, the Seventeenth Earl of Oxford* (London: Palmer, 1920), 533–36.
40. The Flower was touted as the original from which Droeshout had executed his engraving (and similar claims have been made for the Felton, among others). Lee briefly subscribed to the Flower's authenticity, as argued in his 1898 *Life of Shakespeare* (288–90). This position was revised in later editions of the same work (530–32), but Lee continued to use the painting as his frontispiece. Despite Paul Bertram and Frank Cossa's renewed enthusiasm for the authenticity of the picture ("'Willm Shakespeare 1609': The Flower Portrait Revisited," *Shakespeare Quarterly* 37 [1986]: 83–96), Spielmann's masterly discussion of the differences between it and the Droeshout engraving (which exists in more than one state) still, to my mind, incontrovertibly demonstrates that the print preceded the painting rather than the other way around (*Title-Page,* 35–39).
41. Bertram and Cossa, "'Willm Shakespeare 1609,'" 94. The Chandos portrait, on the other hand, seems to have been altered in the opposite direction; as one expert writes, "overpaint, as can be seen clearly in the infra-red photograph, has slightly toned down the uncompromising loft of the dome so marked

in the other two portraits" (Piper, *Image of the Poet,* 18). See also Piper, *Sweet Mr. Shakespeare,* 12–13. Another amusing example appears in the so-called Shakespeare Marriage portrait, where the hair of a bridegroom has been painted out in favor of a Shakespearean bald pate, although Shakespeare was only a teenager when he married Ann Hathaway: see Spielmann, "The 'Shakespeare Marriage Picture' (Part II)," *Connoisseur* 21 (1908): 249.

42. Boaden, *Inquiry,* 72.
43. Charles Lamb and Mary Lamb, *Works,* 7 vols., ed. E. V. Lucas (London: Methuen, 1903–5), 7:573–74.
44. *Plays and Poems,* ed. Malone-Boswell, 1:285–86.
45. Boaden, *Inquiry,* 72.
46. Cited in John Mair, *The Fourth Forger: William Ireland and the Shakespeare Papers* (London: Cobden-Sanderson, 1938), 228.
47. Boaden, *Inquiry,* i. Boaden even intimates that Ireland might have made the Felton head: "I do not know that this picture might not have been intended to appear among the infinite possessions of the *nameless* gentleman [i.e., Ireland's Mr. H.]" (104). Lamb, too, wondered if the young forger had some connection to the Bellows portrait: "It may be a forgery. They laugh at me and tell me Ireland is in Paris, and has been putting off a portrait of the Black Prince. How far old wood may be imitated I cannot say. Ireland was not found out by his parchments, but by his poetry" (*Works,* 7:574). According to J. Parker Norris, *The Portraits of Shakespeare* (Philadelphia: Lindsay, 1885), Ireland was also one of the painting's early owners (228).
48. Boaden, *Inquiry,* ii.
49. Cited in Mair, *Fourth Forger,* 39.
50. William Henry Ireland, *An Authentic Account of the Shakspearian Mss.* (London, 1796; New York: Kelley, 1971), 15.
51. In the folio edition of the same year, the engraving is incorporated among the other facsimiles and there is no frontispiece.
52. See, e.g., Spielmann, *Title-Page,* 33.
53. Malone, *An Inquiry into the Authenticity of Certain Miscellaneous Papers and Legal Instruments . . . Attributed to Shakspeare* (London, 1796; New York: Kelley, 1970), 209.
54. William Henry Ireland, *Confessions* (London, 1805), 109–10.
55. Ireland, *Confessions,* 110–11. Many wondered whether the Droeshout print was also supposed to show Shakespeare in costume. Boaden even suggested the role of (old) Knowell in Jonson's *Every Man in His Humour* (*Inquiry,* 19), since Shakespeare's name is included in the list of players appended to the text as published in 1616: see E. K. Chambers, *William Shakespeare: A Study of Facts and Problems,* 2 vols. (Oxford: Clarendon Press, 1930), 2:71.
56. These drawings appear only in the large folio edition of Samuel Ireland, *Miscellaneous Papers and Legal Instruments under the Hand and Seal of William Shakspeare: Including the Tragedy of King Lear, and a Small Fragment of Hamlet, from the Original Mss. in the Possession of Samuel Ireland, of Norfolk Street . . .* (London, 1796), unpaged. My thanks to Richard Burt for first checking

the text for me, and to Georgianna Ziegler and the staff of the Folger Shakespeare Library for research assistance and help in acquiring photographs. Schoenbaum (*Shakespeare's Lives,* 160) also cites a contemporary defender who argued for the drawings' authenticity precisely because they weren't good enough to be forgeries.

57. Malone, *Inquiry,* 243–44.
58. Ireland, *Confessions,* 112.
59. Ireland, *Authentic Account,* 17–18; *Confessions,* 114.
60. Cited in Schoenbaum, *Shakespeare's Lives,* 150.
61. Samuel Ireland, *Miscellaneous Papers,* 2; emphasis removed.
62. Ireland, *Authentic Account,* 22; *Confessions,* 192.
63. Ireland, *Confessions,* 194.
64. It is a bit ironic, then, that Samuel Ireland's *Picturesque Views on the Upper, or Warwickshire Avon* (London, 1795), published at the same time as his son's forgeries, includes an engraving (by the elder Ireland) of the Stratford monument, which, like so many other eighteenth-century representations, shows a head derived from the Chandos instead. This is all the more revealing in that the accompanying text notes that "this bust, though rudely sculptured, is yet, I have little doubt, a resemblance of the man" (210–11).
65. Ireland, *Confessions,* 84; Malone, *Inquiry,* 143 n. 80.
66. Ireland, *Authentic Account,* 15; *Confessions,* 82.
67. A related bit of confusion occurs in a retelling of Kemble's recollection of the first and only night that *Vortigern* was performed, with the great actor himself in the title role. Young Ireland, we are told, was seated "by the side of Polly Thompson, or some such personage: the person from whose head, as he afterwards confessed, he had cut the identical lock of hair exhibited at the elder Ireland's as a lock from the head of Mrs. Anna Hatherewaye" (cited in Bernard Grebanier, *The Great Shakespeare Forgery: A New Look at the Career of William Henry Ireland* [London: Heinemann, 1966], 225). Someone has forgotten that the lock in question was supposed to come from the head of Shakespeare, not his wife. Coincidentally, an early owner of the Bellows portrait, when having it cleaned, found another picture of a lady underneath and had it covered up again so that the painting could be resold (Lamb, *Works,* 7:574–75). The Flower picture was also painted over a Madonna and Child (Bertram and Cossa, "'Willm Shakespeare 1609,'" 93–94), and another nineteenth-century fake started out as a portrait of an old woman (Spielmann, "The Winstanley Portraits of Shakespeare," *Connoisseur* 22 [1908]: 95).
68. Cf. the verses at the bottom of the print, often omitted in illustrations (including the one provided here), which read in part: "Subscribe but four Guineas as part of my fee, / The first thing I shew you is a relick most rare, / An astonishing Lock of the great Shakspeares hair, / Out of which twenty rings more or less have been made, / Nor a Single Hair misst from this wonderful Braid." Even William Henry ridicules "one Mr. Collet, a hair merchant, [who] was to come in all the pomp of his trade and scrutinise the Shaksperian *curl*" (Ireland, *Confessions,* 84).

69. Malone, *Inquiry,* 143.
70. George Chalmers, *An Apology for the Believers in the Shakspeare-Papers* (London, 1797; New York: Kelley, 1971), 175; emphasis removed.
71. Ireland, *Confessions,* 201–2.
72. Cited in Schoenbaum, *Shakespeare's Lives,* 144n.
73. Ireland, *Confessions,* 202.
74. Cited in Mair, *Fourth Forger,* 93.
75. Samuel Ireland, *Mr. Ireland's Vindication of His Conduct respecting the Publication of the Supposed Shakspeare Mss.* (London, 1796; New York: Kelley, 1970), 36–37. A "MSS. Catalogue of Shakspeare's Library" was included in the sale of Samuel Ireland's effects conducted after his death: see *A Catalogue of the Books, Paintings, Miniatures, Drawings, Prints, and Various Curiosities, the Property of the Late Samuel Ireland, Esq.* (London, 1801), 29.
76. Malone, *Inquiry,* 315–17.
77. Evidently even this drawing left something to be desired in Malone's mind, since he had at one time complained to the artist (in Schoenbaum's summary) that "too much of the white showed in one of the eyes, making Shakespeare appear to squint" (*Records and Images,* frontispiece note).
78. See *Plays and Poems,* ed. Malone-Boswell, 2:510–12.
79. Malone, *Inquiry,* 355–58.
80. Ireland, *Confessions,* 189.
81. Samuel Ireland, *An Investigation of Mr. Malone's Claim to the Character of Scholar, or Critic* (London, 1796; New York: Kelley, 1970), 151.
82. Malone, *Inquiry,* 358–59.
83. Cited in Schoenbaum, *Shakespeare's Lives,* 64. Fabricius illustrates the two portraits together, with the caption: "Father and son?" (*Syphilis in Shakespeare's England,* 252).
84. Boaden, *Inquiry,* 17; Spielmann, *Title-Page,* 27; Piper, *Image of the Poet,* 110–11.
85. Rowse, *William Shakespeare,* 454–55.
86. Rowse, *Shakespeare the Man,* rev. ed. (New York: St. Martin's, 1988), 645. Rowse is also the author of *Homosexuals in History: A Study of Ambivalence in Society, Literature, and the Arts* (New York: Macmillan, 1977), a study in which "heterosexual Shakespeare" (29) is included only for comparison or because he influenced later ("homosexual") writers: "Shakespeare himself was even more than normally heterosexual, for an Englishman" (46).
87. The first edition of Schoenbaum's *Shakespeare's Lives* (Oxford: Clarendon Press, 1970) cites a viewer who saw in Dugdale's Shakespeare a "tired creator of poems, exhausted from lack of sleep" (8). Boaden is unique in finding "a casual expression of hilarity" in Janssen's bust: "The *vis comica* so brightens his countenance, that it is hardly a stretch of fancy, to suppose him in the actual creation of Falstaff himself" (*Inquiry,* 31, 76).
88. Spielmann is hardly exaggerating when he remarks that Droeshout "carried the plate as far as he could—and carried himself over the border-line of sane facial representation" (*Title-Page,* 33).
89. Cf. Schoenbaum, *Records and Images,* 175.

90. To take but one example, with respect to a bald Shakespeare, the most recent edition of *The Riverside Shakespeare* (2d ed., ed. G. Blakemore Evans et al. [Boston: Houghton Mifflin, 1997]) includes—on the cover and spine—a reproduction of the so-called Staunton Janssen (not the Janssen painting but one of a number of copies made after it), but the photo has been radically cropped just above the level of the eyebrows. While perhaps merely just a matter of book design (and my own book is guilty of this too), it is also notable that the most commonly used American undergraduate text "identifies" the bard by ensuring that his baldness is kept safely out of sight.
91. Robert Speaight, *Shakespeare: The Man and His Achievement* (New York: Stein and Day, 1977), 346; Peter Quennell, *Shakespeare: A Biography* (Cleveland: World Publishing, 1963), 65; Honan, *Shakespeare: A Life*, ix.
92. Honan, *Shakespeare: A Life*, 324.
93. Hazelton Spencer, *The Art and Life of William Shakespeare* (New York: Harcourt, Brace, 1940), 388.
94. Even when Shakespeare has been hypothesized as actually having syphilis, as in Fabricius's *Syphilis in Shakespeare's England*, the poet is carefully safeguarded from any hint of sodomy, most of all with respect to the young man of the sonnets. The poems addressed to the young man might "seem to raise friendship to a level more Greek than English" (178)—a strangely Victorian way of putting it—but Fabricius is concerned with the two men only insofar as Shakespeare and W. H. (namely, William Herbert) were "two libertines" *competing* for the affections of the dark lady (183). Herbert is only a "self-projection" of Shakespeare anyway (and the Chandos portrait is compared with one of Herbert in order to prove it), supported by such marvelous coincidences as the fact that they shared the same first name (179). The conclusion to all of this is that "the poet may have been affected with syphilis through a rival who had infected the unfaithful woman they shared" (232), but lest one wonder whether Shakespeare was infected through his *own* relationship to the young man, everything is later clarified as "an act of treachery by a rival who appears to have brought about the poet's infection through a common love object that has proved unfaithful" (243). In other words, Herbert is demonized as the true source of the disease, and Shakespeare remains safely heterosexual. It is only in a caption to an illustration, in fact, and moreover when citing someone else, that Fabricius even alludes to the fact that the sonnets have been interpreted "as rendering a homosexual symbolism" (245). Even Shakespeare's perceived misogyny, which is an example only of "misogyny in heterosexual men," must have been a function of "some traumatic experience at the hands of the opposite sex" ("disregard[ing] the cases in which misogyny appears as a concomitant of certain life styles such as homosexuality") (241). The transmission of syphilis between men is utterly ruled out, not only for Shakespeare but in the text as a whole, and this despite citing warnings from early modern medical commentators that, for instance, the mouth and the anus were equally "dangerous gateways of the body" (45).
95. See, e.g., Schoenbaum, *Shakespeare's Lives*, 338–39.

96. See Martin, *Edmond Malone,* 181. Malone was also probably the first to take painstaking measurements of the features of the print and the bust in order to prove that, proportionally speaking at least, they represent the skull of the same man (Schoenbaum, *Shakespeare's Lives,* 125–26). There are also wonderful anecdotes of viewers measuring their own faces as guides. For example, Spielmann drew a cork moustache above his own upper lip to show that it, like the moustache depicted in the Stratford monument, produced a certain optical illusion of greater breadth (*Title-Page,* 10–11).
97. On these crusades see Schoenbaum, *Shakespeare's Lives,* 339, who also notes the desire to find the leg bones of the "lame" Shakespeare as well, supposedly referred to in sonnets 37 and 89 (341). See also Norris's prefatory essay, "Shall We Open Shakespeare's Grave? A Plea for Ascertaining the True Likeness of the Poet" (*Portraits of Shakespeare,* 1–20).
98. Thanks to Richard Burt for suggesting this term.
99. Our only "evidence" of Shakespeare's appearance comes from Aubrey: "He was a handsome well shap't man: very good company, and of a very readie and pleasant smooth Witt" (cited in Chambers, *William Shakespeare,* 2:253).
100. *Plays and Poems,* ed. Malone-Boswell, 1:254.
101. The most famous modern example is the Grafton painting, advocated by both John Semple Smart and John Dover Wilson despite its admittedly dubious claims to authenticity (see Schoenbaum, *Records and Images,* 191). Even in 1824, Boaden had already noted that previous commentators "usually worked themselves up to the feeling of partizans rather than that of inquirers, and determined to see no marks of authenticity out of the frame of their favourite portrait" (*Inquiry,* 2).
102. Marjorie Garber, *Shakespeare's Ghost Writers: Literature as Uncanny Causality* (New York: Methuen, 1987), 11.

Epilogue

1. Marc Norman and Tom Stoppard, *Shakespeare in Love: A Screenplay* (New York: Miramax, 1998), 169. Further references will be abbreviated *SIL* and cited in parentheses.
2. See, for example, Lynda E. Boose and Richard Burt, eds., *Shakespeare, the Movie: Popularizing the Plays on Film, TV, and Video* (London: Routledge, 1997); and Richard Burt, "*Shakespeare in Love* and the End of the Shakespearean: Academic and Mass Culture Constructions of Literary Authorship," in *Shakespeare, Film, Fin de Siècle,* ed. Mark Burnett and Ramona Wray (London: Macmillan, 2000), 203–31.
3. Cf. Rudolf M. Dekker and Lotte C. van de Pol, *The Tradition of Female Transvestism in Early Modern Europe* (London: Macmillan, 1989), 55: "There was obviously a great difference in the perception of cross-dressing of men and women. Transvestism of men was considered much more objectionable than that of women. The man was demeaned, while the woman strove for something higher."

4. *Shakespeare in Love: The Love Poetry of William Shakespeare* (New York: Miramax, 1998).
5. Cited in S. Schoenbaum, *Shakespeare's Lives,* 2d ed. (Oxford: Oxford University Press, 1991), 225.
6. See Burt, *Unspeakable ShaXXXspeares: Queer Theory and American Kiddie Culture,* rev. ed. (New York: St. Martin's, 1999), xi–xxvi, 1–28.
7. Laurie Rozakis, *The Complete Idiot's Guide to Shakespeare* (New York: Alpha Books, 1999), 34.
8. Rozakis, *Idiot's Guide,* 363–64. For more on the contention that all the sonnets are addressed to a man, see chapter 3.
9. John Doyle and Ray Lischner, *Shakespeare for Dummies* (Foster City, Calif.: IDG Books, 1999), 94.
10. Brandon Toropov, *Shakespeare for Beginners* (New York: Writers and Readers Publishing, Inc., 1997), 3.
11. Toropov, *Shakespeare for Beginners,* 203.
12. Michael Macrone, *Naughty Shakespeare* (New York: Cader Books, 1997), 6–7.
13. Macrone, *Naughty Shakespeare,* 178–80.

Works Cited

Acheson, Arthur. *Shakespeare's Sonnet Story, 1592–1598.* London: Bernard Quaritch, 1922.

Adams, Joseph Quincy. *A Life of William Shakespeare.* London: Constable, 1923.

Amphlett, Hilda. *Who Was Shakespeare? A New Inquiry.* London: Heinemann, 1955; New York: AMS, 1970.

Astington, John. "Malvolio and the Eunuchs: Texts and Revels in *Twelfth Night.*" *Shakespeare Survey* 46 (1994): 23–34.

Aubrey, John. *Brief Lives.* Ed. Oliver Lawson Dick. Ann Arbor: University of Michigan Press, 1957.

Babcock, Robert Witbeck. *The Genesis of Shakespeare Idolatry, 1766–1799: A Study in English Criticism of the Late Eighteenth Century.* Chapel Hill: University of North Carolina Press, 1931.

Bacon, Delia. *The Philosophy of Shakspere's Plays Unfolded.* London: Groombridge, 1857; New York: AMS, 1970.

Bate, Jonathan. *Shakespearean Constitutions: Politics, Theatre, Criticism, 1730–1830* Oxford: Clarendon Press, 1989.

Begley, Walter. *Is It Shakespeare? The Great Question of Elizabethan Literature, Answered in the Light of New Revelations and Important Contemporary Evidence hitherto Unnoticed.* London: Murray, 1903.

Bentley, Gerald Eades. *The Profession of Dramatist in Shakespeare's Time, 1590–1642.* Princeton: Princeton University Press, 1971.

———. *Shakespeare and Jonson: Their Reputations in the Seventeenth Century Compared.* 2 vols. Chicago: University of Chicago Press, 1945.

Bertram, Paul, and Frank Cossa. "'Willm Shakespeare 1609': The Flower Portrait Revisited." *Shakespeare Quarterly* 37 (1986): 83–96.

Bloom, Harold. *Shakespeare: The Invention of the Human.* New York: Riverhead Books, 1998.

Boaden, James. *An Inquiry into the Authenticity of Various Pictures and Prints, Which, from the Decease of the Poet to Our Own Times, Have Been Offered to the Public as Portraits of Shakspeare.* London, 1824; New York: AMS, 1975.

Bodde, Derk. *Shakspere and the Ireland Forgeries.* Cambridge: Harvard University Press, 1930.

Boose, Lynda E., and Richard Burt, eds. *Shakespeare, the Movie: Popularizing the Plays on Film, TV, and Video.* London: Routledge, 1997.

Boswell, John. *Christianity, Social Tolerance, and Homosexuality: Gay People in Western Europe from the Beginning of the Christian Era to the Fourteenth Century.* Chicago: University of Chicago Press, 1980.

Works Cited

Bray, Alan. "Homosexuality and the Signs of Male Friendship in Elizabethan England." In *Queering the Renaissance,* ed. Jonathan Goldberg, 40–61. Durham: Duke University Press, 1994.

———. *Homosexuality in Renaissance England.* London: Gay Men's Press, 1982; New York: Columbia University Press, 1995.

Bredbeck, Gregory W. *Sodomy and Interpretation: Marlowe to Milton.* Ithaca: Cornell University Press, 1991.

Burt, Richard. "*Shakespeare in Love* and the End of the Shakespearean: Academic and Mass Culture Constructions of Literary Authorship." In *Shakespeare, Film, Fin de Siècle,* ed. Mark Burnett and Ramona Wray, 203–31. London: Macmillan, 2000.

———. *Unspeakable ShaXXXspeares: Queer Theory and American Kiddie Culture.* Rev. ed. New York: St. Martin's, 1999.

Butler, Samuel. *Shakespeare's Sonnets Reconsidered, and in Part Rearranged, with Introductory Chapters, Notes, and a Reprint of the Original 1609 Edition.* London: Longmans, 1899; New York: AMS, 1971.

Cady, Joseph. "'Masculine Love,' Renaissance Writing, and the 'New Invention' of Homosexuality." In *Homosexuality in Renaissance and Enlightenment England: Literary Representations in Historical Context,* ed. Claude J. Summers, 9–40. New York: Haworth Press, 1992.

Callaghan, Dympna. *Shakespeare without Women: Representing Gender and Race on the Renaissance Stage.* London: Routledge, 2000.

Campbell, Jill. *Natural Masques: Gender and Identity in Fielding's Plays and Novels.* Stanford: Stanford University Press, 1995.

Carson, James P. "Commodification and the Figure of the Castrato in Smollett's *Humphry Clinker.*" *Eighteenth Century* 33 (1992): 24–46.

A Catalogue of the Books, Paintings, Miniatures, Drawings, Prints, and Various Curiosities, the Property of the Late Samuel Ireland, Esq. London, 1801.

Chalmers, George. *An Apology for the Believers in the Shakspeare-Papers.* London, 1797; New York: Kelley, 1971.

———. *A Supplemental Apology for the Believers in the Shakspeare-Papers.* London, 1799; New York: Kelley, 1971.

Chambers, E. K. *William Shakespeare: A Study of Facts and Problems.* 2 vols. Oxford: Clarendon Press, 1930.

The Character of a Town Gallant, Exposing the Extravagant Fopperies of Some Vain Self-Conceited Pretenders to Gentility and Good Breeding. London, 1675.

Churchill, R. C. *Shakespeare and His Betters: A History and a Criticism of the Attempts Which Have Been Made to Prove That Shakespeare's Works Were Written by Others.* London: Reinhardt, 1958.

Critics and Apologists of the English Theatre: A Selection of Seventeenth-Century Pamphlets in Facsimile. Ed. Peter Davison. New York: Johnson Reprint Corp., 1972.

Dane, Clemence. *The Godson: A Fantasy.* New York: W. W. Norton, 1964.

de Grazia, Margreta. "The Scandal of Shakespeare's Sonnets." *Shakespeare Survey* 46 (1994): 35–49.

———. *Shakespeare Verbatim: The Reproduction of Authenticity and the 1790 Apparatus.* Oxford: Clarendon Press, 1991.

de Grazia, Margreta, and Peter Stallybrass. "The Materiality of the Shakespearean Text." *Shakespeare Quarterly* 44 (1993): 255–83.

Dekker, Rudolf M., and Lotte C. van de Pol. *The Tradition of Female Transvestism in Early Modern Europe.* London: Macmillan, 1989.

DiGangi, Mario. *The Homoerotics of Early Modern Drama.* Cambridge: Cambridge University Press, 1997.

Dobson, Michael. *The Making of the National Poet: Shakespeare, Adaptation, and Authorship, 1660–1769.* Oxford: Clarendon Press, 1992.

Doyle, John, and Ray Lischner. *Shakespeare for Dummies.* Foster City, Calif.: IDG Books, 1999.

Dubrow, Heather. *Captive Victors: Shakespeare's Sonnets and Narrative Poems.* Ithaca: Cornell University Press, 1987.

———. "'Incertainties Now Crown Themselves Assur'd': The Politics of Plotting Shakespeare's Sonnets." *Shakespeare Quarterly* 47 (1996): 291–305.

Duncan-Jones, Katherine. "Much Ado with Red and White: The Earliest Readers of Shakespeare's *Venus and Adonis* (1593)." *Review of English Studies* 44 (1993): 479–501.

Eagle, Roderick L. *The Secrets of the Shakespeare Sonnets.* London: Mitre, 1965.

Earle, John. *Micro-cosmographie; or, A Peece of the World Discovered; in Essayes and Characters.* London, 1628.

Elam, Keir. "The Fertile Eunuch: *Twelfth Night,* Early Modern Intercourse, and the Fruits of Castration." *Shakespeare Quarterly* 47 (1996): 1–36.

Fabricius, Johannes. *Syphilis in Shakespeare's England.* London: Jessica Kingsley, 1994.

Fineman, Joel. *Shakespeare's Perjured Eye: The Invention of Poetic Subjectivity in the Sonnets.* Berkeley: University of California Press, 1986.

Foster, Donald W. *Elegy by W. S.: A Study in Attribution.* Newark: University of Delaware Press, 1989.

Foucault, Michel. *The History of Sexuality.* 3 vols. Trans. Robert Hurley. New York: Pantheon, 1978–86.

Friedman, William F., and Elizabeth S. Friedman. *The Shakespearean Ciphers Examined: An Analysis of Cryptographic Systems Used as Evidence That Some Author Other than William Shakespeare Wrote the Plays Commonly Attributed to Him.* Cambridge: Cambridge University Press, 1957.

Gage, Carolyn. "The Case for Marlowe as the Bard." *Harvard Gay and Lesbian Review* 5:4 (1998): 32–34.

Galland, Joseph S. *Digesta Anti-Shakespeareana.* Unpublished manuscript, 1949; available from UMI Dissertation Service.

Garber, Marjorie. *Shakespeare's Ghost Writers: Literature as Uncanny Causality.* New York: Methuen, 1987.

———. *Symptoms of Culture.* New York: Routledge, 1998.

———. *Vice Versa: Bisexuality and the Eroticism of Everyday Life.* New York: Simon and Schuster, 1995.

"The Ghost of Shakespeare" [roundtable discussion of Oxford as Shakespeare], *Harper's*, April 1999, 35–62.

Gilman, Todd S. "The Italian (Castrato) in London." In *The Work of Opera: Genre, Nationhood, and Sexual Difference*, ed. Richard Dellamora and Daniel Fischlin, 49–70. New York: Columbia University Press, 1997.

Giroux, Robert. *The Book Known as Q: A Consideration of Shakespeare's Sonnets.* New York: Atheneum, 1982.

Goldberg, Jonathan. "*Romeo and Juliet*'s Open Rs." In *Queering the Renaissance*, ed. Goldberg, 218–35. Durham: Duke University Press, 1994.

———. *Sodometries: Renaissance Texts, Modern Sexualities.* Stanford: Stanford University Press, 1992.

———, ed. *Queering the Renaissance.* Durham: Duke University Press, 1994.

Grebanier, Bernard. *The Great Shakespeare Forgery: A New Look at the Career of William Henry Ireland.* London: Heinemann, 1966.

Greenblatt, Stephen et al., eds. *The Norton Shakespeare.* New York: Norton, 1997.

Halliwell-Phillipps, J. O. *Outlines of the Life of Shakespeare.* 2 vols. 7th ed. London: Longmans, 1887.

Halpern, Richard. *Shakespeare among the Moderns.* Ithaca: Cornell University Press, 1997.

Haraszti, Zoltán. "Ireland's Shakespeare Forgeries." *More Books: The Bulletin of the Boston Public Library* 9 (1934): 333–50.

Harbage, Alfred. *Sir William Davenant.* Philadelphia: University of Pennsylvania Press, 1935.

Harman, Edward George. *The "Impersonality" of Shakespeare.* London: Palmer, 1925; New York: Haskell, 1971.

Harris, Frank. *The Man Shakespeare and His Tragic Life-Story.* New York: Mitchell Kennerley, 1909.

———. *The Women in Shakespeare.* New York: Mitchell Kennerley, 1912.

Henderson, Katherine Usher, and Barbara F. McManus. *Half Humankind: Contexts and Texts of the Controversy about Women in England, 1540–1640.* Urbana: University of Illinois Press, 1985.

Hoffman, Calvin. *The Murder of the Man Who Was "Shakespeare."* 1955; New York: Grosset and Dunlap, 1960.

Honan, Park. *Shakespeare: A Life.* Oxford: Oxford University Press, 1998.

Honey, William. *The Life, Loves and Achievements of Christopher Marlowe, Alias Shakespeare.* Vol. 1. London: privately printed, 1982.

Honigmann, E. A. J. *Shakespeare's Impact on His Contemporaries.* London: Macmillan, 1982.

Hope, Warren, and Kim Holston. *The Shakespeare Controversy: An Analysis of the Claimants to Authorship, and Their Champions and Detractors.* Jefferson, N.C.: McFarland, 1992.

Hubler, Edward. *The Sense of Shakespeare's Sonnets.* Princeton: Princeton University Press, 1952.

Ireland, Samuel. *An Investigation of Mr. Malone's Claim to the Character of Scholar, or Critic.* London, 1796; New York: Kelley, 1970.

———. *Miscellaneous Papers and Legal Instruments under the Hand and Seal of William Shakspeare: Including the Tragedy of King Lear, and a Small Fragment of Hamlet, from the Original Mss. in the Possession of Samuel Ireland, of Norfolk Street . . .* Folio ed. London, 1796.

———. *Mr. Ireland's Vindication of His Conduct respecting the Publication of the Supposed Shakspeare Mss.* London, 1796; New York: Kelley, 1970.

———. *Picturesque Views on the Upper, or Warwickshire Avon.* London, 1795.

Ireland, William Henry. *An Authentic Account of the Shakspearian Mss.* London, 1796; New York: Kelley, 1971.

———. *Confessions.* London, 1805.

———. *Vortigern.* London, 1799; New York: Kelley, 1971.

Jacob, Giles. *Poetical Register; or, The Lives and Characters of the English Dramatick Poets.* London, 1719.

Jardine, Lisa, and Alan Stewart. *Hostage to Fortune: The Troubled Life of Francis Bacon.* London: Gollancz, 1998.

Jordan, Mark D. *The Invention of Sodomy in Christian Theology.* Chicago: University of Chicago Press, 1997.

Kahan, Jeffrey. *Reforging Shakespeare: The Story of a Theatrical Scandal.* Bethlehem, Pa.: Lehigh University Press, 1998.

Kowaleski-Wallace, Beth. "Shunning the Bearded Kiss: Castrati and the Definition of Female Sexuality." *Prose Studies* 15 (1992): 153–70.

Lamb, Charles, and Mary Lamb. *Works.* 7 vols. Ed. E. V. Lucas. London: Methuen, 1903–5.

Lee, Sidney. "Edward de Vere." In *Dictionary of National Biography,* ed. Leslie Stephen and Sidney Lee, 20:225–29. Oxford: Oxford University Press, 1921–22.

———. *A Life of William Shakespeare.* 14th ed. London: Macmillan, 1931.

———. "Samuel Ireland." In *Dictionary of National Biography,* ed. Leslie Stephen and Sidney Lee, 10:468–73. Oxford: Oxford University Press, 1921–22.

———. "William Shakespeare." In *Dictionary of National Biography,* ed. Leslie Stephen and Sidney Lee, 17:1286–1335. Oxford: Oxford University Press, 1921–22.

Levin, Richard A. "Shakespeare's Bastard Son." *Notes and Queries* 27 (1980): 177–79.

Levine, Laura. *Men in Women's Clothing: Anti-Theatricality and Effeminization, 1579–1642.* Cambridge: Cambridge University Press, 1994.

Looney, J. Thomas. *"Shakespeare" Identified in Edward de Vere, the Seventeenth Earl of Oxford.* London: Palmer, 1920.

Mackay, Aeneas James George. "George Chalmers." In *Dictionary of National Biography,* ed. Leslie Stephen and Sidney Lee, 3:1354–55. Oxford: Oxford University Press, 1921–22.

Macrone, Michael. *Naughty Shakespeare.* New York: Cader Books, 1997.

Mair, John. *The Fourth Forger: William Ireland and the Shakespeare Papers.* London: Cobden-Sanderson, 1938.

Malone, Edmond. *An Inquiry into the Authenticity of Certain Miscellaneous Papers and Legal Instruments . . . Attributed to Shakspeare.* London, 1796; New York: Kelley, 1970.

———. *Supplement to the Edition of Shakespeare's Plays Published in 1778 by Samuel Johnson and George Steevens.* 2 vols. London, 1780.

Marcus, Leah S. *Puzzling Shakespeare: Local Reading and Its Discontents.* Berkeley: University of California Press, 1988.

Martin, Peter. *Edmond Malone, Shakespearean Scholar: A Literary Biography.* Cambridge: Cambridge University Press, 1995.

Masten, Jeffrey. *Textual Intercourse: Collaboration, Authorship, and Sexualities in Renaissance Drama.* Cambridge: Cambridge University Press, 1997.

McCormick, Ian, ed. *Secret Sexualities: A Sourcebook of 17th and 18th Century Writing.* London: Routledge, 1997.

McFarlane, Cameron. *The Sodomite in Fiction and Satire, 1650–1750.* New York: Columbia University Press, 1997.

Michell, John. *Who Wrote Shakespeare?* London: Thames and Hudson, 1996.

Nethercot, Arthur H. *Sir William D'Avenant: Poet Laureate and Playwright-Manager.* Chicago: University of Chicago Press, 1938.

Norman, Marc, and Tom Stoppard. *Shakespeare in Love: A Screenplay.* New York: Miramax, 1998.

Norris, J. Parker. *The Portraits of Shakespeare.* Philadelphia: Lindsay, 1885.

Ogburn, Charlton. *The Mysterious William Shakespeare: The Myth and the Reality.* New York: Dodd, Mead, 1984.

Orgel, Stephen. "The Authentic Shakespeare." *Representations* 21 (1988): 1–25.

———. *Impersonations: The Performance of Gender in Shakespeare's England.* Cambridge: Cambridge University Press, 1996.

Osborne, Laurie E. "Romancing the Bard." In *Shakespeare and Appropriation,* ed. Christy Desmet and Robert Sawyer, 47–64. London: Routledge, 1999.

The Oxford Companion to English Literature. 5th ed. Ed. Margaret Drabble. Oxford: Oxford University Press, 1985.

Pequigney, Joseph. *Such Is My Love: A Study of Shakespeare's Sonnets.* Chicago: University of Chicago Press, 1985.

Piper, David. *The Image of the Poet: British Poets and Their Portraits.* Oxford: Clarendon Press, 1982.

———. *O Sweet Mr. Shakespeare, I'll Have His Picture: The Changing Image of Shakespeare's Person, 1600–1800.* London: National Portrait Gallery, 1964.

Pointon, Marcia. "Shakespeare, Portraiture and National Identity." *Shakespeare Jahrbuch* 133 (1997): 29–53.

Pressly, William L. "The Ashbourne Portrait of Shakespeare: Through the Looking Glass." *Shakespeare Quarterly* 44 (1993): 54–72.

Quennell, Peter. *Shakespeare: A Biography.* Cleveland: World Publishing, 1963.

Quétel, Claude. *History of Syphilis.* Trans. Judith Braddock and Brian Pike. London: Polity, 1990.

Rendall, Gerald H. *Shakespeare Sonnets and Edward de Vere.* London: Murray, 1930.

Riche, Barnabe. *Riche His Farewell to Militarie Profession.* London, 1581.

Roe, John. "*Willobie His Avisa* and *The Passionate Pilgrim:* Precedence, Parody, and Development." *Yearbook of English Studies* 23 (1993): 111–25.

Rowe, Nicholas. *Works.* 3 vols. London, 1728.

Rowse, A. L. *Homosexuals in History: A Study of Ambivalence in Society, Literature, and the Arts.* New York: Macmillan, 1977.

———. *Shakespeare the Man.* Rev. ed. New York: St. Martin's, 1988 [first ed. 1973].

———. "Shakespeare, the Sexiest Writer in the Language," *The Times,* 24 April 1971, 12.

———. *William Shakespeare: A Biography.* New York: Harper and Row, 1963.

Rozakis, Laurie. *The Complete Idiot's Guide to Shakespeare.* New York: Alpha Books, 1999.

Schoenbaum, S. "Artists' Images of Shakespeare." In *Images of Shakespeare: Proceedings of the Third Congress of the International Shakespeare Association, 1986,* ed. Werner Habicht et al., 19–39. Newark: University of Delaware Press, 1988.

———. "The Ireland Forgeries: An Unpublished Contemporary Account." In *Shakespeare and Others,* 144–53. Washington: Folger Books, 1985.

———. *Shakespeare: His Life, His Language, His Theater.* New York: Signet, 1990.

———. *Shakespeare's Lives.* 2d ed. Oxford: Oxford University Press, 1991.

———. *William Shakespeare: Records and Images.* London: Scolar Press, 1981.

Sedgwick, Eve Kosofsky. *Between Men: English Literature and Male Homosocial Desire.* New York: Columbia University Press, 1985.

———. *Epistemology of the Closet.* Berkeley: University of California Press, 1990.

Sergeant, Philip W. "Young Ireland: An Unappreciated Jester." In *Liars and Fakers,* 239–93. London: Hutchinson, 1926.

Shakespeare, William. *The Norton Shakespeare.* Ed. Stephen Greenblatt et al. New York: Norton, 1997.

———. *Plays and Poems.* 10 vols. Ed. Edmond Malone. London, 1790.

———. *Plays and Poems.* 20 vols. Ed. Edmond Malone and James Boswell. London, 1821.

———. *Poems.* Ed. John Benson. London, 1640.

———. *Poems.* Variorum ed. Ed. Hyder Edward Rollins. Philadelphia: J. B. Lippincott, 1938.

———. *The Riverside Shakespeare.* 2d ed. Ed. G. Blakemore Evans et al. Boston: Houghton Mifflin, 1997.

———. *Shakespeare in Love: The Love Poetry of William Shakespeare.* New York: Miramax, 1998.

———. *Sonnets.* 2 vols. Variorum ed. Ed. Hyder Edward Rollins. Philadelphia: J. B. Lippincott, 1944.

———. *Sonnets.* Ed. W. G. Ingram and Theodore Redpath. New York: Barnes and Noble, 1965.

———. *Sonnets.* Ed. Stephen Booth. New Haven: Yale University Press, 1977.

———. *Sonnets.* Ed. John Kerrigan. Harmondsworth: Penguin, 1985.

———. *Sonnets.* Ed. Katherine Duncan-Jones. London: Thomas Nelson, 1997.

———. *The Tempest.* Variorum ed. Ed. Horace Howard Furness. Philadelphia: J. B. Lippincott, 1892.

The Shakspere Allusion-Book: A Collection of Allusions to Shakspere from 1591–1700. 2 vols. Ed. John Munro et al. London: Humphrey Milford, 1932.

Shapiro, Michael. *Gender in Play on the Shakespearean Stage: Boy Heroines and Female Pages.* Ann Arbor: University of Michigan Press, 1994.

Sherbo, Arthur. *The Birth of Shakespeare Studies: Commentators from Rowe (1709) to Boswell-Malone (1821).* East Lansing: Colleagues Press, 1986.

Sinfield, Alan. *The Wilde Century: Effeminacy, Oscar Wilde and the Queer Moment.* London: Cassell, 1994.

Smart, John Semple. *Shakespeare: Truth and Tradition.* London: Arnold, 1928.

Smith, Bruce R. *Homosexual Desire in Shakespeare's England: A Cultural Poetics.* Chicago: University of Chicago Press, 1991.

Smith, D. Nichol, ed. *Eighteenth Century Essays on Shakespeare.* 2d ed. Oxford: Clarendon Press, 1963.

Sobran, Joseph. *Alias Shakespeare: Solving the Greatest Literary Mystery of All Time.* New York: Free Press, 1997.

Speaight, Robert. *Shakespeare: The Man and His Achievement.* New York: Stein and Day, 1977.

Spencer, Hazelton. *The Art and Life of William Shakespeare.* New York: Harcourt, Brace, 1940.

Spielmann, M. H. "The Portraits of Shakespeare." In *Works of William Shakespeare,* ed. A. H. Bullen et al., 10:373–98. Stratford-on-Avon: Shakespeare Head Press, 1904–7.

———. "The Portraits of Shakespeare." In *Encyclopaedia Britannica,* 24:787–93. 11th ed. New York: Encyclopaedia Britannica, 1910–11.

———. "The 'Shakespeare Marriage Picture' (Part II)." *Connoisseur* 21 (1908): 248–52.

———. *The Title-Page of the First Folio of Shakespeare's Plays: A Comparative Study of the Droeshout Portrait and the Stratford Monument.* London: Humphrey Milford, 1924.

———. "The Winstanley Portraits of Shakespeare." *Connoisseur* 22 (1908): 93–99.

Stallybrass, Peter. "Editing as Cultural Formation: The Sexing of Shakespeare's Sonnets." *Modern Language Quarterly* 54 (1993): 91–103.

———. "Shakespeare, the Individual, and the Text." In *Cultural Studies,* ed. Lawrence Grossberg et al., 593–610. London: Routledge, 1992.

Stanford, Donald E. "Robert Bridges and Samuel Butler on Shakespeare's Sonnets: An Exchange of Letters." *Shakespeare Quarterly* 22 (1971): 329–35.

Stewart, Alan. *Close Readers: Humanism and Sodomy in Early Modern England.* Princeton: Princeton University Press, 1997.

Straub, Kristina. *Sexual Suspects: Eighteenth-Century Players and Sexual Ideology.* Princeton: Princeton University Press, 1992.

Sweet, George Elliott. *Shake-Speare: The Mystery.* Stanford: Stanford University Press, 1956.

Taylor, Gary. "Afterword: The Incredible Shrinking Bard." In *Shakespeare and Appropriation,* ed. Christy Desmet and Robert Sawyer, 197–205. London: Routledge, 1999.

———. *Reinventing Shakespeare: A Cultural History from the Restoration to the Present.* Oxford: Oxford University Press, 1989.

———. "Some Manuscripts of Shakespeare's Sonnets." *Bulletin of the John Rylands Library* 68 (1985): 210–46.

Toropov, Brandon. *Shakespeare for Beginners.* New York: Writers and Readers Publishing, Inc., 1997.

Traub, Valerie. *Desire and Anxiety: Circulations of Sexuality in Shakespearean Drama.* London: Routledge, 1992.

Trumbach, Randolph. "The Birth of the Queen: Sodomy and the Emergence of Gender Equality in Modern Culture, 1660–1750." In *Hidden from History: Reclaiming the Gay and Lesbian Past,* ed. Martin Duberman et al., 129–40. New York: Meridian, 1990.

———. "London's Sapphists: From Three Sexes to Four Genders in the Making of Modern Culture." In *Body Guards: The Cultural Politics of Gender Ambiguity,* ed. Julia Epstein and Kristina Straub, 112–41. London: Routledge, 1991.

———. "London's Sodomites: Homosexual Behavior and Western Culture in the 18th Century." *Journal of Social History* 11 (1977): 1–33.

———. "Sodomitical Subcultures, Sodomitical Roles, and the Gender Revolution of the Eighteenth Century: The Recent Historiography." In *'Tis Nature's Fault: Unauthorized Sexuality during the Enlightenment,* ed. Robert Purks Maccubbin, 109–21. Cambridge: Cambridge University Press, 1987.

Ungerer, Gustav. "Sir Andrew Aguecheek and His Head of Hair." *Shakespeare Studies* 16 (1983): 101–33.

Vendler, Helen. *The Art of Shakespeare's Sonnets.* Cambridge: Harvard University Press, 1997.

Vickers, Brian. *Shakespeare: The Critical Heritage.* 6 vols. London: Routledge, 1974–81.

Wadsworth, Frank W. *The Poacher from Stratford: A Partial Account of the Controversy over the Authorship of Shakespeare's Plays.* Berkeley: University of California Press, 1958.

Waldron, F. G. *Free Reflections on Miscellaneous Papers and Legal Instruments, under the Hand and Seal of William Shakspeare, in the Possession of Samuel Ireland, of Norfolk-Street.* London, 1796.

Wells, Stanley, and Gary Taylor. *William Shakespeare: A Textual Companion.* Oxford: Clarendon Press, 1987.

Whalen, Richard F. *Shakespeare—Who Was He? The Oxford Challenge to the Bard of Avon.* Westport, Conn.: Praeger, 1994.

Wilde, Oscar. "The Portrait of Mr. W. H." In *Complete Works,* 1150–1201. New York: Harper and Row, 1989.

Williams, Gordon. *A Dictionary of Sexual Language and Imagery in Shakespearean and Stuart Literature.* 3 vols. London: Athlone Press, 1994.

Willobie His Avisa. Ed. G. B. Harrison. London: Bodley Head, 1926; New York: Barnes and Noble, 1966.

Wraight, A. D. *The Story That the Sonnets Tell.* London: Adam Hart, 1994.

Zagorin, Perez. *Francis Bacon.* Princeton: Princeton University Press, 1998.

Index